THE
Endangered English
DICTIONARY

THE
Endangered English
DICTIONARY

Bodacious Words Your Dictionary Forgot

DAVID GRAMBS

W. W. NORTON & COMPANY
New York • London

The text of this book is composed in Goudy Old Style with the display
set in Goudy Bold Italic and Goudy Handtooled. Composition by
Crane Typesetting Service, Inc.
Manufacturing by The Haddon Craftsmen, Inc.
Book design by Charlotte Staub.

Library of Congress Cataloging-in-Publication Data

Grambs, David.
    The endangered English dictionary : bodacious words your
dictionary forgot : an exotic, enlightening, and entertaining
companion reference to your trusty Webster's / David Grambs.
        p.   cm.
    1. English language—Obsolete words—Dictionaries.   2. Aureate
terms—Dictionaries.   I. Title.
PE1667.G63   1994
423′.1—dc20   93-32372

ISBN 0-393-03623-5
ISBN 0-393-31606-8 pbk.

W. W. Norton & Company, Inc., 500 Fifth Avenue, New York, N.Y. 10110
W. W. Norton & Company Ltd., 10 Coptic Street, London WC1A 1PU

1 2 3 4 5 6 7 8 9 0

To my affectionate,
generous, ever young, and
dictionary-loving
Aunt Peg

Preface

Endangered whales, snail darters, rain forests—yes, we can all do our part to lessen their peril at the hands of humankind.

Can we also save the lives of a few imperiled, virtually defunct English words, of languished language?

This book aims to give some of the worthier moribund words of our considerable English language a little attention. You'll find some improbable, neglected creatures from our word stock here. You'll find potentially useful old words for whose meanings we have no single-word equivalents in usage today. You'll also find some surprising synonyms (can't we always use an extra synonym or two?) that, over the years or centuries, just got left behind.

An exemplifying phrase or clause accompanies each term, to venture some notion of how such a word might be used in a snatch of contemporary conversation. Let me be the first to admit that dragging—encouraging?—forgotten old words into otherwise idiomatic conversation of today is a curious thing to do, akin to wearing a cummerbund to a beach party. You are not forbidden to smile here. But I hope the conjured-up illustrative phrases at least give you, first, more of a feeling for the word and its meaning and, second, some idea of how or where the words they highlight might conceivably find a place in our chatter or writing today.

Words, when you think about it, *are* creatures of a sort. Words we now consider verbal fossils were once uttered, used in speech and writing, alive. Some (notably, so-called nonce words) may never have taken wing but nevertheless became part of our recorded language. After words fall out of usage, they become the lexical underclass, the silent minority, or, in truth—there are that many—the silent majority. They become endangered, penned in (pun intended) in a few dusty lexicons but ne'er seen by the unsilent majority of us with our comparatively well-worn, pedestrian vocabularies.

The Endangered English Dictionary is particularly for you if your pet dictionary at home or the office is a mere ten-by-seven-inch collegiate edition or a mass-market paperback. Of necessity, our standard or college dictionaries discriminate against the more retired words of our tongue, the so-designated obsolete, archaic, and rare. Chiefly for reasons of space, to be sure, there's a kind of lexical triage. Thousands of interesting and worthy terms never get included in the dictionaries that most Americans and Brits resort to. So many of them are words whose existence cannot but delight. They're words that can also enrich any person's appreciation of the English language and its history—and of its fecundity and possibilities.

I've called this selective collection of alien-looking terms *The Endangered English Dictionary* because I think that's a helpful way of approaching them. All these words are on lexical record. They're not extinct, exactly. But for all we ever glimpse them, they might as well be relegated to the dark side of the moon.

We hear enough about the richness of our great English language, about how many thousands of words more it has than, say, French or even German. Yet few of us have any "eyes-on" sense of just how *many* English words there are, not only out there but back there, forgotten along the waysides of time.

The waysides of time? These, for the word enthusiast, are the musty pages of stout unabridged dictionaries. Most of us own at best a smaller, referral-friendly college-size dictionary, and probably more of us still just a paperback one that is a mere fistful. Alas, such standard, common-parlance glossaries can't give you even an inkling of how much verbal talus lies, forgotten and unused, beneath the ever-changing cliffs of our growing language.

Over the past ten years (in the course of writing other word books), I've ventured through much of this lexical terrain. I haven't merely consulted those thicker dictionaries. I've gone through them page by page from A to Z (more than once). Many words I've happened upon have amazed me— the kinds that bring a smile to the face. So there was—is— a single word conveying *that* meaning! Why did it never come into usage? Why did it fall out of usage? Oh, could we use it *today*!

The words between these covers have almost all been drawn from the gargantuan *Oxford English Dictionary*; *Webster's New International Dictionary*, Second Edition; *Webster's Third New International Dictionary*; and *Funk & Wagnall's Standard Dictionary*. I'm also much indebted to numerous recent books by word-struck authors that have often pointed the way (if sometimes taking updating liberties with the precise meanings of the words).

Popular word books often celebrate the drollness or quaintness of forgotten vocables, the "cuteness" of odd meanings or spellings or pronunciations. I have more quixotic hopes. I'd like people to regard this as a *constant companion* dictionary: a kind of informative and ever-diverting side-by-side volume to go with that reliable pocket or hardcover dictionary you keep on your arm's-reach bookshelf, windowsill, lamp table next to your crossword puzzle chair, or desk at work.

Please consider *The Endangered English Dictionary* a kind of shadow volume or edifying supplement to your main lexical squeeze—a constant reminder of the words that could have been, that fell through the cracks. Or—if you and enough others make imaginative use of this book—that still could become part of our everyday usage.

As a kind of black-sheep sidekick to your everyday lexicon, this book can be, I hope, an enjoyable remembrance of words past. Use your Webster's (whichever version of "Webster's" that may be) to check the meaning of *fractious* or the spelling of *whippoorwill*. Use *The Endangered English Dictionary* for a vintage draught of the historical breadth and depth of your complete national language.

The Endangered English Dictionary differs from other rare-word books chiefly in two respects.

First, it favors common-use, *non*technical words—more correctly, word meanings. That is, the words here are indeed rare but their senses aren't. You'll find few terms from medicine, the physical sciences, history, politics, religion, or the like. But I have included some of these, and some ologies and isms, that I thought might be of interest, if only of humorous interest.

Second, this is a two-way dictionary. Its second part is a complementary glossary of key or cue definitions that will refer you back to the appropriate endangered word you might be seeking. For example, if you're curious about whether there's some rare word meaning "living on handouts," you'll luck out here: you'll find it in the Reverse Glossary alphabetically at "handouts, living on," and you'll learn that the word is *sportulary*. If you want to be the first on the block to know the word for the sort of cavalry trumpet charge one hears played as a rallying cry at major league baseball games, you'll find just the word—it's *tucket*—in the Reverse Glossary at both "cavalry trumpet flourish or signal" and "trumpet flourish or signal."

Or maybe you'd just like to browse and be surprised.

The words here have been selected because, in their meanings, they should be of general interest. They denote (for the most part) things, emotions, actions, or descriptions that pertain to everyday life. Exotic though they look, these nouns, verbs, and modifiers have meanings that would make them quite useful in conversation we hear around us in the year 1993. In this sense, the words are timelessly—I hate to use the word—relevant.

Certainly, many of them have modern-day equivalents, words familiar to us that have the same meaning. But I think unheard-of synonyms are always of interest. Some words we rely on get tired if not tiresome. Maybe we could all use a few spanking old poecilonyms. Poecilonym? It's an old synonym for *synonym* that you'll find in these pages.

But many words in this dictionary have *no* real counterparts in today's English. For example, do you know a single word meaning instinctive parental affection? Time was when people had such a word, and the word was *storge*. Other words here are not so much extremely specific as amusingly specific in meaning, like that for male hysteria (*tarassis*), armed with a noose (*laquearian*), hanging by a thread (*filipendulous*), the space between the thumb and forefinger (*purlicue*), stamping the feet in disapproval (*supplosion*), one and a half times as large (*sesquialteral*), or good writing on a minor subject (*adoxography*).

Other words here are mere curiosities. But it is mere curiosities that often give us a remindful whiff of the past of our great language and civilization. They smell of generations and societies past, possibly of harsher times, or possibly of genuinely kinder and gentler times.

That so many of the words in this book are Latinate is a reminder of the place that a solid classical education once had both in England and in America. Scholars call many such rarefied Latinisms "inkhorn terms" (florid old coinages of pedants) or "aureate language" (those coined by poets). Many such terms are quite facetious. Yet those labels may say more about rarity than about legitimacy: in meaning and potential usefulness, these odd-looking and -sounding words have no apologies to make. When you think about it, many of the Latin-based or Greek-based nouns, adjectives, and verbs we use today aren't really much different in form of pronunciation from their out-of-date cousins resurrected in these pages.

As Lincoln Barnett points out in *The Treasure of Our Tongue*, "The short-lived aureate and inkhorn words, however, represented only a small fraction of the total Graeco-Latin invasion. A quantitative study by the late Professor George Lyman Kittredge of Harvard disclosed that out of all the words listed in a standard Latin dictionary one out of every four or five had moved over into the English dictionary and there lives on as a permanent resident today."

A few other comments regarding this book. Definitions are simplified. (For more detail, go to your nearest *Oxford English Dictionary*.) A great many of these words have several general meanings and occur as different parts of speech, but I've usually borrowed just one inflectional form (sometimes two), the one I thought might have the most potential usefulness in or application to life today. There are only a few dialectal words and Scotticisms, and I've generally not included Anglo-Indian terms or slang.

About Pronunciations

I t's been said, in the case of the English language, that anybody who takes hyphens seriously will surely go mad. The same could be said of the fine points of word pronunciations, particularly as they are rendered in all their phonetic intricacies and variations in unabridged dictionaries.

To spare the reader having to deal with phonetic marks (or printed pronunciations that can sometimes look like arcane mathematical equations), this book uses the imperfect but simpler system based on sound-approximating syllables. It reads like a kind of slow-motion word division.

The syllable receiving the main stress in a word appears in capital letters. For example, "apricate (AP-ri-kayt)."

Unaccented syllables and their subleties are a vexing problem in any pronunciation system. Throwing in silent *h*'s after vowels (as one finds in many books using this reader-friendly approach) doesn't really solve the problem (which vowel pronunciation, for example, does the syllable "wah" represent?); and in lieu of endless and sometimes questionable "ah's" and "uh's," I've kept as close to the word's actual spelling as possible.

My chief but not sole guide for pronunciations has been *Webster's New International Dictionary*, Second Edition.

I have deliberately not cluttered up the text—of a book I've all along wanted to present in as straightforward a style as possible—with variant pronunciations (though there are a few), which I think would confuse rather than benefit the reader. Let it merely be noted that alternative pronunciations are sometimes possible. So always, of course, are regional pronunciational variations. Human beings have a way of articulating words the way they want to or can't help. Possibly this is even truer where rare, unfamiliar words—today never heard in conversation or even seen in print—are concerned. Moreover, even in their day, many of the words collected in *The Endangered English Dictionary* appeared in print only scantly and were probably uttered only once or twice if at all.

When all is said and done, speech is a natural or instinctive activity. This book's diacritic-free, trans-lit-er-a-ted pronunciation system plus common sense should work fine for you. The STRESSED syllable is usually the key: in most if not all cases (correct vowel sounds cannot always be guessed), when you know which syllable in a word has the main stress, the rest of the word's pronunciation falls into place. In many instances, alien as these dusty English words are to us nowadays, you'll probably be able to guess the correct pronunciation. Most of these words are Latinate—but so are many other familiar polysyllabic words that are part of our contemporary speech.

THE
Endangered English
DICTIONARY

THE
Endangered English
DICTIONARY

A

abditive (AB-di-tiv) hidden or hiding
a fear of his new partner's abditive agenda

abditory (AB-di-tor-ee) a hiding place for goods
a chocoholic codependent's clever abditory

abdominous (ab-DOM-i-nus) having a large belly
the prospect of dancing with her gross, abdominous uncle

abearance (uh-BAIR-ens) behavior
appalling abearance at a social occasion

abequitate (ab-EK-wi-tayt) to ride away
no sunset for me to abequitate into

abilitate (a-BIL-i-tayt) to enable
some money that will abilitate Dennis to quit his second job

aberuncate (ab-er-UNG-kayt) to pull up by the roots; extirpate
a neighborhood dog that aberuncated some of her prize garden plants

abhominality (ab-hom-i-NAL-i-tee) a cruel or inhuman deed
the cold-blooded abhominalities of a serial killer

1

abiological (ay-by-o-LOJ-i-kal) pert. to the study of inanimate things
a psych major with no interest in the abiological sciences

abjunct (ab-JUNGT) disconnected or severed
a tangle of abjunct colored wires in the switch box

abjunctive (ab-JUNK-tiv) exceptional, isolated, or disconnected
only a rare and abjunctive phenomenon

ablactate (ab-LAK-tayt) to wean from the breast
the process of ablactating twins

ablatitious (ab-la-TISH-us) lessening, diminishing, or subtractive
a pie in the face being ablatitious to one's self-esteem

ablegate (AB-le-gayt) to send away or abroad
when he ablegated two very special agents

abligurition (ab-lig-yoor-ISH-un) lavish spending on food and drink
a prodigal nephew notorious for his late-night abligurition

ablocate (AB-lo-kayt) to rent out
plans to ablocate a metal canoe to cross the lake

ablude (ab-LYOOD) to differ (from) or not be in keeping with
some crude lines that ablude from the general tone of the script

abonné (ab-uh-NAY) a subscriber
those lucky opera season abonnés

abraid (a-BRAYD) to awake, arouse, or startle
tiptoeing around so as not to abraid his napping grandfather

abscede (ab-SEED) to move away or go elsewhere; lose contact
an older sister who absceded to California when Jane was fourteen

absit (AB-sit) a pupil's brief leave of absence
a delinquent student deserving no further absits

2

absonant (AB-so-nant) discordant or unharmonious; unnatural or unreasonable
a gaffe that struck an absonant note

abstriction (ab-STRIK-shun) loosening or unbinding
an overdue abstriction of the community's old blue laws

abuccinate (ab-YOO-si-nayt) to proclaim like a fanfare
wanting to abuccinate his love for her

abundary (a-BUN-da-ree) an abundant source or
fountainhead
*some county annals that are an abundary for interesting
anecdotes*

abvolate (AB-vo-layt) to fly away
poking into the bird feeder and abruptly abvolating

acataleptic (a-kat-a-LEP-tik) not knowable for certain
areas of genetics that are acataleptic

acates (or acatery) (a-KAYTS) (a-KAY-te-ree) things
bought
a wonderful trip with many acates as souvenirs

acatharsia (or acatharsy) (ak-a-THAR-see-a) (AK-a-thar-
see) filth
the eyesore of urban acatharsia

accerse (ak-SERS) to summon
dreading being accersed by one's accurst boss

accinge (ak-SINJ) to apply oneself, as to a task
a worker not known for conspicuous accingeing

accismus (ak-SIZ-mus) pretended refusal of something
one wants
using the accismus ploy once too often

accolent (AK-o-lent) neighboring or living nearby
a girl not only attractive but conveniently accolent

accoy (ak-KOY) to quiet or soothe
desperate lies that will not accoy my outrage

3

accrescent (ak-KRES-ent) growing continuously or ever-increasing
the problem of the government's accrescent deficit

accurance (ak-KYOOR-anse) caring for or solicitude
showed a touching accurance for the three children of somebody else

aceldama (a-SEL-da-ma) a scene of bloodshed
the homicide squad finding the bedroom a veritable aceldama

acervation (a-ser-VAY-shun) an accumulation or heaping up
an article with a relentless acervation of telling details

acetarious (a-se-TAIR-ee-us) used in salads
a stop at the supermarket for some acetarious vegetables

acherontic (ak-er-ON-tik) infernal or hellish
the acherontic working conditions of a factory in Eastern Europe

aclinal (a-KLY-nal) horizontal
the old house's not quite aclinal floors

acolastic (ak-o-LAS-tik) incorrigible
a talkative waiter who was an acolastic punster

acolaust (AK-o-lawst) a sensualist
luxury hotels catering to your every need and turning you into an acolaust

acomous (a-KO-mus) bald
the uncomfortably acomous who wear hats indoors

acopic (a-KOP-ik) relieving weariness
resting his head in his wife's warm and acopic lap

acturience (ak-TYOO-ree-ense) the desire for or impulse to act
the lack of acturience in a paralyzed organization

acuate (AK-yoo-ayt) sharp-pointed
handily acuate elbows that get him many offensive rebounds

acupunctuate (ak-yoo-PUNG-tyoo-ayt) to prick or poke (with a pin or needle)
used a sewing needle to acupunctuate the paper

addubitation (ad-doob-i-TAY-shun) the suggestion of a doubt
some hedgings and phrasings that sounded a note of addubitation

adephagous (a-DEF-a-gus) voracious
her sister's sadly adephagous vacation appetite

adeps (AD-eps) animal fat
a concern about ingesting any form of adeps

adhorn (ad-HORN) to make a cuckold of
the actor's celebrated adhorning of other celebrity husbands

adiaphoron (ad-i-AF-or-on) a matter of indifference ethically
a consideration that's no adiaphoron where I'm concerned

ad interim (ad IN-ter-im) temporary
an ad interim but expeditious solution

adipsous (a-DIP-sus) quenching thirst
the most adipsous of beverages being pure water

adjectament (ad-JEK-ta-ment) an addition
the questionable adjectament of second garage

adjutator (ad-JOO-tay-ter) a helper or assistant
the magician's equally adroit adjutator

adjutorious (ad-joo-TO-ri-us) helpful
an adjutorious German-English dictionary

adjuvant (AD-joo-vent) helpful, auxiliary, or contributory
your daughter's adjuvant role in its success

admarginate (ad-MAR-ji-nayt) to note in the margin
when she heavily admarginated his midterm paper

adminicular (ad-min-IK-yoo-ler) corroborative
the hole in the deceased's left temple being more than adminicular evidence

adonize (AD-o-nyz) to beautify or dandify
her regrettable attempts to adonize her very young son

5

adoxography   (ad-ok-SOG-ra-fee) good writing on a minor
subject
early McPhee works for adoxography par excellence

adscititious   (ad-sit-TISH-us) additional or supplemental
an adscititious dessert as a fillip

adulterine   (a-DUL-ter-in) an illegitimate child
the old stigma of being a forlorn adulterine

adumbered   (ad-UM-berd) overshadowed
*an important news item regrettably adumbered by the election
coverage*

adunation   (ad-un-AY-shun) making into one
the term for literary adunation being conflation

advectitious   (ad-vek-TISH-us) imported
a longtime dealer in advectitious kitsch

advesperate   (ad-VES-pe-rayt) to get dark or late
to see the day advesperate with wintry swiftness

advigilate   (ad-VIJ-i-layt) to watch diligently
hired as an overseer to advigilate the transfer of the goods

advolution   (ad-vo-LYOO-shun) a rolling toward
the relentless advolution of Germany's panzer divisions

aeolistic   (EE-o-lis-tik) long-winded
the aeolistic interviewer being the worst kind

aequor   (EE-kwor) a flat surface; the sea
to have some sort of portable aequor to write on

aequorial   (ek-WAR-ee-ul) oceanic; marine
either marine biology or the navy for aequorial adventure

aerarian   (eh-RAIR-ee-an) fiscal
rash and unwise aerarian policies

aerose   (er-ROS) (EE-ros) brassy or coppery
a skin color less brown than aerose

aerumnous   (air-OOM-nus) full of trouble
to avoid getting involved in their aerumnous politics

aesthesics (es-THEEZ-iks) pronunciation
murdering the English language with slurvian aesthesics

affabrous (AF-a-brus) workmanlike or well-made
a shelter not jerry-built but clearly affabrous and solid

affiche (af-FEESH) a poster or placard
a graffito-ridden affiche for a rock concert

affidation (af-fi-DAY-shun) a vow to be faithful and
true
paused during their walk to declare his affidation to her

affinal (af-FY-nal) related by marriage
their purely affinal but not at all awkward relationship

afflated (af-LAY-ted) inspired
a poet more inflated than afflated

affrontee (af-frun-TEE) an insulted person
*a politically correct atmosphere swelling the numbers of
affrontees*

affrontive (af-FRUN-tiv) insulting
the hostess's typically affrontive remarks

agaçant (ag-a-SAN) exciting or provocative
her rather agaçant mermaid costume

agacerie (a-gas-REE) coquetry
her coyness and agacerie at the office

agamy (AG-a-mee) absence of marriage
the youth and agamy of the staff

Aganippe (ag-a-NIP-ee) a source of poetic inspiration
a poetry prize as her chief Aganippe

agapet (a-ga-PET) a ladies' man
the practiced overtures of a self-styled agapet

agathism (AG-a-thiz-um) the belief that things tend to
work out for the better
a little agathism regarding the controversial budget

agathokakological (ag-ath-o-kak-o-LOJ-i-kal) comprising or showing both good and evil
a dramatization that in the end was an agathokakological and balanced interpretation

agennesis (a-je-NEE-sis) impotence
a television special on marital agennesis

agerasia (a-jer-AY-zha) youthful appearance
a longing for face-lifts and chronic agerasia

aggerose (AJ-er-ose) in heaps
a quantity of agerose foreign coins

aggregable (AG-gre-ga-bul) collectible into one mass
clumps of aggregable molding clay for kindergarteners

agminate (AG-min-ayt) grouped together in a cluster
agminate red, blue, and white poker chips around the table

agnition (ag-NI-shun) recognition or acknowledgment
their reluctant agnition of his feat

agnosy (AG-no-see) ignorance
the deadly combination of ideology and agnosy

agnoiology (ag-noy-OL-o-jee) the study of human ignorance
the ever-expanding field of agnoiology

agomphious (a-GOM-fee-us) toothless
the drooling, agomphious caretaker at the beginning of the movie

agrestal (a-GRES-tal) living or growing in the wild
a posy of agrestal flowers

agrestic (a-GRES-tik) rural and uncouth
agrestic, backwoods types up in the hills

agrypnotic (a-grip-NOT-ik) something to prevent sleep
his sad search for a voluptuous and agrypnotic bedmate

aischrolatreia (ice-kro-la-TRY-a) the cultish worship of obscenity or filth
modern pornography and ancient aischrolatreia

aknee   (a-NEE) on one's knee or knees
aknee and digging furiously at a corner of the backyard

alabandical   (al-a-BAN-di-kal) barbarous
alabandical atrocities

alamodality   (a-la-mo-DAL-i-tee) fashionableness
the cyclical alamodality of short skirts

albiculi   (al-BIK-yoo-ly) white people (derogatory)
an older population of albiculi

aleiptic   (a-LAYP-tik) pert. to physical or gymnastic
training
an impossible aleiptic regimen

alembicated   (a-LEM-bi-kay-ted) overly subtle or refined in
thought or expression
an essay so alembicated and allusive that I couldn't understand it

aletude   (AL-e-tyood) obesity
the aletude of his ego

alexipharmic   (a-lek-si-FAR-mik) an antidote for poison
*that all mystery writers were less knowledgeable about
alexipharmics*

algefacient (or **algific**)   (al-je-FAY-shent) (al-JIF-ik)
cooling
some effective algefacient balm for her sunburn

algetic   (al-JET-ik) pert. to or causing pain
the algetic feelings of parting

algific   (al-JIF-ik) making cold
a touch like a witch's algific finger

alienigenate   (ay-lee-en-IJ-en-et) foreign-born
their alienigenate parents who were nonetheless very patriotic

alieniloquy   (ay-lee-en-IL-o-kwee) rambling or evasive
talk
the unctuous alieniloquy of the head of personnel

aliety   (a-LEE-i-tee) being different
the aliety of the newcomers

9

alimentotherapy (a-li-ment-o-THER-a-pee) dietary therapy for disease
the importance of postoperative alimentotherapy

alimonious (al-i-MO-nee-us) nourishing
tasty but hardly alimonious junk food

aliud (AY-lee-ud) something else or another thing
putting off for now dealing with the exceptions and the aliuds

aliunde (ay-lee-UN-dee) from elsewhere or another source
a couple of aliunde boxes of a different color

allagrugous (al-a-GROOG-us) grim and ghastly
your unwelcome and allagrugous countenance

allatrate (al-la-TRAYT) to bark like a dog
a promise not to allatrate on the wedding night

allégresse (al-lay-GRES) gaiety or lightheartedness
a dark, backstreet world devoid of all allégresse

alliaceous (al-lee-AY-shus) garlic- or onion-smelling
the knockout, alliaceous breath of a fellow straphanger

alliciency (al-LISH-en-see) attractiveness or enticement
to rely on her tried and true alliciency skills and wiles

allicient (al-LISH-ent) attractive
an allicient, elevated site for the new cottage

alligation (al-li-GAY-shun) attachment
a steadfast sibling alligation

allision (al-LIZH-un) an intentional ship collision
the legalities of what may have been a case of allision

alloerotism (al-lo-ER-o-tiz-um) loving another sexually as an object
feminist strides against all-pervasive alloerotism

allogeneous (al-lo-JEE-nee-us) different in kind
the ark's allogeneous animals

allograph (al-lo-GRAF) a signature or writing for another person
her hurried allograph for Anthony's package

allopath (or **allopathist**) (al-lo-PATH) (al-LOP-a-thist) a physician
the allopath's Hippocratic oath

alluvium (al-LOO-vee-um) an overflow or flood
the fear of a levee alluvium

alogy (al-o-GEE) unreasonableness or absurdity
the alogy of such a concocted explanation

alpenglow (al-pen-GLO) a reddish lumination around mountaintops
her silhouette against the Rockies' alpenglow

alphenic (al-FEN-ik) sugar candy
the ludicrousness of dietetic alphenic

alterity (awl-TER-i-tee) (al-TER-i-tee) being different; otherness
his placing a premium on his precious alterity

altivolant (al-TIV-o-lant) flying high
an altivolant hawk

alture (AL-tyoor) height
a spire of considerable alture

alviducous (al-vi-DOO-kus) purgative
the remedy of alviducous prunes

alvine dejections (AL-vyn dee-JEK-shuns) excrement
the dog's alvine dejections in the snow

amadelphous (a-ma-DEL-fus) gregarious
an amadelphous pest

amanous (AM-a-nus) having no hands
the challenge of amanous foreplay

ambagious (am-BAY-jus) not straightforward; circumlocutory; roundabout
typically smarmy and ambagious

ambilevous (am-bi-LEE-vus) clumsy
an ambilevous but determined athlete

ambisinister   (am-bi-SIN-ist-er) clumsy with both hands
to end up as an ambisinister dishwasher

amblosis   (am-BLO-sis) abortion
the moral and political issues surrounding amblosis

ambsace   (AYM-zase) (AM-zase) something worthless or
unlucky
a class ring he now considered an ambsace

amenage   (a-me-NAZH) to domesticate or tame
a new preserve to amenage wild game

ament   (AY-ment) a mentally deficient person
lively but definitely a lifelong ament

amiture   (AM-i-tyoor) friendship
their deep but troubled amiture

ammophilous   (am-MOF-il-us) sand-loving
too amophilous and landlubbing to be a surfer

amnic   (AM-nik) pert. to a river
both of them painters of amnic landscapes

amort   (a-MORT) lifeless, as if dead, or spiritless
an overblown Broadway production virtually amort

amphierotic   (am-fee-er-ROT-ik) sexually attracted to
either sex
has been called an amphierotic rubbernecker

amphierotism   (am-fi-ER-o-tiz-um) bisexuality
an anthropological treatise on tribal amphierotism

amphoric   (am-FOR-ik) like the sound of blowing across
an empty bottle
whispering her amphoric sweet nothings into my ear

amphorous   (am-FOR-us) hollow-sounding
Mr. Ward's amphorous reassurances

amplexation   (am-plek-SAY-shun) embracing
the usual airport amplexations

amplivagant (or amplivagous)   (am-PLI-va-gant) (am-PLI-va-gus) large or wide in scope; extensive
the old building's amplivagant courtyard

ampollosity   (am-pol-LOS-i-tee) bombast
political sloganeering and ampollosity

amyctic   (a-MIK-tik) irritating or excoriating
an uncomfortably shaggy and amyctic sweater

amylaceous   (am-i-LAY-shus) starchy
generous but doughily amylaceous food

anabathrum   (a-NA-bath-rum) a pulpit
like telling tasteless jokes from a cathedral anabathrum

anabiotic   (an-a-by-OT-ik) tonic or stimulating
your ever anabiotic interruptions

anacalypsis   (an-a-ka-LIP-sis) an unveiling or revealing
removing her scarf in the manner of some great anacalypsis

anacardic   (an-a-KAR-dik) pert. to cashews
an anacardic flavor

anacatharsis   (an-a-ka-THAR-sis) vomiting
a messy backseat anacatharsis while en route

anaclitic   (an-a-KLIT-ik) overly dependent
as anaclitic as a petrified limpet

anagraph   (AN-a-graf) a record or register
a year-by-year anagraph of clients

analeptic   (an-a-LEP-tik) restorative or invigorating
like an analeptic slap in the face

analphabet   (an-AL-fa-bet) an illiterate person
volunteer work with older analphabets

anandrious   (an-AN-dree-us) impotent
aging, anandrious, and aggravating

anaphroditous   (an-af-ro-DY-tus) lacking sexual desire
a properly anaphroditous chaperone

anapologetical (an-a-pol-o-JET-i-kal) inexcusable
an absolutely anapologetical failure to show up

anaudia (an-AW-dee-a) loss of voice
frustrating anaudia by the seventh inning

ancipitous (an-SIP-it-us) doubtful
of ancipitous authenticity

anderun (an-de-ROON) a harem
his fantasies of a double-shift anderun

andic (AND-ik) involving males
the antique andic occasion of a bachelor's party

androcentric (an-dro-SEN-trik) dominated by males
a novel with a distinctly androcentric flavor

androphagous (an-DROF-a-gus) man-eating
a myth replete with androphagous monsters

anfracture (an-FRAK-cher) a mazy winding
the labyrinthine anfracture of its back alleys

angelophany (ayn-je-LOF-a-nee) the apparition of an
angel (on earth)
a blind date who was no angelophany

Anglice (ANG-li-see) in English or in plain English
esprit de l'escalier or, Anglice, staircase wit

anguria (ang-YOOR-ee-a) a gourd or watermelon
a head like a bewigged anguria

angustate (ang-US-tayt) narrowed or contracted
the cleared but somewhat angustate roads in the blizzard

anhedonia (an-he-DO-nee-a) the inability to be happy
whether affluence is a cure for anhedonia

anhedonic (an-he-DON-ik) incapable of experiencing
happiness or pleasure
one of those stand-up comics with an anhedonic shtick

anhelous (an-HEE-lus) short of breath or panting
with his happy, anhelous comments after their jog

14

anicular (an-IK-yoo-ler) old-womanish
a sergeant with strangely anicular traits

annomination (an-nom-i-NAY-shun) punning
(paronomasia)
a penchant for ponderous annomination

annonary (an-NO-na-ree) pert. to provisions
*the community's annonary concerns before the predicted
hurricane*

annosity (an-NOS-i-tee) length of life
the surprising annosity of parrots

annotinous (an-NOT-in-us) one year old (biologically)
a cuddly annotinous beagle

anoetic (a-no-ET-ik) conscious but passive and
unthinking
the dreariness of an anoetic existence

anopisthographic (an-o-piz-tho-GRAF-ik) bearing writing on only one side
the preferred anopisthographic postcard

anorchous (an-OR-kus) lacking testicles
Larry's anorchous unwillingness to confront him

another-guess (a-NUTH-er-ges) of another type or sort
as opposed to an another-guess job

ansal (AN-sal) two-edged; cutting both ways
political patronage being an ansal business

anteambulate (an-tee-AM-byoo-layt) to walk in front of
or before
a great help in surveillance work when the quarry anteambulates

antecedaneous (an-tee-se-DAY-nee-us) preceding in time
unaware of a greater battle that was antecedaneous

antefact (AN-tee-fakt) an earlier or previous act
*whether his crime should be judged in the light of his related
antefacts*

antelucan (an-tee-LOO-kan) before dawn
their antelucan rendezvous at lakeside

antenuptial (an-tee-NUP-shul) premarital
some antenuptial nervousness

antetype (AN-tee-typ) a prototype or earlier example
a remarkable invention with no antetype

antevenient (an-tee-VEE-nyent) preceding in time
an antevenient rather than resultant event

anthropomorphosis (an-thro-po-MOR-fo-sis) changing
into human form
the final anthropomorphosis of the creature

anthropopithecus (an-thro-po-pi-THEE-kus) the missing
link
the guy on the varsity they called the anthropopithecus

anthropotomy (an-thro-POT-o-mee) human anatomy
female anthropotomy

anthropurgic (ab-thro-PER-jik) done or acted upon by
humans
anthropurgic factors in the ecosystem

antiethnic (an-tee-ETH-nik) anti-Gentile
antiethnic suspicions of anti-Semitism

antiorgastic (an-tee-or-GAS-tik) acting as a sedative
a monotonously antiorgastic speech

antipudic (an-tee-PYOO-dik) covering private parts
a not quite antipudic bathing suit

antisocordist (an-tee-so-KOR-dist) an opponent of laziness and stupidity
*a bureaucracy needing a good antisocordist who will really crack
the whip*

antistasis (an-TIS-ta-sis) defense of something that prevented something worse
an editorial that is an overdue and much appreciated antistasis

16

antithalian (an-tee-thay-LEE-an) opposed to merriment and festivity
your antithalian library assistant

antitwilight (an-tee-TWY-lyt) the sky's pink or purple glow after sunset
the right colors for painting the sky at antitwilight

antitypy (an-TIT-up-ee) resistance of matter to penetration
the degree of antitypy of a bulletproof vest

any-lengthian (en-ee-LAYNTH-ee-an) unscrupulous
a bunch of any-lengthian zealots justifying their means

aosmic (ay-OZ-mik) odorless
a longing for the days when glossy magazines were aosmic

apanthropy (ap-AN-thro-pee) love of solitude
the distinction between apanthropy and misanthropy

apellous (a-PEL-us) circumcised (or skinless)
the prevalence of apellous males in a particular culture

aperient (a-PEER-ee-ent) a laxative
a standard, over-the-counter aperient

aphilanthropy (af-il-AN-thro-pee) a dislike for social intercourse
the crusty aphilanthropy of a stolid New Englander

aphotic (ay-FO-tik) lightless
a noisy and almost aphotic below-sidewalk bar

aphronia (ay-FRO-ni-a) lack of good practical judgment
the CEO's very quirky aphronia and lapses

aphthong (AF-thong) an unpronounced letter or letter combination
a difficult name with two aphthongs

apodictic (a-po-DIK-tik) utterly certain
my apodictic and incontestable conclusion

apolactize (a-po-LAK-tize) to kick aside or away
careful to apolactize any associations that might jeopardize his election

apolaustic   (a-po-LAW-stik)   pleasure-loving or self-indulgent
Nathalie's apolaustic nephew

aponic   (ay-PON-ik)   free of pain
distrustful of the worth of aponic exercise

apopathetic   (a-po-pa-THET-ik)   showing-off
apopathetic machismo

apopemptic   (a-po-PEMP-tik)   pert. to leaving or departing; valedictory
spared the usual apopemptic platitudes

aporetic   (a-po-RET-ik)   skeptical or doubting
not sufficiently aporetic in this case

apositic   (a-po-SIT-ik)   taking away the appetite
a truly apositic dish

apostil   (ap-OS-til)   a marginal note
too many illegible apostils

apotelesm   (a-POT-el-ez-um)   the casting of horoscopes
an apostle of apotelesm

appaumé   (a-po-MAY)   with the palm outstretched
standing there hunched over and appaumé

appersonation   (ap-PER-so-nay-shun)   the delusion that one is a famous person
over the edge into actual appersonation

appetition   (ap-pe-TISH-un)   desire or yearning
old feelings and vagaries of appetition

apprecation   (ap-re-KAY-shun)   a devout wish
birthday candles and a secret apprecation

appropinquity   (ap-pro-PING-kwi-tee)   nearness
the fortunate appropinquity of the hospital

appropriament   (ap-PRO-pree-a-ment)   an individual characteristic
your own perfect and unmatchable appropriaments

18

appulse (ap-PULSE) a driving or running toward
the appulse of the rabid crowd

apricate (AP-ri-kayt) to bask in the sun or to sunbathe
to apricate happily wearing nothing but headphones

aprosexia (ap-ro-SEK-see-a) the inability to sustain
attention
*a classroom of kids who all seem to have aprosexia and loud
voices*

apsychia (ap-SIK-ee-a) unconsciousness
the cultural apsychia of an entire generation

aquabib (AK-wa-bib) (AYK-wa-bib) water drinker
marathon racers as aquabibs on the run

aquosity (ak-WOS-i-tee) moisture
parched and devoid of aquosity

arbitrament (ar-BIT-ra-ment) free will or free choice;
decisiveness
her newfound feeling of individual arbitrament

arbuscle (ar-BUS-kyool) a dwarf tree
an atrium exhibit of beautiful arbuscles

archaeolatry (ar-ki-OL-a-tree) worship of anything
archaic
the characteristic archaeolatry of a reactionary cult

arcifinious (ar-si-FIN-i-us) having a natural boundary as a
defensive frontier (law)
the arcifinious security of the small kingdom

ardent spirits (ar-dent SPEER-its) strong liquor
some ardent spirits brewed in the hills

arefy (AR-e-fy) to dry up
told him to arefy and blow away

argotic (ar-GOT-ik) pert. to slang
the argotic colorfulness of the underworld dialogue

arietation (ar-i-et-AY-shun) butting like a ram (as a bat-
tering ram)
police raids and violent arietations of apartment doors

ariolate (AR-i-o-layt) to prophesy or foretell
an astrologer who ariolated the second earthquake

aristology (ar-is-TOL-o-jee) the science of dining
the hostess with the mostest in aristology

arithmocracy (ar-ith-MOK-ra-see) rule of the numerical majority
a group of survivors operating by simple arithmocracy

arles (arls) money to bind a bargain; earnest money or money up front
a deal requiring some arles

armilla (ar-MIL-la) a bracelet
her playing a slave girl with the usual jangly armillas

arreptitious (ar-rep-TISH-us) given to raptures; possessed or mad
a disturbed and arreptitious young man

artigrapher (ar-TIG-ra-fer) a grammarian
an old-fashioned English teacher and strict artigrapher

ascriptitious (as-krip-TISH-us) added to a list; ascribed or attributed
the ascriptitious addition of his name

aselgeia (as-el-JEE-a) lasciviousness
their mentor's horror of any kind of aselgeia

asmatographer (as-ma-TOG-ra-fer) a songwriter
an ambitious but unoriginal asmatographer

aspectable (as-PEK-ta-bul) visible; fair or fit to look upon
Steve's improved but not as yet aspectable appearance

asperge (as-PERJ) to sprinkle
to asperge the shirt before ironing it

aspernate (AS-per-nayt) to reject or condemn
a reader who wrote in to aspernate the paper's editorial

asperous (AS-per-us) rough or rugged
their asperous mountain training

aspheterism   (as-FET-er-iz-um) communism
the unlikeliness of the complete extinction of aspheterism

assation   (as-SAY-shun) roasting or baking
the redolence of assation at Christmastime

assentation   (as-sen-TAY-shun) rote or insincere
agreement
wanting more than their mere assentation

asseth   (as-SETH) satisfaction or amends
a crime for which there can be no satisfactory asseth

asteism   (AS-ti-iz-um) a cleverly polite insult
a master of the offhand asteism

astorgy   (AST-or-jee) lack of natural affection
the evident astorgy of the boy's stepfather

astrict   (as-TRIKT) to tie up, bind, or restrict
to astrict further the hands of apathetic bureaucrats

astriferous   (as-TRIF-er-us) starry
the wonderfully astriferous night sky

ataraxy (or ataraxia)   (AT-er-ak-see) (at-er-AK-si-a) unfazability; intellectual detachment
a top-notch mercenary with stony ataraxy

ateknia   (a-TEK-ni-a) childlessness
ateknia and infant mortality statistics

athanasia   (ath-a-NAY-zha) immortality
the theme of athanasia in mythology

athetize   (ATH-e-tyz) to reject as spurious
to summarily athetize two particular assertions

atrament   (AT-ra-ment) ink
powdered atrament

atrichia   (at-RIK-ee-a) baldness
many women finding atrichia in man quite appealing

attinge   (at-TINJ) to touch; to affect or influence
a story that attinged many younger people as well

attingent   (at-TIN-jent) touching or in contact with
a not yet attingent red wire on the bomb

attrahent   (AT-ra-hent) attracting or magnetic
a most well-spoken and attrahent receptionist

audient   (AW-dee-ent) listening or paying attention
raptly audient bystanders

aurantiicortex   (or-ran-shee-ai-KOR-teks) orange peel
a skin wizened like dried-out aurantiicortex

auricomous   (aw-RIK-o-mus) golden-haired
the auricomous bad guy who was the real psychopath

aurific   (aw-RIF-ik) producing gold
the aurific fixations of westward migrants

aurulent   (AW-roo-lent) golden in color
a kind of aurulent syrup

austerulous   (aw-STER-yoo-lus) somewhat harsh
the austerulous but not unbearable climate of the islands

austral (or austrine)   (AW-stral) (AW-strin) southern
bound for austral climes

autacoidal   (aw-ta-KOY-dal) hormonal
a personality more autacoidal than charismatic

autolatry   (aw-TOL-a-tree) self-worship
the not-so-subtle autolatry of her supposed celebrity interviews

automorphic   (aw-to-MOR-fik) patterned after oneself;
ascribing one's traits to another
her transparently automorphic main character

autophilia   (aw-to-FIL-ee-a) self-love or narcissism
the autophilia of decadent aesthetes

autophoby   (aw-TOF-o-bee) fear of referring to oneself
the shy neurotic's ever-increasing autophoby

autoptic   (aw-TOP-tik) based on personal observation
recommendations drawn from her autoptic fieldwork

autoschediaze (aw-to-SKEE-dee-ayz) to improvise
how to autoschediaze in an emergency

autotelic (aw-to-TEL-ik) for its own sake
Ken's purely curious and autotelic participation

auturgy (aw-TER-jee) independent activity
the auturgy of one special patient

aval (AY-vul) grandparental
strong aval ties

avanious (av-AY-nee-us) extortionate
the avanious markup on that medicine

averruncate (av-er-RUN-kayt) to avert or ward off
a good political stratagem to averruncate the usual detractors

avulse (a-VULSE) to tear away or pluck
compulsively avulsing and devouring seedless grapes

B

Baalism (BAY-a-liz-um) idolatry
the show business Baalism of the modern world

babblative (BAB-la-tiv) tending to babble or prattle
to dismiss a babblative psychiatrist

baculine (BAK-yoo-lyn) pert. to punishment by whipping
the baculine rites of the English public school

baisemains (bez-maah) one's respects or compliments
the fulsome baisemains of her backstage flunkies

balatron (BAL-a-tron) a contemptible buffoon
a born balatron as a camp counselor

balatronic (bal-a-TRON-ik) buffoonish
the flat jokes of a balatronic yuppie

balbutient (bal-BYOO-shent) stammering
an unnerved and balbutient suspect

23

balneal (BAL-nee-al) pert. to warm baths
the spa's balneal delights

banausic (ba-NAW-sik) practical, functional, or
utilitarian
an all-purpose banausic tool

baragouin (ba-ra-GWAN) gibberish
the pseudosincere baragouin of some self-help books

barbate (BAR-bayt) bearded
barbate Berbers as extras in the scene

barbatulous (bar-BAT-yoo-lus) having a small beard
a wizened, barbatulous grandmother

barbigerous (bar-BI-jer-us) bearded or hairy
reports of the barbigerous Yeti

bardocucullated (bar-do-kuk-UL-ay-ted) wearing a cowled
cloak
*a finale with a chase through the cave by the villain's bardocu-
cullated followers*

bariolage (ba-ree-o-LOJ) a medley
your standard piano-bar bariolage

barr (bar) to utter an elephant's cry
to barr mightily when in pain

basiate (BAY-zee-ayt) to kiss
a statue for patriots to basiate

basilic (ba-SIL-ik) royal or kingly
getting advice on the unfamiliar basilic protocols

batata (ba-TA-ta) the sweet potato
you say "potato" and I say "batata"

bathyal (BATH-ee-al) deep-sea
bathyal mysteries of the Pacific Ocean

bathycolpian (bath-i-KOL-pee-an) having deep cleavage
between the breasts
describing her bathycolpian assets as a veritable lover's leap

bating (BAY-ting) with the exception of; excepting
bating the present company, of course

battailous (BAT-i-lus) ready for battle or warlike
young but battailous troops

battology (bat-OL-o-jee) needless verbal repetition
a radio talk-show host who heads off the slightest battology

battue (bat-TOO) (bat-TYOO) a massacre or slaughter
dreadful battues attributable to the rival warlords

bavardage (ba-var-DAZH) small talk or chitchat
an impatience with inane bavardage about shopping

bavian (BAY-vee-an) a baboon
the doglike faces of bavians

Bavian (BAY-vee-an) a malicious poetaster
an unpublished Bavian

beauish (BO-ish) foppish or dandyish
a beauish denizen of downtown clubs

bechic (BEEK-ik) a cough remedy
a menthol bechic

bedight (be-DYT) (bee-DYT) to deck out or array
bedighting both her daughters for a Halloween party

bedrabble (bed-RAB-ul) (bee-DRAB-ul) to befoul with
rain and mud
an unpleasant excursion that bedrabbled one and all

begrutten (be-GRUT-en) having a face swollen from
weeping
the begrutten face of her husband at her bedside

belamour (bel-a-MOR) a glance of love
furtive belamours at the dinner table

belcher (BEL-cher) a spotted kerchief
a Western shirt and yellow-and-blue belcher

belgard (bel-GARD) a loving look
*thrilled by the open belgards of the girl at the back of the
classroom*

bellibone   (BEL-i-bone) an attractive girl
distracted by a spectacular bellibone in the lobby

bellipotent   (bel-LIP-o-tent) mighty in war
the two bellipotent superpowers

bellitude   (BEL-i-tyood) beauty
a vanity table stocked with all the colorings and pastes to enhance bellitude

belluine   (BEL-yoo-in) brutal
the belluine treatment of those captured

belute   (bee-LOOT) to cover or spatter with mud or dirt
not only beluted but sideswiped the other car

benedicence   (be-NED-i-sense) kindliness or considerateness in speech
mollified by the apologies and benedicence of the store's owner

beneplacit   (be-nee-PLAY-sit) pleased or satisfied
a beneplacit and generous contributor

bethphany   (BETH-fa-nee) turning water into wine
no miraculous bethphany in the offing

bevue   (bee-VYOO) an inadvertent error
a minor bookkeeping bevue

bezoardic   (bez-o-AR-dik) antidotal
a bezoardic home remedy for a hangover

biduous   (BID-yoo-us) lasting two days
a biduous out-of-town conference

Biedermeier   (BEE-der-my-er) artistically conventional, bourgeois, or vulgar
the Biedermeier taste of a self-made vulgarian

bigential   (by-JEN-shul) comprised of two races
essentially a bigential island

biliment   (BIL-i-ment) an article of women's clothing
her seasonal biliments and jewelry

bionomics   (by-o-NOM-iks) ecology
a lecture on bionomics and our shrinking planet

biota   (by-O-ta) living things (of a region); flora and fauna
not the geology but the biota of the Great Plains

bivious   (BIV-i-us) leading two ways
a bivious point along the trail

bizarrerie   (bee-zar-re-REE) bizarreness
the bizarrerie of the city's most exotic quarter

blench   (blench) a trick, wile, or strategem
not above unscrupulous bluffs and blenches

blesiloquent   (bles-IL-o-kwent) stammering or stuttering
one of those gruff and blesiloquent types like Dr. Watson

bloviation   (blo-vi-AY-shun) talking windily
the bloviation of the equally uncompelling candidates

blunderly   (BLUN-der-lee) badly or clumsily made
made fun of his playmate's blunderly snowman

blype   (BLYPE) a piece or shred of skin
a fingernail biter gnawing on this or that blype

boation   (bo-AY-shun) bellowing or roaring
the deafening boation of the home-team fans

bombilate   (BOM-bi-layt) to hum or buzz; bombinate
machines that thrummed, chugged, whirred, and bombilated

bombus   (BOM-bus) a buzzing in the ears or stomach
a residual bombus from the sounds of the construction work

bombycine (and **bombycinous**)   (BOM-bi-sin) (bom-BIS-i-nus) silken
sheer and bombycine lingerie

bonamano   (bo-na-MON-o) a tip (gratuity)
a generous bonamano for the carriage driver

borasca (or borasco)   (bo-ROS-ka) (bo-ROS-ko) a thunderstorm or squall
a borasca coming over the headland

borborology   (bor-bor-OL-o-jee) filthy talk
the macho borborology of two waterfront workers

borborygm   (BOR-bo-rim)   a growling in the stomach
embarrassing borborygms during the chamber concert

boreal   (BO-ree-al)   northern
the boreal cold of the North Pole

borecole   (BOR-kole)   kale
a store selling collard greens but no borecole

borne   (bor-NAY)   narrowmindedly provincial or
hidebound
the borne burghers of this benighted town

bottega   (bo-TAY-ga)   a workshop or studio; atelier
an advanced class in a large and drafty bottega

bougie   (boo-ZHEE)   a suppository
a painkiller in bougie form

brachyskelic   (brak-i-SKEL-ik)   short-legged
a brachyskelic and quick halfback

bradypeptic   (brad-i-PEP-tik)   slow to digest
a diligent but slow and bradypeptic reader

brephic   (BREF-ik)   pert. to an early stage of growth; young
the brephic behavior of chimpanzees

bridewell   (BRYD-wel)   a prison
an exurban bridewell built like a fortress

brigue   (breeg)   to gain by intrigue
a Machiavellian aptitude for anticipating and briguing

brimborion   (brim-BO-ree-on)   a foolish charm or
ornament
the sentimental value of an old brimborion

brontide   (BRON-tyd)   a sound like distant thunder
the brontides of artillery a few miles away

brumal   (BROO-mal)   wintry
brumal gusts rattling the windows

brummagem   (BRUM-a-jem)   gaudy and cheap
brummagem costume jewelry

brumous   (BROO-mus) foggy
a gray, brumous dawn

bruslery   (BRUS-le-ree) disturbance
a bruslery attracting a crowd near the Ferris wheel

brusquerie   (BROO-ske-ree) bluntness or brusqueness
an in-your-face brusquerie that clients find abrasive

buccan   (BUK-an) a barbecue
a buccan of mouth-watering steaks on the terrace

buccula   (BUK-yoo-la) double chin
with pouched eyes and a bit of a baby-fat buccula

bugiard   (BUG-yard) a liar
not only a disingenuous person but a shrewd bugiard

buldering   (BUL-de-ring) hot and muggy
an oppressively buldering July afternoon

bumbaste   (bum-BAYST) to spank
to bumbaste the children only after a second warning

C

cabotinage   (ka-bo-ti-NAJH) obvious theatricality or playing to the crowd
a production weakened by the star's campy cabotinage

cache-sex   (kash-SEKS) a skimpy loincloth
an exotic dancer in a cache-sexe and too much mascara

cachexia   (ka-KEK-see-a) a chronically bad outlook or way
of thinking
the unfortunate cachexia of a crime-ravaged community

cacique   (ka-SEEK) a political boss
a corrupt cacique of the back room

cacodoxy   (KAK-o-dok-see) wrong belief or opinion
mere justifications for arrant cacodoxy

cacoeconomy   (ka-ko-ee-KON-o-mee) bad economy or economic management
the debacle of our cacoeconomy

cacogastric   (kak-o-GAS-trik) having bad digestion
a cacogastric, myopic, and misanthropic geezer

cacology   (ka-KOL-o-jee) bad pronunciation or diction
a grammar stickler and real critic of people's cacology

cacotrophy   (ka-KOT-ro-fee) deficient nutrition
infant cacotrophy in a backward region

caducity   (ka-DYOO-si-tee) transitoriness; senility
the caducity and meaninglessness of much media celebrity

cafardise   (ka-far-DEEZ) hypocrisy; humbug
a sanctimonious gathering that will be pure cafardise

calenture   (KAL-en-tyoor) passion; zeal
the cooling of calenture with age

calicrat   (KAL-i-krat) an ant
children's eternal fascination with busy colonies of calicrats

caliginous   (kal-I-jen-us) dark or obscure
the caliginous dungeon

callid   (KAL-id) cunning or crafty
a callid and calculating spymaster

callipygian   (kal-i-PIJ-yun) having beautiful buttocks
a male stripper described as callipygian

callisteia   (kal-i-STY-a) beauty prizes
the awarding of callisteia that's really for local boosterism

callithumpian   (kal-i-THUMP-yun) boisterous and noisy
a callithumpian wedding party

calodemon   (KAL-o-dee-mon) a good spirit
time to conjure up the calodemons

calophantic   (kal-o-FAN-tik) deceiving or pretending by a show of excellence
like the calophantic demonstration of a snake-oil salesman

30

calumet (KAL-yoo-met) a peace pipe
offered a calumet of apologies and flatteries

calvous (KAL-vus) bald
a hulking and calvous bodyguard

camisated (ka-mi-SAY-ted) wearing a shirt on the outside
(over other clothing)
the camisated Chinese citizenry

canaster (ka-NAS-ter) coarse smoking tobacco
an emergency stash of cheap canaster

candent (KAN-dent) glowing white
a wizard holding some kind of candent wand

canicular (kan-IK-yoo-ler) pert. to the dog days
adrift during those canicular weeks

caniculture (KAN-i-kul-cher) raising dogs
a veterinarian's book on caniculture

cap-a-pie (kap-a-PEE) from head to foot
sartorial elegance cap-a-pie

capax (KAY-paks) legally competent
a failing widow who is no longer capax

capelocracy (kap-e-LOK-ra-see) shopkeepers
the capelocracy of England

capitose (KAP-i-tose) large-headed
a short and capitose figure in the shadows

capitulant (kap-IT-yoo-lent) a surrenderer
a capitulant who will see a better day

capripede (KAP-ri-peed) a satyr
a short man with the goaty ears of a capripede

capruncle (KAP-run-kul) an earthen vessel
a crafts class for making handsome capruncles

caprylic (ka-PRIL-ik) smelling like an animal
the steamy and caprylic locker room

31

captation (kap-TAY-shun) speaking or flattering to curry favor
shameless and contemptible captation

carcanet (KAR-ka-net) a gold or jeweled necklace
dancing girls with carcanets and castanets

carceral (KAR-ser-al) pert. to prison
carceral reform

cardialgia (kar-di-AL-juh) heartburn
a little postdelicatessen cardialgia

cardophagus (kar-DOF-a-gus) a donkey
a childhood ride on a cardophagus

carious (KAR-i-us) decayed
the carious carcass of a run-over squirrel

carminative (kar-MIN-a-tiv) (kar-min-AY-tiv) relieving flatulence
tap dancing at home as a terrific carminative exercise

carnifex (KAR-ni-feks) an executioner
the company's de facto carnifex

carnous (KAR-nus) fleshy
the cook's raw and carnous forearms

castorial (kas-TO-ri-al) pert. to a hat
castorial feathers and silver pins

castrensian (kas-TREN-shun) pert. to a camp or campsite
angry about castrensian litter

catachthonian (or **catachthonic**) (kat-ak-THO-ni-an) (kat-ak-THON-ik) underground or subterranean
a whole catachthonian network of escape routes

catadupe (KAT-a-dyoop) a waterfall
the precipice of a spectacular catadupe

cataglottism (kat-a-GLOT-iz-um) tongue-kissing
finding cataglottism in public repugnant

catamenial (kat-a-MEE-nee-al) menstrual
a pill for catamenial discomfort

cataphatic   (kat-a-FAT-ik) affirmative
a mostly cataphatic response

cataskeuastic   (kat-a-skyoo-AS-tik) constructive
a play doctor much in demand for his imagination and cataskeu-astic know-how

Catharan   (KATH-ar-an) a puritan
an illiberal Catharan

catholicon   (ka-THOL-i-kon) a panacea
a ridiculous mail-order catholicon

cauponate   (KAW-po-nayt) to traffic or trade in for profit
a smooth talker who cauponates and corrupts the name of religion

causatum   (kaw-ZAY-tum) an effect or result
an unforeseen and happy causatum

cautela   (kaw-TEE-la) a cautionary rule or reminder
a parting cautela

cautelous   (KAW-tel-us) cautious or prudent; crafty or sly
investors who are reckless rather than cautelous

caveat actor   (KAY-ve-at AK-tor) let the doer beware
unsafe sex, or caveat actor

cavillation   (ka-vil-LAY-shun) the raising of quibbles
a person who can always be counted on for some annoying cavillation

cebocephalic   (see-bo-se-FAL-ik) monkey-headed
a short haircut that made him look cebocephalic

cecity   (SEE-si-tee) blindness
their ideological cecity

ceduous   (SED-yoo-us) fit (a tree) to be felled
an old and ceduous oak

celation   (see-LAY-shun) concealing pregnancy or childbirth
the tragedy of third-world celation

celative (SEL-a-tiv) adapted for concealment
a beautifully celative weapon

celibatarian (se-li-ba-TAIR-i-an) a bachelor
a celibatarian but not at all a self-reliant one

celsitude (SEL-si-tyood) high position or rank
the fat prerogatives of political celsitude

centoculated (sen-TOK-yoo-lay-ted) hundred-eyed
the seemingly centoculated security forces

centuple (SEN-tyoo-pul) a hundredfold
quite vindictive and wishing him centuple miseries

centuply (SEN-tyoo-plee) a hundredfold
to increase profits centuply

cepaceous (see-PAY-shus) onionlike
an unmistakeable cepaceous odor

cepivorous (se-PIV-or-us) onion-eating
the breath of cepivorous peasants

cervicose (SER-vi-kose) having a strong neck
a couple of brawny and cervicose moving men

cervisial (ser-VIZ-ee-al) pert. to beer
a stale cervisial smell

chalastic (ka-LAS-tik) laxative
the chalastic effect of coffee

chalybeus (ka-LIB-ee-us) steel blue
an elegant chalybeus cigarette case

chantage (shan-TAZH) blackmail
microphones, photography, and the technology of chantage

chaogenous (kay-OJ-en-us) born amid chaos
a provisional, chaogenous treaty

chapter of accidents (CHAP-ter uv AK-si-dents) a series
of chance occurrences
in retrospect an astonishing chapter of accidents

charactery (KAR-ak-te-ree) writing
the charactery of some alien language

charientism (KAR-ee-en-ti-zum) an artfully veiled insult
charientisms that sailed over his head

chartaceous (kar-TAY-shus) papery
a delicate and almost chartaceous pastry

chaumière (sho-mi-AYR) a thatched cottage
picturesque chaumières in the countryside

checkle (CHEK-ul) to laugh violently
the chilling feeling at hearing him checkle

chersonese (KER-so-neez) (KER-so-neese) peninsula
a windswept chersonese

cherte (CHER-te) tenderness or affection
a warm display of cherte that really surprised her

chinch (chinch) a bedbug
a children's story about an anemic chinch

chirognostic (ky-rog-NOS-tik) able to distinguish right from left
not chirognostic enough to give reliable directions

chirography (ky-ROG-ruf-ee) handwriting or penmanship
third-grade chirography

chirotony (ky-ROT-o-nee) voting by a show of hands
the old town-hall meeting tradition of chirotony

choller (CHOL-er) a double chin
tickling her bow-tied uncle's choller

choragus (ko-RAY-gus) a choirmaster or bandleader
an experienced choragus who can get the most out of mediocre voices

chrematistic (kree-ma-TIS-tik) preoccupied with becoming rich
a horde of chrematistic yuppies

chreotechnics (kree-o-TEK-niks) the science of the useful arts (e.g., commerce and farming)
more attention from economists to chreotechnics

chryselephantine (kris-el-ef-AN-tin) (kris-el-ef-AN-tyn) of gold and ivory
a chryselephantine amulet

chrysostomic (kry-so-STO-mik) golden-tongued (eloquent)
a chrysostomic poet of the streets

chthonian (THO-ni-an) infernal
the chthonian depths of poverty

ci-devant (see-de-VON) former or erstwhile
a ci-devant museum curator

cibation (si-BAY-shun) feeding or taking food
some initial cibation just to feel human

cicurate (SIK-yoo-rayt) to tame or to make mild
the patience necessary to cicurate the three cubs

circumambulate (ser-kum-AM-byoo-layt) to approach indirectly; beat around the bush
to return warily and slowly circumambulate

circumbendibus (ser-kum-BEN-di-bus) a roundabout process; circumlocution
the circumbendibuses and catch-22s of bureaucracy

circumcrescent (ser-kum-KRES-ent) growing around
an old park statue with circumscrescent vines

circumforaneous (ser-kum-for-AY-nee-us) wandering from market to market
happily circumforaneous in springtime Paris

circumfulgent (ser-kum-FUL-jent) shining around
a circumfulgent glow around the top of the building

circummure (ser-kum-MYOOR) to wall in or around
to circummure the swimming pool for safety reasons

circumvest (ser-kum-VEST) to clothe or enwrap
circumvested herself in her boyfriend's bathrobe

clairsentient (klair-SEN-she-ent) perceiving the normally unperceivable
a believably clairsentient housewife

clancular (KLAN-kyoo-ler) secret, private, or underhand
clancular negotiations at the palace

clarigation (klar-i-GAY-shun) a recital of wrongs before declaring war
a ringing clarigation to unite the people

clastic (KLAS-tik) having separable pieces; take-apartable
one of those clastic toy puzzles of wood

clatterfart (or **clatterfert**) (KLAT-er-fart) (KLAT-er-fert) a chatterer or babbler
making a big journey in a little car with a bunch of clatterfarts

claudicant (KLAW-di-kent) limping
a scary movie about some cloaked and claudicant stalker

claviature (KLAV-ee-a-tyoor) a piano or organ keyboard
claviatures that no longer have ivory keys

clerisy (KLER-i-see) intellectuals, literati, or scholars
a difficult book of interest only to members of the modern-day clerisy

clinamen (kly-NAY-men) an inclination or bias
the obvious racial clinamen of her constituency

clipsome (KLIP-sum) nicely embraceable
my lovely and clipsome wife

clivose (KLAI-vose) hilly or steep
a route more rugged and clivose

clou (kloo) a center of attention; cynosure
the unmistakeable clou of the dance—the belle of the ball

clysmic (KLIZ-mik) washing or cleansing
a clysmic solution

clyssus (KLIZ-us) quintessence
the very clyssus of mediocrity

37

clyster   (KLIS-ter) an enema
embarrassed to ask in the pharmacy for a clyster bag

coacervate   (ko-a-SER-vayt) (ko-AS-er-vayt) piled up or collected into a crowd
where you'll please find all your coacervate belongings

coact   (ko-AKT) to work together
learning to coact and communicate

coactive   (ko-AK-tiv) compulsory or obligatory
sort of a coactive favor

coadjument   (ko-AJ-oo-ment) mutual assistance
to begin a process of coadjument to benefit both parties

cochleare   (kok-lee-AY-ree) a spoonful (medicinally)
a healthy cochleare of chicken soup

codon   (KO-don) a small bell
a codon affixed to the Dutch door

coeliginous   (see-LI-jen-us) heaven-born
somehow not aware that she was not only ethereal but coeliginous

coenaculous   (see-NAK-yoo-lus) supper-loving
too coenaculous to spoil things with a late-afternoon snack

coetaneous   (ko-e-TAY-nee-us) coming into existence at the same time
their coetaneous inventions

coevality   (ko-e-VAL-i-tee) equality of age
kept emphasizing their coevality and supposed compatibility

cogitabund   (KOJ-it-a-bund) deep in thought or pensive
a person looking particularly cogitabund of late

cohonestation   (ko-ho-nes-TAY-shun) honoring another with one's company
my ever-generous cohonestation

coinonomic   (ko-in-o-NOM-ik) pert. to joint or combined enterprise or management
the potential coinonomic problems of a hasty merger

collabent   (ko-LAY-bent) collapsing in the middle or sunken
a collabent kayak

collibration   (kol-i-BRAY-shun) comparison
a simple collibration of the two car models

collop   (KOL-op) a small piece or slice
a succulent collop of mango

colluctation   (kol-uk-TAY-shun) struggling, contention, or wrangling
the colluctation of two massive egos

collugency   (kol-LOO-jen-see) mutual sorrow or mourning
an assassination that brought about a collugency of the two enemies

collutory (or collutorium)   (KOL-yoo-to-ree) (kol-oo-TOR-ee-um) mouthwash
a small slug of collutory before the concert

colluvies   (kol-OO-vi-eez) collected garbage or filth
the reek of curbside colluvies

comestion   (ko-MES-chun) eating
seemed too busy even for comestion

commentitious   (kom-en-TISH-us) fabricated or untruthful
a colorful but commentitious anecdote

commere   (KOM-air) a gossiping woman
avoiding the nattering of the porch-front commeres

commoratory   (KOM-or-a-to-ree) a place to live or dwell; habitation
using an abandoned barge as an emergency commoratory

compatchment   (kom-PACH-ment) a thing patched together
a speech that was kind of a ridiculous compatchment of platitudes

compathy   (KOM-pa-thee) shared feeling
compathy among the disaster's victims

compellation   (kom-pel-LAY-shun) a way of addressing or calling upon somebody
getting used to the U.S. Marines' raw style of compellation

compellative   (kom-PEL-a-tiv) one's (addressed) name
much preferring the compellative Rocky

compendiate   (kom-PEN-dee-ayt) to sum up concisely
to compendiate the two-part article nicely

comperendinate   (kom-per-EN-di-nayt) to procrastinate
a vow not to comperendinate until tomorrow

compital   (KOM-pi-tal) pert. to a crossroads
one of those compital moments in life

complanate   (KOM-pla-nayt) to place in a horizontal or level position
a mechanism to complanate the ramp

compotation   (kom-po-TAY-shun) drinking together
an enjoyable downtown compotation with the girls

comprecation   (kom-pre-KAY-shun) a praying together
the team's private comprecation before the game

compursion   (kom-PER-shun) pursing (one's lips)
the million-dollar cover girl's seductive compursions

concionator   (KON-shun-ay-ter) a haranguer or preacher
a familiar concionator ranting at the edge of the park

conclamant   (kon-KLAY-ment) calling out in unison
a conclamant response

concoquent   (kon-KO-kwent) digestive
some concoquent distress after gorging himself on mushrooms

concubinage   (kon-KYOO-bi-nij) cohabitation of the unmarried
his generation's frowning on—or envy of—concubinage

concubitus   (kon-KYOO-bi-tus) sexual intercourse; coitus
senior citizens accused of overage concubitus

conculcation   (kon-kul-KAY-shun) a treading under foot
the government's conculcation of subversive elements

40

concupiscence   (kon-KYOO-pi-sens) lust
a concupiscence unfortunately not reciprocated

concupiscible   (kon-KYOO-pi-si-bul) to be longed or
lusted after; most desirable
a pleasant but hardly concupiscible date

condecent   (KON-de-sent) fit, appropriate, or becoming
a garish wreath that was not at all condecent

condisciple   (kon-di-SY-pul) a fellow student
certain responsibilities to one's condisciples

conductitious   (kon-duk-TISH-us) for hire; hired
a conductitious boat to get upriver

confariation   (kon-far-i-AY-shun) conversation
*the hypocritical confariation of people who basically dislike each
other*

confarreation   (kon-fa-re-AY-shun) marriage or a wedding
a well-attended alfresco confarreation

confelicity   (kon-fe-LIS-i-tee) joy or pleasure in another's
happiness
his gift for spontaneous altruism and confelicity

congaudence   (kon-GAWD-ense) a celebrating or rejoicing together
their noisy congaudence after passing the bar exam

congenerous   (kon-JEN-er-us) akin in nature or character;
of the same kind
congenerous hardware from different computer manufacturers

congustable   (kon-GUS-ta-bul) having a similar flavor or
taste
bad scotch and congustable iodine

connictation   (kon-nik-TAY-shun) a winking or twinkling
with the eye
the practiced connictation of a roué

conquassate   (kon-KWAS-sayt) shake violently
fear when an elevator begins to conquassate

41

consectaneous (or **consectary**) (kon-sek-TAY-nee-us) (kon-SEK-ta-ree) following as a consequence
a second accident that was definitely consectaneous

consenescence (kon-se-NES-ense) growing old together
a contented consenescence in Florida

consiliary (kon-SIL-i-a-ree) giving counsel
a helpfully consiliary paralegal

consociate (kon-SO-shee-ayt) to introduce (people)
hoping to consociate Bill and Eleanor at his party

consopite (KON-so-pyt) to lull to sleep or stupefy
some murmurous white noise to consopite her

conspectable (kon-SPEK-ta-bul) obvious
his off-kilter and conspectable toupee

conspue (kon-SPYOO) to spit upon
angrily conspued the compromising photograph

conspurcated (kon-SPER-kay-ted) corrupted or defiled
conspurcated and ultimately jaded by all the bribery

consternate (KON-ster-nayt) to dismay or terrify
a weird guest who thoroughly consternated the help

constringe (kon-STRINJ) to squeeze or compress
one of those huge machines to constringe wrecked cars

constuprate (KON-stoo-prayt) to violate or deflower
punishment for irregulars who constuprated prisoners

consuetude (KON-swe-tyood) social custom or convention
the taboos of island consuetude

contabulate (kon-TAB-yoo-layt) to use boards for flooring
to contabulate the new bathhouses

contesserate (kon-TES-er-ayt) allied in friendship
once estranged but now contesserate

conticent (KON-ti-sent) silent
uneasy in the presence of the conticent visitor

contignation (kon-tig-NAY-shun) a timber framework
the inn's very old contignation

contortuplicate (kon-tor-TOO-pli-kit) twisted and
entangled
a contortuplicate wad of thread

contraconscientious (or **contra-conscient**) (kon-tra-kon-
shee-EN-shus) (kon-tra-KON-shee-ent) against conscience
*a vote that she would consider to be personally
contraconscientious*

contralateral (kon-tra-LAT-er-al) on the opposite side (of
the body)
a pistol and a contralateral knife

contranitent (kon-tra-NI-tent) struggling in opposition
two irreconcilably contranitent factions

contrapletal (kon-tra-PLEE-tal) polar and complementary
contrapletal viewpoints or a kind of dualism

contrectation (kon-trek-TAY-shun) touching or fingering
*increased contrectation in the push-button, computer keyboard
age*

contrist (or **contristate**) (kon-TRIST) (kon-TRIS-tayt)
to sadden
a needless war to contrist all involved

contrude (kon-TROOD) to crowd or jam together
unwise to contrude healthy people with patients in a small room

coprolalia (kop-ro-LAYL-yuh) foul speech
the gratuitous coprolalia of much cable-TV comedy

coprology (kop-ROL-o-jee) filthy or obscene literature
coprology in the form of cheap pulp paperbacks

coriaceous (ko-ri-AY-shus) leathery or leatherlike
a coriaceous but fake upholstery

cornuted (kor-NYOO-ted) cuckolded
finally confronted by her cornuted husband

corrivate   (KAR-i-vayt) to cause to run or flow together
a plan to corrivate the three tributaries

corvée   (kor-VAY) an unpleasant but unavoidable job or
task
the corvée of breaking the bad news

corybantic   (kor-i-BAN-tik) a frenzied dance
*a spectator jumping in among the drummers and doing a
whirling corybantic*

costive   (KOS-tiv) constipated
as saddle-sore as a costive cowboy

covinous   (KUV-i-nus) fraudulent or deceitful
a covinous health-club contract

crassitude   (KRAS-i-tyood) stupidity or ignorance;
thickness
the probable crassitude of scandal-sheet readers

crastin   (KRAS-tin) the morrow or the day after
arrive Tuesday and begin work on the crastin

creatic   (kree-AT-ik) pert. to flesh
a painter's knowledge of creatic hues

crebrous   (KREE-brus) frequent
a crebrous occurrence

credenda   (kre-DEN-da) things to be believed
the denomination's requisite credenda

crembalum   (KREM-ba-lum) Jew's-harp
the folksy twang of the crembalum

cresty   (KRES-tee) afflicted with hemorrhoids
the cresty agonies of a taxi driver in the city of potholes

crève-coeur   (KRAYV-ker) heartbreak
recovering slowly from the doldrums of crève-coeur

cribration   (krib-RAY-shun) sifting
the careful cribration of data from many sources

crine   (KRYNE) hair or a head of hair
seeking treatments to enhance his sparse crine

crinicultural   (krin-i-KUL-tyoor-al) pert. to hair care or growth
skeptical about the product's crinicultural claims

crinkum   (KRING-kum) venereal disease
about as welcome as tertiary crinkum

crisic   (KRY-sik) pert. to a crisis
thinking ahead to possible crisic options and a worse-case scenario

crocodility   (krok-o-DIL-i-tee) false reasoning
the crocodility of base racial propaganda

cruciation   (kroo-shi-AY-shun) torment or torture
a forced conversation that was a form of cruciation for each of them

cruentous   (kroo-EN-tus) bloody
as cruentous as a thriving abattoir

cryptodynamic   (krip-to-dy-NAM-ik) pert. to or having hidden power
the cryptodynamic intrigues of a gray eminence

cubicular   (kyoo-BIK-yoo-ler) pert. to the bedroom
cubicular secrets

cultellated   (KUL-te-lay-ted) having a knifelike edge
a large paper clasp with almost cultellated edges

cunctipotent   (kung-TIP-o-tent) all-powerful
a cunctipotent despot

cunctitenant   (kung-TIT-en-ant) possessing or holding all things
a planned air attack on a cunctitenant supply depot

curple   (KER-pul) buttocks
working on firming up her thighs and her curple

cursitate   (KER-si-tayt) to run here and there; flit
to get together on Saturday mornings and cursitate at the farmer's market

curtate   (KER-tayt) comparatively short in time
  complaining about their curtate foreplay

cyanotype   (sy-AN-o-typ) a blueprint
  a cynotype for reform of the city's school system

cymotrichous   (sy-MOT-ri-kus) having wavy hair
  the cymotrichous Breck girl

cynocephalous   (sy-no-SEF-a-lus) dog-faced or -headed
  a squat, cynocephalous first sergeant

Cyprian   (SIP-ree-en) a prostitute
  a onetime truck-stop Cyprian

D

dacity   (DAS-i-tee) ability; activity; energy
  his prodigious dacity

dactylogram   (DAK-ti-lo-gram) a fingerprint
  a modern painting looking like an ornate dactylogram

dactyloid   (DAK-ti-loyd) fingerlike
  some kind of dactyloid Italian pastry

Daphnean   (DAF-nee-an) shy or bashful
  a hesitant, Daphnean smile

darg   (darg) a day's work
  happy to get in a full darg

dasypygal   (das-i-PY-gal) having hairy buttocks
  museum watercolors of dasypygal cave people

dation   (DAY-shun) giving that is not voluntary
  twist-your-arm dation worded as "suggested contribution"

deacon   (DEE-kun) to pack fruit so that the best is on top
  greengrocers who deacon their peaches and plums daily

dealbate   (dee-AL-bayt) to bleach
  thoughts of dealbating his grizzled mustache

debarrass (dee-BAR-us) to disembarrass or relieve
to debarrass Nancy of her extra chocolate bar

debellator (de-bel-AY-ter) a subduer or conqueror
the ruthless debellators of the Dark Ages

deblaterate (de-BLAT-er-ayt) to prate
finding a traveling companion who doesn't continually deblaterate

debord (dee-BORD) to overflow
fears that rain would cause the stream to debord

decadescent (dek-a-DES-ent) beginning or tending to decay
a decadescent floral spray

decatize (DEK-a-tyz) to moisten or steam to uncurl
hoping to decatize their old and brittle family photographs

decoct (dee-KOKT) to boil down
to decoct the report to its essentials

decollation (dee-kol-AY-shun) beheading
capital punishment by decollation

decubation (dek-yoo-BAY-shun) lying down
a comfortable employees' room for rest breaks and decubation

decubitus (dee-KYOO-bi-tus) a way of lying down
often falling asleep in a fetal decubitus

decumbent (dee-KUM-bent) lying down or stretched at length
a cavalry squad decumbent on the ridge

decumbiture (dee-KUM-bi-tyoor) confinement to a sickbed
his stubbornness during his decumbiture

decuple (DEK-up-ul) tenfold
a decuple margin of profit

dedition (de-DISH-un) surrender
her reluctant dedition of an important piece of evidence

defervescence   (dee-fer-VES-ens) a cooling down
a period of defervescence for the lovers

defluxion   (dee-FLUK-shun) a runny nose
sniffles and defluxion

defossion   (dee-FOSH-un) burial alive
a horrible nightmare about accidental defossion

defunct   (dee-FUNKT) a dead person
a gory film about walking defuncts

defunction   (dee-FUNG-shun) death
marking the final defunction of an unforgettable era

defunctive   (dee-FUNG-tiv) pert. to death
well-planned defunctive arrangements

dégagé   (day-ga-ZHAY) casual or easygoing
wearing a plaid cap with a dégagé air

deglutition   (dee-gloo-TISH-un) swallowing
chewing gum not being intended for deglutition

dégringolade   (day-gran-go-LOD) a speedy decline or deterioration; downfall
the dégringolade of a profligate playboy

dehort   (dee-HORT) to loudly or strongly advise against or dissuade from
repeatedly had to dehort her from quitting her job

deipotent   (day-I-po-tent) having divine power
a supervisor who thinks she's deipotent

deisidaimonia   (dy-si-dy-MO-nee-a) fear of supernatural powers
the childlike deisidaimonia of certain primitive tribes

deivirile   (day-IV-ir-il) both divine and human
a fantasy film with an animated puppet as a deivirile sage

dejecta   (dee-JEK-ta) excrement
dodging clumps of dejecta on the park grass

delassation   (del-a-SAY-shun) weariness or fatigue
good overtime pay but incredible delassation

deletitious   (del-e-TISH-us) pert. to erasing or erasure
a comprehensive and deletitious rewrite

delibate   (DEL-i-bayt) to taste or sip
the bartender's invitation to delibate a cocktail he had created

delibation   (del-i-BAY-shun) a slight taste or knowledge of something
gave him a delibation of life in an office

deligible   (DEL-i-ga-bul) worthy to be chosen
a candidate definitely deligible

delitescent   (del-i-TES-ent) lying hidden or latent
to throw light on its delitescent cause or explanation

delubrum   (de-LU-brum) a shrine or sanctuary
a home that became a kind of musical delubrum for young composers

démêlé   (day-me-LAY) a debate, argument, or quarrel
a stupid démêlé about their hotel accommodations

demephitize   (dee-MEF-i-tyz) to remove or purify of foul air
a railroad that should demephitize its stale old smoking cars

demission   (dee-MISH-un) a relinquishing or resignation
the demanded demission of congressional special privileges

demonette   (DEE-mo-net) a little demon
a wild younger son who is a demonette in training

demulcent   (dee-MUL-sent) soothing or softening
a minty, demulcent cream

dendrophilous   (den-DROF-i-lus) living in trees or tree-loving
the dendrophilous koala

denegate   (DEN-e-gayt) to deny or refuse
their unwillingness to denegate their younger girl anything

dentagra   (den-TAG-ra) a toothache
a pulsating dentagra

dentigerous   (den-TI-jer-us) having teeth
an old man but still dentigerous

dentiscalp   (DEN-ti-skalp) a toothpick
a gangster who kept colored dentiscalps in his upper pocket

denudate   (dee-NYOO-dayt) to strip or lay bare
a developer's plan to denudate the tract

deoppilate   (dee-OP-i-layt) to free of an obstacle or obstruction
to deoppilate the outer lane after the crash

deordination   (dee-or-di-NAY-shun) a disorder or abnormality
a slight deordination in his walk

deosculate   (dee-OS-kyoo-layt) to kiss affectionately
not too shy to deosculate in public

depatriate   (dee-PAY-tree-ayt) to renounce residence in one's country; expatriate oneself
criticized the country so much he should have depatriated

depauperate   (dee-PAW-pe-rayt) poor or impoverished
the city's most depauperate quarter

dépaysé   (day-pay-ee-ZAY) in unfamiliar surroundings or out of one's element
feeling old and a little dépaysé at a riotous rock concert

depilous   (DEP-i-lus) hairless
a small depilous dog

depone   (dee-PONE) to swear under oath
unable to depone to a single one of the allegations

deprehension   (dep-re-HEN-shun) catching in the act
the satisfying deprehension of a neighborhood burglar

deracinated   (dee-RAS-in-ay-ted) uprooted
a deracinated survivor of the war

deric   (DER-ik) pert. to skin
the deric art of tattooing

derisable (dee-RIZ-a-bul) deserving mockery or mockable
a halfhearted and derisable attempt

desiderium (des-i-DEER-ee-um) a feeling of yearning or loss
an abandonment that left the child with an overwhelming desiderium

desinent (DES-i-nent) terminal or closing
the desinent phase of the operation

desipient (de-SIP-ee-ent) foolish, silly, or trifling
a self-important columnist with desipient opinions

despiciency (des-PISH-en-see) contempt
a cowardly act deserving only despiciency

desponsate (des-PON-sayt) married
despondent about not being desponsate

desucration (dee-soo-KRAY-shun) depriving of sugar
the desucration of a reformed chocoholic

détraqué (day-tra-KAY) a deranged person
a wretched détraqué incapable of holding a job

deuterogamy (dyoot-er-OG-a-mee) one's second marriage
my partner in deuterogamy

deutoplasm (DYOOT-o-plaz-um) egg yolk
the cholesterol in deutoplasm

deversary (de-VER-sa-ree) a lodging house or inn
a rustic but comfortable deversary up in the mountains

devorative (dee-VOR-a-tiv) swallowable whole
succulent and devorative cherrystone clams

diallelous (dy-a-LEE-lus) arguing in a circle
your clever but clearly diallelous argument

diaskeuast (dy-a-SKYOO-ast) an editor
a middling writer but a terrific diaskeuast

didascalic (did-as-KAL-ik) pert. to a teacher; didactic; preceptive
didascalic recordings in intermediate French

51

dies faustus   (DY-eez FAW-stus) lucky day
her pipe dreams of some all-solving dies faustus

diffareation   (dif-far-ee-AY-shun) divorce
separation followed by eventual diffareation

diffidation   (dif-i-DAY-shun) a severing of peaceful
relations
their not so reluctant diffidation

digitigrade   (DIJ-it-i-grayd) tiptoeing or on tiptoes
digitigrade stagehands backstage during the performance

digladiation   (dy-glad-i-AY-shun) verbal wrangling
some pretty good digladiation at the debate

dilaniate   (di-LAY-nee-ayt) to tear to pieces
Joe's impatience to dilaniate the steak tartare

dimication   (di-mi-KAY-shun) fighting or strife
frowning on any dimication or even disagreement

dimidiate   (di-MID-ee-ayt) to divide in half
an agreement to dimidiate the proceeds

dimissory   (DIM-i-so-ree) giving permission to go
mother's dimissory nod

dioristic   (dy-o-RIS-tik) distinguishing, distinctive, or
defining
a dioristic but not gonzo approach in his journalism

di petto   (dee PET-o) sung in a natural (rather than falsetto) voice
the falsetto and di petto mixture in doo-wop

dipsetic   (dip-SET-ik) thirst-causing
a cleverly dipsetic bowl of salty peanuts on the bar

dirigent   (dir-i-JENT) guiding or directive
a helpfully dirigent floor plan

discalced   (dis-KALST) barefoot
discalced picnickers dancing on the grass

disceptation   (di-sep-TAY-shun) debate or disputation
a matter of some disceptation

discinct (di-SINGT) loosely dressed or partly undressed
discinct actors and actresses backstage

disconscient (dis-KON-shent) lacking conscience; unconscientious
an opportunistic and disconscient political hack

discruciate (dis-KROO-shi-ayt) to torment or torture
discruciated the other tenants nightly with his heavy-metal CDs

dishabille (di-sa-BEEL) loosely dressed or partly undressed
came to the front door yawning and dishabille

dispendious (dis-PEN-di-us) expensive
a known but more dispendious brand

dispunct (dis-PUNGT) to mark for erasure; to distinguish or set off
zestfully dispuncted all of Paul's editorial additions

dissight (dis-SYT) an eyesore
a discordant, ultramodern annex that was an architectural dissight

dissympathy (dis-SIM-pa-thee) indifference
impossible to exaggerate her utter dissympathy

distrait (dis-TRAY) worriedly preoccupied or absent-minded
a tour guide who appeared to be a little distrait

ditation (di-TAY-shun) financial enrichment
the ditation of greedy and undeserving people

ditionary (DISH-i-ner-ee) under rule or domination
a ditionary population that all along resisted the Occupation

diurnation (dy-er-NAY-shun) sleeping during the day
the night watchman's life of diurnation

diuturnal (dy-yoo-TER-nal) lasting
a diuturnal memorial

divellent (di-VEL-lent) causing to separate or come apart
had a divellent influence

diversiloquent   (dy-ver-SIL-o-kwent) speaking in different ways
the diversiloquent gifts of a leader with different constituencies

diversivolent   (dy-ver-SIV-o-lent) wanting trouble or contention
the disruption of a diversivolent outsider

diversory   (di-VER-so-ree) a place of shelter along the way
a cousin's home as a convenient diversory

divitiate   (di-VISH-i-ayt) to enrich
a generous gift that will certainly divitiate the museum's Impressionist collection

divulgate   (di-VUL-gayt) published
divulgate personal letters

doctiloquent   (dok-TIL-o-kwent) speaking learnedly
the doctiloquent and deep-voiced moderator

dolent   (DO-lent) sad or sorrowful
such a dolent face

dolichoderous   (dol-i-KOD-er-us) having a long neck
those swanlike, dolichoderous models

dolichopodous   (dol-i-KOP-o-dus) having long feet
some kind of dolichopodous dinosaur

dolichoproscopic   (dol-i-ko-pro-SOP-ik) having a long and narrow face
a dour and dolichoproscopic maitre d'

doli incapax   (DO-ly IN-ka-paks) incapable of guilt
a career criminal and psychopath deemed doli incapax

dolorific   (dol-er-IF-ik) causing pain, anguish, or grief
a death that was a dolorific loss for an entire community

dolorifuge   (do-LOR-i-fyooj) something that dispels grief
news of his inheritance seeming to be quite a dolorifuge

dominial   (do-MIN-ee-al) pert. to ownership
all of his various dominial papers in a strongbox

---

dominical   (do-MIN-i-kal) pert. to Sunday
dominical family outings to the country

dorbel   (DOR-bel) a dull-witted pedant
a tenured and fully ensconced dorbel

do ut des   (do ut deez) tit for tat
an unwritten organization policy of do ut des

dulcarnon   (dul-KAR-non) dilemma
a painful dulcarnon

durance   (DYOOR-ans) imprisonment or confinement
a long term of durance as a prisoner of war

dysnomy   (DIS-no-mee) a bad legal system or bad
legislation
talk of dysnomy when the crime rate goes up

dysphoria   (dis-FO-ri-a) a general bad feeling
a growing dysphoria among the residents

dysthymic   (dis-THY-mik) morbidly anxious or dejected
a dysthymic loner but no criminal

E

---

eburnean   (eb-OR-ne-an) (eb-ER-ne-an) ivorylike
a slightly yellowish, eburnean disk of glow-in-the-dark plastic

ecceity   (ek-SEE-i-tee) the quality of being present
a reminder that on the stage ecceity sometimes has to be taught

ecchymotic (or ecchymosed)   (ek-i-MOT-ik) (EK-i-most)
black-and-blue
arms that were ecchymotic from his first parallel-bars class

ectal   (EK-tal) exterior, external, or outside
a better ectal design

edacious   (ee-DAY-shus) pert. to eating
a boor with the edacious manners of an anteater

edea (ed-EE-a) the external genitals
*anatomically incorrect male and female dolls still not showing
the edea*

edentulous (ee-DEN-tyoo-lus) toothless
a rubbery, edentulous smile

educand (ED-yoo-kand) a student
textbooks and a classroom but no educands

effigiate (ef-FIJ-i-ayt) to make a picture or sculpture of;
portray
a proposal to effigiate the town war hero

efflagitate (ef-FLAJ-i-tayt) to desire or demand eagerly
a couple who always efflagitated the best seats in the house

effraction (ef-FRAK-shun) a breaking into; burglary
an effraction of the locked storage room

egest (ee-JEST) to defecate
fortunately egested the bad food within an hour

egestuous (ee-JES-tyoo-us) very poor and needy
not homeless but egestuous

egolatrous (ee-GOL-a-trus) self-worshiping
an egolatrous, second-rate crooner

egritude (or **aegritude)** (EG-ri-tyood) sickness
an enjoyable retirement free of egritude or second thoughts

egrimony (EG-ri-mo-nee) deep sorrow
a sense of egrimony throughout the congregation

eidolism (ai-DO-liz-um) belief in ghosts
occultism and eidolism

ejulate (EJ-yoo-layt) to wail or lament
the terrible sound of mistreated animals ejulating in their cages

eleemosynate (el-lee-MOS-i-nayt) to give out alms or
handouts
always carried some loose change so she could eleemosynate

eloin (or **eloign**)   (ee-LOIN) to remove (oneself) to a distance
a determination to eloin herself after their breakup

elozable   (el-LO-za-bul) open to flattery
a very insecure and elozable widow

elumbated   (ee-LUM-bay-ted) weakened in the loins
a bit punchy and elumbated after their honeymoon

emacity   (ee-MAS-i-tee) an itch to buy
an uncontrollable emacity on payday

embrocate   (EM-bro-kayt) to rub linament on (an afflicted area)
a nice nurse to embrocate her sore leg

embusqué   (on-bus-KAY) one trying to get out of military service
accused of being a Vietnam embusqué

emesis   (EM-e-sis) vomiting
sounds of convulsive emesis in the rest room

emication   (em-i-KAY-shun) sparking or sputtering
the flare's brilliant emication in the rain

emiction   (ee-MIK-shun) urine or urination
a little vial of emiction as a laboratory sample

empasm   (em-PAZ-um) fragrant powder
an after-shower dash of empasm

emperiment   (em-PER-i-ment) physical deterioration
not just general wear-and-tear but more serious emperiment of the park's gazebos

empleomania   (em-plee-o-MAY-nee-a) a craving for holding public office
a case of small-town empleomania

emporeutic   (em-po-ROO-tik) pert. to merchandise
many emporeutic shipments that created an actual surplus

emporté (on-por-TAY) irritated beyond self-possession or "losing one's cool"
imperative not to become emporté in this situation

empressement (on-pres-MON) a show of affection
the hollow empressements and gush of show biz

emptional (EMP-shun-ul) buyable
display goods that were not emptional

emptitious (em-TISH-us) corruptible or capable of being bought
your classic banana republic's ever emptitious customs officials

empyreuma (em-pi-ROO-ma) a burnt smell
an acrid empyreuma in the cellar

emunction (ee-MUNG-shun) nose wiping
a drippy cold requiring his constant and discreet emunction

emunctory (ee-MUNG-to-ree) pert. to nose blowing
the kids' laughter at Uncle Larry's deafening emunctory fanfares

enatic (ee-NAT-ik) related on the mother's side
enatic cousins

enceinte (on-SANT) (on-SAYNT) pregnant
a girl young but visibly enceinte

encratic (en-KRAT-ik) self-controlled or abstinent
admirably encratic for the first two weeks

endimanché (on-di-mon-SHAY) dressed up in Sunday clothes; in festal attire
parks teeming with endimanché strollers

enfelon (en-FEL-un) to infuriate
a male unresponsiveness that increasingly enfeloned Mary

engleim (en-GLAYM) to make sticky or slimy
a humid atmosphere that only engleimed the new coat of white paint

ennomic (en-NOM-ik) lawful or within the law
irritating but ennomic transgressions

ensorcell (en-SOR-sel) to put a spell on
thinking of ways to ensorcell Mike's handsome brother

ensynopticity (en-sin-op-TI-si-tee) the ability to take a general or overall view
possessing the qualities of both ensynopticity and compassion

ental (EN-tal) inner, interior, or inside
the vehicle's revolutionary ental design

entêté (on-te-TAY) extremely stubborn
an entêté school principal who should have retired ten years earlier

entheos (EN-the-os) inspiration or actuating power
a sense of great entheos in his poetry

entregent (on-tre-ZHAN) social intercourse
the famously witty entregent of the Algonquin Round Table

entremets (ON-tre-may) side dishes
a potluck feast with splendid entremets

envergure (on-ver-GYOOR) a stretch or span of the outstretched arms (anthropology)
stretched and formed an envergure to describe its length

eoan (ee-O-an) pert. to dawn or the east
the red bruise of the eoan horizon

epergne (e-PERN) (ee-PAIRN) a central ornament on a table
a long table needing an epergne or at least a bowl of flowers

ephebic (e-FEE-bik) entering manhood
his ephebic younger son nearing his bar mitzvah

ephectic (e-FEK-tik) always suspending judgment
being patiently ephectic only up to a point

ephemeron (e-FEM-er-on) anything short-lived
a glorious day in the sun that proved to be an ephemeron

epicedial (or **epicedian**) (ep-i-SEE-dee-al) (ep-i-SEE-dee-an) elegiac or funereal
the epicedial tone of the symphony's last movement

epicurity   (ep-i-KYOOR-i-tee) sensual or luxurious living
dreams of carefree epicurity in sunny Mexico

epideistic   (ep-i-dee-IS-tik) zealously religious
an epideistic splinter group

epimyth   (EP-i-mith) the moral of a story
a long-winded account with no epimyth as a payoff

epinician   (ep-i-NISH-an) in celebration of victory
an impromptu epinician parade along the boardwalk

epiphenomenon   (ep-i-fen-OM-e-non) a secondary or resultant phenomenon
the phenomenon of drought and the epiphenomenon of disease

epipolic   (ep-i-POL-ik) pert. to a surface; fluorescent
an epipolic inspection before deeper probing

epitimesis   (ep-i-te-MEE-sis) censure
an epitimesis by the members that was far from unanimous

epithumetic   (ep-i-thyoo-MET-ik) sensual or pert. to human appetites and desires
*paintings with grotesques depicting all the epithumetic tendencies
of humankind*

epitonic   (ep-i-TON-ik) overstrained
the library's epitonic ESL resources

epulation   (ep-yoo-LAY-shun) feasting
the joys of holiday epulation

equaeval   (e-KWEE-val) of equal age or of the same period
three equaeval furniture pieces

equiparate   (e-KWIP-a-rayt) to treat as on the same level
a president who would equiparate all her appointees

equipollent   (e-kwi-POL-lent) equal in power or validity
a different but equipollent job title

equiponderate   (e-kwi-PON-de-rayt) equal in weight
the two carry-on bags being equiponderate

erept (ee-REPT) to snatch or take away
a new commanding officer who promptly erepted all weekend passes

erethism (ER-e-thiz-um) morbid overactivity
his odd crotchets that are now in a state of erethism

ergasia (er-GAY-zhee-a) disposition toward activity; work
those applicants having an enthusiastic ergasia

ergogenic (er-go-JEN-ik) enhancing abilities for work
new lighting in the office that is both cheery and ergogenic

ergusia (er-GYOO-zee-a) (er-GYOO-see-a) vitamin A
increased ergusia to minimize night blindness

erotetic (er-o-TET-ik) interrogatory
an unfriendly, erotetic meeting that he resented

erubescent (e-roo-BES-ent) blushing
a self-conscious, erubescent young boy

erugate (ER-oo-gayt) wrinkleless
lustrous skin that is both tan and erugate

erumpent (ee-RUM-pent) bursting open or apart
an erumpent carton that had been overpacked

escamotage (es-ka-mo-TAZH) sleight of hand or trickery
persuasion that was more like seductive escamotage

esculent (ES-kyoo-lent) edible
church supper leftovers but eminently esculent ones

esemplastic (es-em-PLAS-tik) molding into a unified whole
possessing esemplastic genius as an artist

esquillous (ES-ki-lus) splintery
dangerously esquillous lumber

essentic (es-SEN-tik) showing emotion outwardly and naturally
a healthily receptive and essentic personality

essorant   (ES-o-rant) soaring in spirit
the essorant poetic rhapsodies of a man in love

estall   (es-TALL) to arrange payment in installments
relieved at being able to estall her debt

estaminet   (es-ta-mi-NAY) a bistro
a smoke-filled estaminet at the end of the little street

estellation   (es-tel-AY-shun) astrology
critical of the hedged generalizations of some practioners of estellation

esthesia   (es-THEE-zhee-a) ability to feel; sensibility
to reclaim and sharpen one's innate esthesia

estuate   (ES-tyoo-ayt) to boil
to estuate all contaminated dishware

estuous   (ES-tyoo-us) having surging or agitated feelings; welling with passion
darting, estuous glances

estus   (ES-tus) a glow of passion
a glint of estus in his eyes

etesian   (ee-TEE-zhan) periodic or annual
the region's etesian downpours

etourderie   (ay-TOR-de-ree) thoughtless action
tired of their shallowness and childish etourderies

euclionism   (YOO-klee-on-iz-um) stinginess
the man's lifelong euclionism

eucrasia (or **eucrasy)**   (yoo-KRAY-zha) (YOO-kra-see) good health or soundness
the reported eucrasia of yogurt-eating Asian peoples

eugeny   (YOO-je-nee) nobleness of birth
Twain's treatment of eugeny in The Prince and the Pauper

eumoirous   (yoo-MOY-rus) lucky in being happily innocent and good
thankful for having had a eumoirous rather than a troubled childhood

eumorphous (yoo-MOR-fus) well-shaped
a eumorphous and unbreakable kitchen utensil

eunomy (YOO-no-mee) civil orderliness under good rule
or good laws; good administration
a postwar recovery and general feeling of eunomy

euonymous (yoo-ON-i-mus) named aptly
the euonymous characters in Dickens's novels

eupatrid (yoo-PAT-rid) an aristocrat
a utopia in which there is no place for eupatrids

eupeptic (yoo-PEP-tik) having good digestion
eupeptic since cutting out the heavy foods

eupsychics (yoo-SY-kiks) good education
eupsychics, after health and safety, as the second social priority

eurygnathic (or eurygnathous) (yoo-rig-NATH-ik) (yoo-
RIG-na-thus) having a wide jaw
the eurygnathic side of our family

eurythmy (yoo-RITH-mee) harmonious proportion or
movement
the eurythmy of the Parthenon

eutaxy (YOO-tak-see) good or established order or
arrangement
*the importance of both the amassing and the eutaxy of gathered
evidence*

euthycomic (yoo-thi-KOM-ik) having straight hair
an ancient, euthycomic South American people

eutrophic (yoo-TROF-ik) nutritional
packaged foods that are at least somewhat eutrophic

eutrophy (YOO-tro-fee) good nutrition
the eutrophy of his diet while held a prisoner

evagation (ee-va-GAY-shun) impropriety or extravagance;
mental wandering; digression
evagations that show what a hedonist he is

evirate (EE-vi-rayt) (EV-i-rayt) to castrate or emasculate
an extreme proposal to evirate convicted rapists

evulgation (ee-vul-GAY-shun) publication
the bimonthly evulgation of an additional magazine

exanimate (eg-ZAN-i-mut) lifeless
a desolate and apparently exanimate island

exauctorate (eks-AWK-to-rayt) to dismiss or fire
to exauctorate a proven incompetent

excogitous (eks-KOJ-i-tus) inventive
a quick, unconventional, and excogitous mind

excreate (eks-kree-AYT) to spit out or cough up
getting the dog to excreate whatever it had put into its mouth

excubant (EKS-kyoo-bant) keeping watch or on one's
guard
two excubant bruisers

exegematic (eks-e-jem-AT-ik) explanatory
an introduction helpfully exegematic but far too long

exfodiate (eks-FO-di-ayt) to dig out
up in the attic exfodiating his old love letters

exgorgitation (eks-gor-ji-TAY-shun) matter vomited
a colorful patty of frozen exgorgitation near the curb

exhimious (eg-ZIM-i-us) select or excellent
a round gift box of exhimious cheeses and smoked meats

exiconize (eks-IK-on-aiz) to represent, portray, or depict
artistically
murals to exiconize the struggle of the country's underclass

exitious (or exitial) (eks-ISH-us) (eks-ISH-ul) destructive
or fatal
*the Donner party's alternative route that turned out to be
exitious*

exlegal (eks-LEE-gal) lawless
*the whim of two teenagers that grew to be a considerable exlegal
enterprise*

exoteric (ek-so-TER-ik) readily understandable to most people
an exoteric and minimally technical introduction to the science

exousiastic (eks-ooz-ee-AS-tik) pert. to authority
exousiastic trappings and perquisites

expergefacient (eks-per-je-FAY-shent) awakening
a lost spaceship with its now expergefacient crew

experrection (eks-per-REK-shun) waking up; awakening
clock radios, wristwatch alarms, and other experrection aids

expiscate (eks-PIS-kayt) to find out or fish out
a plucky reporter's ability to expiscate that crucial fact

exprobrate (EKS-pro-brayt) to censure or upbraid
not at all hesitant to exprobrate surly waiters

exsanguine (eks-SANG-gwin) anemic or bloodless
an exsanguine response that suggested a coverup

exsensed (eks-SENST) out of one's senses
must be totally exsensed to be going out with such a person

exsert (eks-SERT) to protrude
a floor lamp that exserted the car's open back window

exsertile (eks-SER-til) protruding
an exsertile platform where the first three rows of seats were

exsibilate (eks-SIB-i-layt) to hiss (someone) off the stage
an awful stand-up comic impervious to the crowd's hooting and exsibilating

exspuition (or **expuition**) (ek-spyoo-ISH-un) spitting out
the child's furtive expuition of the medicine

exsputory (eks-SPYOO-to-ree) spit out or ejected
a plate for the exsputory fishbones

exter (eks-TER) to dig up
loved to exter rare mushrooms in the woodland

extimate (EKS-ti-mayt) the most distant; outermost or uttermost
the extimate planet

extonious (eks-TO-nee-us) astonishing
a circus feat that was nothing short of extonious

exulant (EKS-yoo-lent) living in exile
the exulant Napoleon

F

facia (FASH-ee-a) a storefront name-plate
a gaudier, more attention-getting facia

facinorous (fa-SIN-or-us) extremely wicked
some facinorous delinquents

facrere (fa-KRER-re) deception as an art; make-believe
the dazzling facrere of movie special effects

facture (FAK-tyoor) something made, constructed, or created
varied student factures made in the handicrafts class

facund (FAK-und) (fa-KUND) eloquent
a poised and facund class officer

faex (feks) sediment or dregs (of a liquid)
the brownish cider faex

faithworthy (FAYTH-wer-thee) worthy of trust or belief
the value of two or three faithworthy volunteers

falbalas (FAL-ba-las) finery or frippery
her sister's expenditures for frivolous falbalas

fallaciloquent (fal-a-SIL-o-kwent) speaking deceitfully
a glibly fallaciloquent ladies' man

falsidical (fawl-SID-i-kal) suggesting as true what is false
the revisionist text's falsidical influence on schoolchildren

famigerate (fa-MIJ-er-ayt) to divulge or disseminate
an obscene salary that he would be embarrassed to famigerate

fanal (FAY-nal) (fa-NAL) a lighthouse or beacon
*a scenic coastline of rocky promontories and the occasional
white fanal*

fantigue (fan-TEEG) a state of excitement, anxiety, or
tension
in a fantigue about the coming holiday

farctate (FARK-tayt) stuffed with or full of food
*crashed the party with the sole intent to become farctate and
soused*

fastuous (FAS-tyoo-us) haughty, overbearing, pretentious, or showy
the club's smug and fastuous members

fatidic (fa-TI-dik) prophetic
a casual remark that later seemed fatidic

fatiloquent (fa-TIL-o-kwent) prophetic
the fatiloquent claims of an astrologer

fatiscent (fa-TIS-ent) having cracks or clefts; chinky
the ruin's fatiscent walls

favillous (fa-VIL-us) like ashes
some favillous powder on the floor

feak (feek) a dangling curl of hair
a quite-becoming forehead feak

featous (FEET-us) well-formed or -proportioned;
handsome
a featous and statuesque model

febricula (fe-BRIK-yoo-la) a slight fever
some aching muscles and a febricula

febrifacient (fe-bri-FAY-shent) producing fever
a febrifacient tropical climate

febriferous (fe-BRIF-er-us) producing fever
a sweltering, febriferous region

feculent (FEK-yoo-lent) covered with filth
a feculent old mattress

fedifragous (fe-DIF-ra-gus) agreement-breaking
historically a fedifragous government

fedity (FED-i-tee) foulness or vileness; turpitude
the garish fedity of the city's prurient nightlife

feneration (fen-er-AY-shun) usury
moneylenders and feneration

feracious (fe-RAY-shus) prolific or fruitful
a feracious crop for voracious consumers

feriation (fe-ri-AY-shun) celebrating a holiday
a welcome midwinter feriation

ferine (FEE-ryn) (FEE-rin) like a wild beast
a ferine roar

ferity (FER-i-tee) barbarity
the ferity of using any form of torture

fernticled (FERN-ti-kuld) extremely freckled
the shifting dapples of sunlight on her fernticled face

ferruminate (fe-ROO-mi-nayt) to cement together
ferruminating photos and magazine cutouts for the collage

fescinnine (FES-i-nyn) (FES-i-neen) obscene or scurrilous
a parody that was unacceptably fescinnine

festinate (FES-ti-nat) hasty
festinate introductions

festucine (FES-tyoo-sin) straw-yellow in color
a cheap festucine wig that belonged on a clown

feu de joie (fe-de-ZHWA) a bonfire
a feu de joie being a component of the ritual

fico (FEE-ko) the (obscene) finger
the old highway fico as a parting shot

fictile (FIK-til) a molded object
possibly a prehistoric fictile

fidicinal (fi-DI-sin-al) pert. to stringed instruments
the fidicinal lushness of mood music

fidimplicitary   (fy-dim-PLI-si-ter-ee)   having implicit faith
an important fidimplicitary gesture

filipendulous   (fil-i-PEN-dyoo-lus)   hanging by a thread
her filipendulous promotion

fimetic   (fi-MET-ik)   excremental
a fimetic deal

finitor   (fi-NI-tor)   the horizon
clouds extending all the way to the finitor

fissilingual   (fi-si-LING-wal)   fork-tongued (zoology)
fissilingual PR people

flabellation   (fla-be-LAY-shun)   fanning
flabellation not being one of his duties

flagitate   (FLA-ji-tayt)   to importune
the shame of having to flagitate that man

flagitious   (fla-JISH-us)   vilely wicked
a handsome but flagitious mercenary

flamfew   (FLAM-fyoo)   a trinket or bauble
a top drawer filled with costume-jewelry flamfews

flavescent   (fla-VES-ent)   turning pale yellow
the swimmer's flavescent teeth

flebile   (FLEB-il) (FLEB-ile)   tearful or doleful
a profuse and flebile apology

flexanimous   (fleks-AN-i-mus)   able to change others' minds;
affecting or moving
a mightily flexanimous orator

flob   (flob)   to move in a clumsy or aimless way
watching Janet, still sleepy, flob around the kitchen

floccify   (FLOS-i-fy)   to value little or consider worthless
not to floccify your kind gift, but . . .

floccipend   (FLOK-si-pend)   to treat as if of trifling value
underestimated, even floccipended their contribution

focillate   (FOS-si-layt) to refresh or comfort
a reception party to focillate the new arrivals

fodient   (FO-di-ent) burrowing or digging
a fodient animal

footle   (FOO-tul) (FOOT-ul) to talk or behave foolishly
footling in the balcony all during the concert

forcible-feeble   (FOR-si-bul FEE-bul) seemingly vigorous but really weak
a forcible-feeble tribal elder

forfex   (FOR-feks) a pair of scissors
an army knife with a foldout forfex

foudroyant   (foo-DROY-ant) (foo-dra-YAN) dazzling or stunning
a perfectly foudroyant cabaret singer

foveate   (FO-vi-ut) pitted or pockmarked
the foveate surface of the marble

fracid   (FRAS-id) rottenly ripe
a fracid peach left in the glove compartment

frappant   (fra-PON) striking or impressive
looking quite frappant on horseback

freinage   (fre-NAJH) interference by workers with the orderly processes
some freinage by the disgruntled night shift

fremescent   (fre-MES-ent) becoming murmurous or noisy
a fremescent crowd

frendent   (FREN-dent) gnashing one's teeth
an outraged loser who was tight-lipped and frendent

frescade   (fres-KAYD) a cool walkway or a shady place
bicycling over the pine needles of a lovely frescade

friand   (fri-AN) a dainty
viands and friands

frigolabile   (frig-o-LAY-byl) easily affected by cold
a delicate and frigolabile plant

frigorific (fri-gor-IF-ik) cooling
a frigorific draft just inside the cave's entrance

frixory (FRIKS-o-ree) a frying pan
an old cast-iron frixory

frustraneous (frus-TRAY-nee-us) vain or unprofitable
a frustraneous conversation

frustrum (FRUS-trum) a part or fragment
a mere frustrum and hence worthless

fubsy (FUB-zee) squatly fat
his younger and fubsy cousin

fulgor (FUL-ger) a splendid or dazzling brightness
the fulgor of the fire on the deck

fuliginous (fu-LIJ-i-nus) smoky or sooty
a fuliginous old furnace room

fumacious (fyoo-MAY-shus) fond of smoking
avoiding the fumacious crowd at the other end of the bar

funambulate (fu-NAM-byoo-layt) to walk or dance on a
rope
a clown who could funambulate admirably

fundament (FUN-da-ment) buttocks or anus
following his wobbly fundament up the ladder

funipendulous (fyoo-ni-PEN-dyoo-lus) hanging from a
rope
a red-boxed bar of funipendulous soap as a Christmas gift

furibund (FYOOR-i-bund) furious or raging
a sudden and furibund storm

furacious (fu-RAY-shus) given to stealing
a skulking, furacious vagrant

furcula (or furculum) (FER-kyoo-la) (FER-kyoo-lum) the
wishbone
a medal with a design like a furcula

furfuraceous (fer-fyoo-RAY-shus) covered with dandruff
his furfuraceous black comb

G

galeophobia (gay-le-o-FO-bi-a) fear of sharks
the lasting galeophobia induced by Jaws

Gallice (GAL-i-see) in French or per French usage
the word being a double entendre or, Gallice, double entente

gash-gabbit (GASH gab-bit) having a chin that projects
a husky, gash-gabbit talk-show host

gastrimargy (gas-TRIM-er-jee) gluttony
the deadly sin of gastrimargy

gastrosoph (GAS-tro-sof) an expert or refined eater
a gastrosoph who never picks up the check

gaucherie (go-she-REE) (GO-she-ree) a socially awkward, tactless, or crude act
his mocking toast considered by all present to be a gaucherie

gelasin (JEL-a-sin) a smile dimple
smitten with his fetching eyes and gelasins

gelastic (je-LAS-tik) laughable
a designer outfit that was unfortunately ludicrous and gelastic

gelogenic (jel-o-JEN-ik) funny
nothing gelogenic about material in bad taste

gerendum (je-REN-dum) something to be done
a most urgent gerendum for this afternoon

gerocomical (jer-o-KOM-i-kal) pert. to the medical treatment of the aged
a community with excellent gerocomical care

gerontogeous (je-ron-to-JEE-us) Old Worldish or pert. to the Eastern Hemisphere
gerontogeous traditions brought across the sea

gestant (JES-tant) pregnant or laden
fields gestant with ripened crops

72

gesten   (GES-ten) to welcome as a guest
stayed near the door to gesten all visitors

geusioleptic   (jee-ooz-ee-o-LEP-tik) pleasant-flavored
a geusioleptic lipstick for her boyfriend

gignate   (JIG-nayt) to originate or produce
*hard to believe a young person could gignate such a mature
novel*

glabrous   (GLAY-brus) bald
a large and glabrous professional basketball player

glaciarium   (glay-shee-AIR-i-um) an ice skating rink
an ankle sprained at the busy glaciarium

gleet   (gleet) sticky, slimy, or greasy filth
gleet in the grease trap

gloriation   (glo-ri-AY-shun) triumphant exultation or
boasting; vainglory
the gang's bumptious gloriation after the killing

glossal   (GLOS-al) pert. to the tongue
picking his teeth with slow glossal movements

gluteal   (gloo-TEE-al) (GLOO-te-al) pert. to the buttocks
sitting so long he felt a gluteal tingling when he got up

glycipricon   (gly-SIP-ri-kon) something that is bittersweet
to prefer a chocolaty glycipricon as dessert

gnathonic   (na-THON-ic) sycophantic or parasitic
too many gnathonic opportunists as her aides

gnomologic (or gnomological)   (no-mo-LOJ-ik) (no-mo-
LOJ-i-kal) sententious
the vapidly gnomologic dialogue of a bad martial arts melodrama

goelism   (GO-el-iz-um) blood vengeance
primal goelism

goety   (GO-e-tee) the black arts or necromancy; black
magic
a priestess of lugubrious goety

gracilescent   (gra-si-LES-ent) narrowing or becoming slender
the arcade's gracilescent supports

gradatim   (gra-DAY-tim) step by step or gradually
a methodic and gradatim investigation

grand (or great) climacteric   (grand kly-MAK-ter-ik) (grayt kly-MAK-ter-ik) the sixty-third or eighty-first year of one's life
totally unaware that she was approaching her grand climacteric

grandevity   (gran-DEV-i-tee) great or old age
the grandevity of the few remaining Civil War veterans

grandinous   (GRAN-di-nus) pert. to hail
when the precipitation became grandinous

grandisonant   (gran-DI-so-nant) stately sounding
such a grandisonant name

Grandisonian   (gran-di-SO-ni-an) gentlemanly, exemplary, or heroic
an old-fashioned man with Grandisonian qualities

gravedinous   (gra-VED-i-nus) drowsy
gravedinous from the heat and stuffiness of the air in the theater

gravedo   (gra-VEE-do) a head cold
a gravedo that made him feel partially deaf

graveolence   (gra-VEE-o-lens) a strong and offensive smell
the gamy graveolence of the nearby stockyards

graveolent   (gra-VEE-o-lent) stinking or rank
cooking some graveolent foreign meat dish

gravid   (GRAV-id) pregnant
discalced and gravid

gravidate   (GRAV-i-dayt) impregnate
to gravidate livestock by artificial means

gremial   (GREE-mi-al) pert. to the lap or bosom
standing up and brushing off gremial cookie crumbs

gressible (GRES-i-bul) able to walk
a patient progressing but not yet gressible

gride (gryd) to make a grating sound
when the old boat grided against the dock's edge

griffinage (GRIF-i-nedge) the state of being a newly arrived white person in India
the excitement and uncertainties of her griffinage

griffonage (gree-fo-NAZH) illegible handwriting
the proverbial physician's griffonage

grivoiserie (gri-VWAZ-er-ee) improperly licentious behavior
cabin fever and grivoiserie at the remote office

grumous (GROO-mus) thick or clotted
gobs of grumous matter

gubbertushed (GUB-er-tusht) buck-toothed
a goofy, gubbertushed cowboy

guimbard (GIM-bard) a Jew's harp
a vague memory of buying a red-painted guimbard in a candy store

gurgulation (ger-gyoo-LAY-shun) a rumbling in the bowels
kept clearing his throat to cover the bleating of his gurgulation

guttatim (gut-TAY-tim) drop by drop
medicine carefully administered guttatim

guttulous (GUT-yoo-lus) in the form of small drops
guttulous residue on the glass slide

gymnosophy (jim-NOS-o-fee) nudism
an old black-and-white film on gymnosophy

gynaecocoenic (jin-e-ko-SEE-nik) (gy-nee-ko-SEE-nik) having women in common
a society not only patriarchal but gynaecocoenic

gynaecomania (jin-ik-o-MAY-nee-a) sexual craving for women; satyriasis
the gynaecomania of marooned men

75

gynethusia   (jin-e-THOO-zha) (jy-ne-THOO-zha) a sacrifice of women
plant layoffs that this time will not be a form of sexist gynethusia

gynics   (JIN-iks) (JY-niks) knowledge of women
callow and ill-informed in the lifelong subject of gynics

H

habile   (HAB-il) able or skillful
a habile and chattering Japanese chef

habitacle   (HAB-i-ta-kul) a dwelling place
a restless family changing its habitacle every year

haematocryal   (hem-at-o-KRY-al) cold-blooded
a pretty haematocryal snub of her in-laws

halfpace   (HAF-payse) a small staircase landing
a tiny rug on the halfpace

halieutic   (hal-ee-YOO-tik) pert. to fishing
the longing for a rural halieut c retreat

halimous   (HAL-i-mus) pert. to salt; marine
halimous blood-pressure and diet concerns

haliography   (hal-i-OG-ra-fee) a description of the sea
the evocative haliographies of Conrad and Melville

hallucal   (HAL-yoo-kul) pert. to the big toe
the hallucal pain of his gout

haptic   (HAP-tik) pert. to touch
a form of holistic healing that is partly haptic

harageous   (ha-RAY-jus) cruel or violent
a truly harageous disposition

harbergage   (HAR-ber-ga-je) lodging; entertainment
a town without any decent harbergage

76

hardydardy   (HAR-dee-DAR-dee) foolish daring or willful recklessness
the hardydardy of the picaresque swashbuckling hero

hariolate   (HAR-i-o-layt) to prognosticate
a pompous tendency to hariolate

hebamic   (he-BAM-ik) pert. to Socratic reasoning; maieutic
venturing a hebamic, less emotional argument

hebdomadal   (heb-DOM-a-dal) lasting or occurring every seven days; weeklong or weekly
the cleaning lady's hebdomadal visit

hebetate   (HEB-e-tayt) to become or to make dull, obtuse, or stupid
ever soporific, hebetating television

hebetude   (HEB-e-tyood) stupidity or dullness
her almost deliberate and schooled hebetude

hebetudinous   (heb-e-TYOO-di-nus) dull or obtuse
hebetudinous even where small talk is concerned

hecatomped   (hek-a-TOM-ped) a hundred feet square
a perfect hecatomped studio

helcosis   (hel-KO-sis) ulceration
a job guaranteeing a lifetime of helcosis

heliochromy   (HEE-li-o-kro-mee) color photography
a calendar celebrating Alpine heliochromy

hemerology   (hem-er-OL-o-jee) a calendar
checking his busy social hemerology

hemophobia   (hee-mo-FO-bi-a) aversion to the sight of blood
an extreme hemophobia you wouldn't expect in such a large man

heredipety   (her-e-DIP-e-tee) legacy hunting
the long-term, covert scheming that goes along with heredipety

herile (HER-il) (HER-ile) pert. to a master
the herile cruelties of the old plantation system

Hesperian (hes-PEER-i-an) western or occidental
a reawakened interest in the Hesperian viewpoint

hesternal (hes-TER-nal) pert. to yesterday
our hesternal gate receipts

hesychastic (hes-i-KAS-tik) soothing or calming (esp. music)
a most hesychastic lullaby

heterize (HET-er-ize) to make different or transform
the continually heterized Greek gods

heterolith (HET-er-o-lith) a hair ball
the unflattering epithet of "heterolith"

heterophemy (or **heterophemism**) (HET-er-o-fe-mee) (het-er-OF-em-iz-um) a Freudian slip
a howling heterophemy that broke everybody up

hexicology (hek-si-KOL-o-jee) ecology
new threats to world hexicology

hexiology (hek-see-OL-o-jee) the study of the effect of environment on creatures
a pioneer in freshwater hexiology

hiant (HY-ant) gaping
her hiant incredulity

hibernacle (HY-ber-na-kul) a winter retreat
a log cabin as a Spartan hibernacle

hibernal (hy-BER-nal) wintry
a landscape that was a hibernal wonderland

hiccius doccius (HIK-she-us DOK-she-us) a juggler
a children's show complete with hiccius doccius

hiemal (HY-e-mal) wintry
hiemal Christmas scenes

hierurgy (HY-er-er-jee) a religious rite
with all the seriousness of a hierurgy

higgaion (hi-GAY-yon) (hi-GY-yon) resounding music; meditation
a moving choral higgaion in a very old church

hilasmic (hi-LAZ-mik) propitiatory
a dozen roses as a hilasmic overture

hinnible (HIN-i-bul) able to whinny
a prankish and hinnable young boy

hippiater (HIP-i-ay-ter) horse doctor
insulted by being called a horrendous hippiater

hippic (HIP-ik) pert. to horses or horse racing
the issue of a state government's resorting to hippic income

hippomachy (hip-POM-ma-kee) a fight on horseback
an exciting, clanky hippomachy between the good knight and the bad knight

hircinous (HER-si-nus) goat-smelling; goaty
bedraggled and hircinous infantry

hircosity (her-KOS-i-tee) lewdness or goatishness; lust
the retired magician's known hircosity

hirrient (HER-i-ent) trilled
the mannerism of his hirrient r's

hobhouchin (hob-HOO-chin) an owl
a Halloween cutout of an orange-and-black hobhouchin

hodiernal (ho-di-ER-nal) pert. to today or this day
told to concentrate on his hodiernal responsibilities

holmgang (HOME-gang) a duel to the death
what police suspect was a holmgang between the two bank robbers

hominiform (ho-MIN-i-form) human in shape
a suspiciously hominiform extraterrestrial

homodox (or **homodoxian)** (HOM-o-doks) (hom-o-DOK-si-an) having the same opinion
her complaisant, homodox friends

homoglot (HO-mo-glot) (HOM-o-glot) of the same language
interested in some additional homoglot curses

homophylic (ho-mo-FIL-ik) (hom-o-FIL-ik) of the same race
a homophylic civil war

hontous (HON-tus) ashamed or shameful
a painfully hontous part of his past

horal (HO-ral) hourly
with horal telephone check-ins from the front desk

horripilate (ha-RIP-i-layt) to give one goose bumps or make the flesh creep
an outlandish outfit specifically chosen to horripilate her parents

hortulan (HOR-tyoo-lan) pert. to gardening
the happy prospect of a hortulan retirement

hospitize (HOS-pi-tyz) to extend hospitality to
a wariness about hospitizing the mysterious new neighbors

hubristic (hyoo-BRIS-tik) insolent or contemptuous
a handsome and hubristic fighter pilot

hufty-tufty (HUF-tee TUF-tee) swaggering
a security guard with a hufty-tufty gait

humdudgeon (hum-DUJ-un) an imaginary ailment or pain
his very detailed humdudgeons being his favorite topic of conversation

humicubation (hyoo-mik-yoo-BAY-shun) lying on the ground, especially in penitence or prayer
the humicubation of devout Moslems

hyaline (HY-a-lin) (HY-a-lyn) glassy or glasslike
a partition made of some hyaline synthetic material

hyblaean (hy-BLEE-an) smooth-talking
a hyblaean and conservatively dressed pimp

hydrophanous (hy-DROF-a-nus) transparent in water
the hydrophanous sea creature

hyetal (HY-e-tal) pert. to rain
annual hyetal figures for the state

hygeiolatry (hy-jee-OL-a-tree) obsession about health or health matters
whether hygeiolatry could be an unhealthy obsession

hylactic (hy-LAK-tik) like barking
a high and hylactic voice

hyperdisyllable (hy-per-di-SIL-a-bul) a word of more than two syllables
a stuffy writer given to hyperdisyllables and rhetorical questions

hyperosmic (hy-per-OZ-mik) having a keen sense of smell
more hyperosmic than a deluxe smoke alarm

hyperphysical (hy-per-FIZ-i-kal) supernatural
a total disbelief in hyperphysical visitations

hyperpiesis (hy-per-py-EE-sis) high blood pressure; hypertension
obesity and hyperpiesis

hypertrophic (or **hypertrophied**) (hy-per-TROF-ik) (hy-PER-tro-feed) overdeveloped or overgrown
my hypertrophic but kissable earlobes

hypnagogic (hip-na-GOJ-ik) causing sleep
a droning, hypnagogic voice

hypnobate (HIP-no-bayt) a sleepwalker
claimed that they first met as colliding hypnobates

hypnopompic (hip-no-POM-pik) causing to wake up
complaining about her husband's hypnopompic snoring

hypobulia (hy-po-BYOO-li-a) difficulty in making decisions
a dithering hypobulia from a young age

hypokoristikon (hip-o-kor-IST-i-kon) a pet name
a catchy hypokoristikon instead of her difficult given name

hypomnematic (hy-po-nem-AT-ik) consisting of notes or memoranda
an anthology including even her hypomnematic writings

hyponoia (hip-o-NOY-a) hidden significance
the eternal controversy over possible Old Testament hyponoia

hypophrenic (hy-po-FREN-ik) feebleminded
the dull, hypophrenic copy for a lowbrow ad

hyposthenic (hy-pos-THEN-ik) physically weak
a tryout for a hyposthenic but determined kid

hypotypic (hy-po-TIP-ik) (hip-o-TIP-ik) not perfectly
typical; subtypical
a similar but hypotypic house

hypotyposis (hy-po-ty-PO-sis) (hy-po-ti-PO-sis) vivid
description
the necessity for a detail or two in voice-over hypotyposis

hyppish (HIP-ish) somewhat low in spirits or depressed
her roommate's hyppish mood

hypsicephalic (hip-si-se-FAL-ik) having a high skull
the cartoon's hypsicephalic Daddy Warbucks

hypsiphobia (hip-si-FO-bi-a) fear of heights; acrophobia
a dangerous mountain road to reawaken his hypsiphobia

hypsophonous (hip-SOF-o-nus) having a high and clear
voice
a single, hypsophonous cry from somebody in the crowd

I

ichnography (ik-NOG-ra-fee) a ground plan
a doodler unskilled in ichnography

iconoplast (ai-KON-o-plast) an image maker
the PR man as iconoplast

idee-force (ee-day-FORS) an influential idea
an idee-force promulgated by the losing candidate

ideoplastia (id-ee-o-PLAS-tee-a) (ai-de-o-PLAS-tee-a)
suggestability to hypnotism
an eye-movement test to determine a person's ideoplastia

idiasm (ID-ee-az-um) a peculiarity or idiosyncrasy
trying to single out some personal idiasm as a key to the woman

idoneous (ai-DO-nee-us) suitable or apt
reasonably idoneous accommodations for the weekend

ignavia (or **ignavy**) (ig-NAY-vee-a) (IG-na-vee) idleness
or sloth
the spectre of growing ignavia in the welfare state

ignotism (IG-no-tiz-um) a mistake due to ignorance
foreign-language gaffes that were understandable ignotisms

ikary (IK-a-ree) caviar
champagne and ikary

illachrymable (il-LAK-ri-ma-bul) not able to cry
a stolid and illachrymable man

illapse (il-LAPS) a gradual advance
the illapse of the floodwaters

illaqueate (il-LAK-wee-ayt) to trap or ensnare
to safely illaqueate various endangered species

illation (il-LAY-shun) deduction or inference
a questionable illation

illaudatory (il-LAWD-a-to-ree) not praising or
complimentary
a letter of reference strangely illaudatory

illecebrous (il-LES-i-brus) alluring
distracted by an illecebrous night nurse

illepid (il-LEP-id) unpleasant
a thoroughly illepid outing to an overcrowded beach

illocal (il-LO-kal) having no location in space
the planet's illocal and elusive threat in the story

83

illth (ilth) economic misery or poverty
the road to illth and disease

illude (il-LOOD) to ridicule or mock
a political cartoon being the perfect way to illude the mayor's arrogance

illutation (il-yoo-TAY-shun) a mud bath
special illuations at the spa

imbenignity (im-be-NIG-ni-tee) unkindness
a hospitable town in which you'd not encounter any imbenignity

imberbe (or imberbic) (an-BAIRB) beardless
the one imberbe member of the sect

imbonity (im-BON-i-tee) the lack of good qualities
his vast and unmatchable imbonity

imbreviate (im-BREE-vi-ayt) to register or enroll
imbreviated four more names in the book

immarcesible (or immarcessible) (im-mar-SES-i-bul) imperishable or indestructable
an employee with an immarcesible bad attitude

immiserization (im-mi-zer-i-ZAY-shun) the making (one) miserable
giving credit where credit is due for his marital immiserization

impassible (im-PASS-i-bul) incapable of pain or suffering; insensitive or unfeeling
an impassible and impossible troop leader

impavid (im-PAV-id) fearless
an impavid warrior

impeccant (im-PEK-ant) without sin
not being impeccant myself

impenitible (im-PEN-i-ti-bul) incapable of repentance or remorse
a coldhearted, impenitible military officer

imperdible (im-PER-di-bul) not losable or destroyable
basic, solid qualities that are imperdible

imperscriptable (im-per-SKRIP-ti-bul) unrecorded
the author's imperscriptable utterances

impetition (im-pe-TISH-un) an accusation or charge
a formal impetition

impletion (im-PLEE-shun) filling up or making full
the impletion of the drug lord's coffers

impravable (im-PRAYV-a-bul) incorruptible
venal local politicos who are far from impravable

impretiable (im-PRET-ee-a-bul) invaluable or priceless
an impretiable relic

imprevisible (im-pre-VIZ-i-bul) unforeseeable
an imprevisible mishap during the ceremony

improcerous (im-pro-SER-us) short in stature
the only improcerous member of the family

improcreant (im-PRO-kree-ant) impotent
a new therapy for my improcreant husband

improficuous (im-pro-FIK-yoo-us) unprofitable
a strategy improficuous for the airline

imprompt (im-PROMPT) unready or unprepared
a cousin who was always maddeningly imprompt

impubic (or impuberal) (im-PYOO-bik) (im-PYOO-
ber-al) immature
very impubic behavior for a graduating senior

impudicity (im-pyoo-DI-si-tee) shamelessness
Margerie's flagrant impudicity with four-letter words

incalescent (in-ka-LES-ent) growing warm
an incalescent metal container

incede (in-SEED) to advance
to incede no farther into the rubble of the building

incogitant (in-KOJ-i-tant) thoughtless
an incogitant and thoughtless decision

incondite   (in-KON-dit) badly constructed (esp.
artistically)
an incondite and confusing second act

incrassate   (in-KRAS-ayt) dulled or made gross
young minds incrassate from television addiction

increpation   (in-kre-PAY-shun) a chiding, rebuke, or
reproof
a young teacher called in for a carefully worded increpation

incruent   (IN-kroo-ent) bloodless
an incruent android

inculpate   (in-KUL-payt) (IN-kul-payt) to accuse or blame
a vow to inculpate the higher-ups as well

indagate   (IN-da-gayt) to search into or investigate
Joan's well-meaning intent to indagate their family history

indefeasible   (in-de-FEE-zi-bul) not undoable
a fateful and indefeasible change in procedure

indefectible   (in-de-FEK-ti-bul) perfect and everlasting;
infallible
the indefectible vision and values of one who is enlightened

indigitate   (in-DIJ-i-tayt) to declare or proclaim
when you indigitate your full approval

indocible (or indocile)   (in-DOS-i-bul) (in-DOS-il)
unteachable as a pupil
her idealistic refusal to regard any student as being indocible

indoles   (IN-do-leez) one's natural or innate character or
disposition
bahavior that would somehow go against his temperate indoles

indult   (in-DULT) a special privilege or license
needing some indult or password for admission

indument   (IN-dyoo-ment) clothing or a garment
an inmate wearing a robelike indument

indurate   (IN-dyoor-ayt) hardened
the indurate attitude of a war-weary veteran

inennarable (in-e-NAR-a-bul) indescribable or
unrelatable
an inennarable atrocity

inesculent (in-ES-kyoo-lent) not edible
a colorful but inesculent mushroom

in esse (in ES-ee) in actual existence
that such a missing link could be in esse

infand (or infandous) (in-FAND) (in-FAN-dus) unspeakable or unmentionable
accusations that were outrageously infand

infelicific (in-fee-li-SIF-ik) causing unhappiness
*to persuade teenagers that drugs are ultimately—or soon—
infelicific*

inferoanterior (in-fer-o-an-TEER-ee-or) below and in front
the external damage being inferoanterior

inficete (in-fi-SEET) not amusing or witty
some strained and inficete introductory remarks

inflorescent (in-flo-RES-ens) blossoming
brilliantly inflorescent cherry trees

infra-angelic (in-fra-an-JEL-ik) human
the fallibilities and foibles of all who are infra-angelic

infract (in-FRAKT) broken or violated
an infract contract

infriction (in-FRIK-shun) rubbing (ointment) in
requiring vigorous infriction for the salve to have any effect

infrunite (IN-froo-nyt) senseless or tasteless
hung up in the dorm a poster infrunite if not offensive

ingannation (in-gan-NAY-shun) a deception or fraud
*untrue casualty figures that were the result of governmental
ingannation*

ingeminate (in-GEM-i-nayt) to repeat or reiterate
ingeminated her very words

ingenit   (in-JEN-it) innate or inherent
a persecuted people's ingenit skepticism

ingluvious   (in-GLOO-vi-us) gluttonous or piggish
Don's ingluvious grabbing at the buffet table

ingordigious   (in-gor-DI-jus) greedy
no need to be ingordigious

ingram   (ING-ram) one who is ignorant
a gullible listenership mostly of trailer-park ingrams

ingurgitate   (in-GER-ji-tayt) to swallow up or gulp down
thirstily ingurgitated juice from the smashed gourd

ingustable   (in-GUS-ta-bul) having no detectable taste
his ingustable processed-cheese casserole

inhume   (in-HYOOM) to bury
watching Michael reverently inhume his expired pet hamster

innascible   (in-NAS-i-bul) without beginning or always existing (as God)
the paradox of an innascible cause

innominate   (in-NOM-in-ut) unnamed
innominate contributors

inodorous   (in-O-der-us) without smell
preferring the inodorous version of the lotion

inopinate (or **inopine**)   (in-OP-in-ayt) (IN-o-pyn) unexpected
the inopinate thrill of finding that book in the library

inopious   (in-OP-ee-us) financially needy
a burned-out family now inopious

inosculate   (in-OS-kyoo-layt) to unite, blend, or grow together
vines that inosculate

in posse   (in POS-see) potentially but not actually
a perfect resort in posse

inquinated   (IN-kwi-nay-ted) corrupted or defiled
an already inquinated junior official

inquirendo (in-kwy-REN-do) (in-kwi-REN-do) an inquiry
shocking vandalism calling for an informal inquirendo

inscient (IN-shi-ent) (IN-shent) discerning or insightful
a caring and very inscient social worker

insenescible (in-se-NES-i-bul) that cannot grow old
our insenescible love

insessor (in-SES-or) one who sits in or upon
a welcome female insessor at the meeting

insipient (in-SIP-ee-ent) unwise or foolish
a rash response that would definitely be insipient

isochrous (ai-SOK-ro-us) of the same color throughout
an unusual but isochrous substance

inspissated (in-SPIS-say-ted) thickened
a fog inspissated at the curves in the road

instauration (in-staw-RAY-shun) restoration or renewal (to former excellence)
funding for the instauration of the old train station

insuccate (in-SUK-ayt) to soak or steep
to insuccate the tea bag only half a minute

insudate (in-SYOO-dayt) causing or characterized by sweating
a good, insudate workout

insufflate (in-SUF-layt) (IN-suf-layt) to blow or breathe upon
carefully insufflating the embers

insulse (in-SULSE) witless
a predictable and insulse sitcom

intabulate (in-TAB-yoo-layt) to inscribe or enroll (on a list)
to intabulate fifty more people as subscribers

intarrisable (in-TAR-is-a-bul) incapable of being dried up; inexhaustible
an intarrisable supply

intemerate (in-TEM-er-it) undefiled
intemerate by the inevitable cynicism of city dwellers

intenerate (in-TEN-er-ayt) to soften or make tender
using water to intenerate the clay

interaural (in-ter-OR-al) between the ears
a person mentally possessing an interaural void

intercur (in-ter-KER) to run or come between
when a stream of visitors from the right intercurred between them

interemption (in-ter-EMP-shun) destruction or killing
the bloody interemption in the country's capital

interfector (in-ter-FEK-tor) a planet bringing death
an apocalyptic novel about an exploding interfector

intergern (in-ter-GERN) to snarl back
amused at seeing the far smaller dog intergern

interlucent (in-ter-LYOO-sent) shining between others
mostly green with an interlucent streak of gold

intermure (in-ter-MYOOR) to wall in
new high-rises that virtually intermured them and their view

interturb (in-ter-TERB) to disturb by interrupting
their constantly interturbing what would have been

invaginated (in-VAJ-i-nay-ted) turned in or folded inside out
a discarded, invaginated garment

invex (IN-veks) concave
a stereo with slightly invex speakers

invictive (in-VIK-tiv) unbeatable
an obnoxious and invictive contestant

invious (IN-vi-us) trackless or pathless; without roads
an invious coastal jungle

invultuation (in-vul-tyoo-AY-shun) the witchcraft stabbing of a person's image
such malicious folkways as black magic and invultuation

inwit (IN-wit) conscience or a sense of remorse
a cad's underdeveloped inwit

ipseity (ip-SEE-i-tee) self-identity or selfhood
an abused child badly needing ipseity

iracund (AI-ra-kund) easily angered
an iracund but fair person

irascent (ai-RAS-ent) growing angry
the frustrated and irascent populace

irrefrangible (ir-re-FRAN-ji-bul) inviolable
Dorothy's irrefrangible integrity

irreptitious (ir-rep-TISH-us) creeping in or insinuated
into (esp. into a text)
irreptitious innuendos

irrespirable (ir-re-SPY-ra-bul) (ir-RES-per-a-bul) not
breathable
irrespirable highway fumes

ismy (IZ-mee) switching from one faddish doctrine or theory to another
a credulous and ismy counterculture type

isonomy (ai-SON-o-mee) equal political rights
the struggle for female isonomy in backward countries

izzat (IZ-at) honor, credit, or reputation
a blotch on his professional izzat

J

jactation (jak-TAY-shun) boasting
the pathetic jactation of nostalgic has-beens

jactitate (JAK-ti-tayt) to toss and turn
to jactitate and get little sleep

jannock (JAN-uk) straightforward or genuine
a refreshingly jannock individual

91

janua (JAN-yoo-a) a door
an unlockable janua for minimal privacy

jecoral (JEK-o-ral) pert. to the liver; hepatic
jecoral damage from alcoholism

jejunation (je-joo-NAY-shun) fasting
some periodic jejunation to accelerate weight loss

jentacular (jen-TAK-yoo-ler) pert. to breakfast
her jentacular grouchiness

jentation (jen-TAY-shun) breakfast
an especially sumptuous Sunday morning jentation

jobation (jo-BAY-shun) tedious criticism or scolding
Rick's epic and entertaining jobation on his answering machine

jorum (JO-rum) a large drinking vessel
a makeshift jorum for them to share around the campfire

jouissance (JOO-i-sans) use or enjoyment
full jouissance of all the hotel's offerings

jubate (JOO-bayt) having long hair or a mane
a jubate and muscular male model

Judophobism (joo-DOF-o-biz-um) anti-Semitism
a scholarly history of Judophobism in medieval Europe

jumelle (joo-MEL) twin or paired
a pub sign showing jumelle bears

juncate (JUNK-et) cheesecake (the edible kind)
a tempting piece of strawberry juncate

juramental (JOOR-a-men-tal) pert. to an oath
a formal promise of almost juramental force

juste-milieu (zhoost-mi-LYUH) the golden mean
a getting back to the old ideal of the juste-milieu

juvencle (joo-VEN-kul) a girl or young woman
a former halfway house for wayward juvencles

juvenescent (joo-ven-ES-ent) growing young
a feeling of juvenescent vigor

K

kakistocracy (kak-i-STOK-ra-see) government by the worst element
a political vacuum unfortunately filled by a kakistocracy

kalokagathia (kal-o-ka-GATH-i-a) personal nobility of character
a leader possessing some measure of kalokagathia

kalon (KAL-on) beauty more than skin-deep
a tall woman with exotic and magnetic kalon

kef (kayf) a dreamy and peaceful state; languor
balmy days of kef on his yacht

kenodoxy (KEN-o-dok-see) the love or pursuit of self-aggrandizement or vainglory; vanity
disgust with the endemic kenodoxy of Hollywood

kenspeckle (KEN-spek-ul) easily recognized
a familiar delivery truck with its kenspeckle markings

kerygmatic (ker-ig-MAT-ik) pert. to preaching
an aversion to kerygmatic bluster

kosmokrator (koz-MOK-ra-tor) a ruler of the world
Chaplin in the role of a daffy kosmokrator

L

labefy (LAB-e-fy) to weaken or impair
a layoff that would labefy her upper body strength

laboriferous (lab-or-IF-er-us) painstaking; persevering through difficulty
a laboriferous but worthwhile experience

labrose (LAY-brose) thick-lipped
a mask of a thin-nosed, labrose face

laches (LACH-ez) carelessness, negligence, or slackness
the laches of a discouraged work force

lacuscular (la-KUS-kyoo-ler) pert. to small pools
a lacuscular wetland

laetation (le-TAY-shun) manuring or manure
the laetation of endless farm fields

lagan (LAG-an) goods sunk (and the spot marked) at sea
sailing out to retrieve the lagan

lambitate (LAM-bi-tayt) to lick
a puppy that lambitates the face of one and all

lamiaceous (lay-mee-AY-shus) minty
her lamiaceous kisses

languescent (lang-GWES-ent) becoming faint or tired
a languescent fellow passenger

laniate (LAY-nee-ayt) to savage with one's teeth
cursed and impatiently laniated the wrapper on the prophylactic

lapactic (la-PAK-tik) a laxative
warned by his teammates against taking a lapactic before the game

laquearian (lak-wee-AIR-ee-an) armed with a noose
a rowdy, laquearian mob of good old boys

largeour (LARJ-or) width
the largeour of the river at that point

larmoyant (lar-MOY-ant) weepy
the larmoyant contingent at the wedding

lassate (LAS-ayt) tired or weary
a lassate single mother

lasslorn (LAS-lorn) jilted by one's girlfriend
a lasslorn guy on the rebound

lateritious (lad-er-ISH-us) like brick
the tavern's lateritious wallpaper

latibule (LAT-i-byool) a hiding place
a perfect latibule for her husband's birthday gift

latitant (LAT-i-tent) hidden or lurking
the child's desperate fear of latitant monsters at night

latitudinarian (lat-i-TYOO-di-nair-i-an) broad-minded
a latitudinarian and understanding official

latrant (LAY-trant) barking
a loud, latrant electronic alarm

latrede (la-TRED) slow or tardy
an infuriatingly latrede waiter

latrocination (lat-ro-sin-AY-shun) highway robbery
the evils of latrocination and carjacking

lautitious (law-TISH-us) sumptuous (esp. meat)
a lautitious poolside barbecue

lectual (LEK-tyoo-al) confining to a bed (as a disease)
a slight but not lectual fever

ledgit (LEJ-it) a label or memo slip projecting from a book's pages
a tattered Bible stuffed with ledgits

leech-finger (LEECH-fing-er) the finger next to the little finger
you say ring finger, I say leech-finger

leggiadrous (lej-ee-AD-rus) graceful or elegant
a leggiadrous pergola

leguleian (leg-yoo-LEE-yan) (leg-yoo-LEE-an) a lawyer
a powerful confraternity of corporate leguleians

leighster (LAY-ster) a female liar
a runaway who is a compulsive leighster

leiotrichous (ly-OT-ri-kus) having straight hair
a large, leiotrichous dog

lenify (LEN-i-fy) to soften
to lenify John's harsh criticisms of Alex

lenity (LEN-i-tee) lenience or mercy
a court not known for its lenity

lenocinant (len-OS-i-nant) tempting or enticing to evil
with her sister as a steadily lenocinant influence

lentiginous (len-TIJ-i-nus) extremely freckled
an old woman with shriveled, lentiginous arms

lentitude (LENT-i-tyood) slowness or sluggishness
an impatience with the lentitude of the adoption process

lentor (LEN-tor) slowness or sluggishness
the elephantine lentor of the bureaucracy

leptochrous (lep-TOK-rus) delicately thin-skinned
a rare, leptochrous marine organism

leptodactylous (lep-to-DAK-ti-lus) having slender toes
footprints of somebody leptodactylous in the sand

lestobiotic (les-to-by-OT-ik) living by covertly stealing others' food
the elusive identity of the lestobiotic guest

Lestrigon (LES-tri-gon) a cannibal
an isthmus inhabited by reputed Lestrigons

lethiferous (or **lethiferal**) (leth-IF-er-us) (leth-IF-er-al) deadly
the lethiferous dimension of a fully automatic weapon

levigate (LEV-i-gayt) to polish or make smooth
an order to levigate all brass fixtures

levining (LEV-i-ning) lightning
distant zigzags of levining

lexiphanic (leks-i-FAN-ik) pretentious or bombastic in speech
the lexiphanic senator from the Midwest

libence (LY-bense) willingness
a plea gauged to inspire not only compliance but libence

libkin (LIB-kin) a place to sleep
a broad, cushioned window seat that makes a cozy libkin

ligiament (LEEZH-ya-ment) an act of allegiance
*a deed that in the world of organized crime constituted a
ligiament*

ligniperdous (lig-ni-PER-dus) injurious or destructive to
wood
a raw and ligniperdous climate

limitrophe (LIM-i-trofe) on the frontier or border
rugged limitrophe outposts

linctus (LINGK-tus) cough syrup
a bitter-tasting but effective menthol linctus

lingacious (ling-AY-shus) talkative
a lonely and lingacious bus driver

lingible (LING-i-bul) meant to be licked
some lingible name labels

linguipotence (ling-GWI-po-tense) mastery of languages
the impressive linguipotence of a widely traveled lecturer

linguished (LING-wishd) skilled in languages
*fantasies of being a cosmopolitan and linguished citizen of the
world*

lipothymic (ly-po-THIM-ik) tending to faint or swoon
those lipothymic Victorian heroines

litaneutical (lit-a-NYOO-ti-kal) pert. to a litany
her mother-in-law's litaneutical complaints

litation (li-TAY-shun) sacrificing or sacrifice
a call for great economic litation

literose (LIT-er-ose) pretentiously or self-consciously
literary
the obscure allusions of insufferably literose academics

littlemeal (LIT-ul-meel) little by little
catching up to them littlemeal

lochetic (lo-KEE-tik) waiting in ambush for a victim
vicious, lochetic muggers

locuplete (LOK-yoo-pleet) rich and complete or plentifully stocked
a locuplete family larder

logodaedaly (log-o-DED-a-lee) cleverness in using wordplay
James Joyce's prodigious logodaedaly

logofascinated (LO-go-fas-i-nay-ted) fascinated by words
a logofascinated crossword addict

logogogue (LOG-o-gog) one who legislates where words are concerned
an intellectual gadfly and self-proclaimed logogogue

loimic (LOY-mik) pert. to the plague
loimic population losses

longanimity (long-a-NIM-i-tee) patient forbearance or suffering
a remarkable prisoner with great longanimity

longevous (lon-JEE-vus) long-lived
the longevous parrot

loricate (LOR-i-kayt) to enclose or cover protectively
specifications for loricating the fragile instrument

lovertine (LUV-er-tyn) addicted to making love
just a lovertine fool

lucrifaction (loo-kri-FAK-shun) the process of becoming rich
the patient lucrifaction of Florida treasure salvors

lucripetous (loo-KRIP-e-tus) money-hungry
an aversion to dealing with lucripetous middlemen

luctation (luk-TAY-shun) a struggling to overcome
a valiant luctation under great duress

luctiferous (luk-TIF-e-rus) bringing sorrow or gloom
the regions's tragic and luctiferous drought

luctual (LUK-tyoo-al) mournful or sorrowful
the luctual look of a pious attendant

ludification (loo-di-fi-KAY-shun) deriding
a well-deserved ludification by satirists

luition (loo-ISH-un) payment of ransom
the kidnapper's instructions regarding the luition

lupanarian (loo-pa-NAIR-i-an) pert. to a brothel
the Hungarian roué's lupanarian pursuits

lustration (lus-TRAY-shun) spiritual or moral purification
lustration through self-denial

lutaceous (loo-TAY-shus) muddy
a lack of traction on the lutaceous playing field

lutescent (loo-TES-ent) yellowing
torn and lutescent old posters

Lutetian (loo-TEE-shun) Parisian
the Lutetian romance of cafe music

lutose (LOO-tose) covered with mud
lutose houses, some of them caved in

lymphate (LIM-fayt) diluted with water
nothing like a stein of stale and lymphate beer

lymphate (LIM-fayt) to drive mad
if your blathering doesn't lymphate me before that

M

macarism (MAK-a-riz-um) joy or pleasure in another's happiness
her genuine macarism rather than petty envy

macarize (MAK-a-ryz) to bless or congratulate
a crowd gathered to macarize the crew

macilent   (MAS-i-lent) thin or lean
a macilent but not bony adolescent

mackabroin   (MAK-a-broyn) an old hag
a nasty, cigarette-smoking mackabroin in the ticket booth

mackeler   (MAK-e-ler) a broker
the comfortable income of a successful mackeler

macrobian   (ma-KRO-bee-an) a person who lives long
a family of hale macrobians

macromeritic   (mak-rom-er-IT-ik) visible to the naked eye
macromeritic insects on the tree trunk

macroscian   (ma-KROSH-ee-an) casting a long shadow
an unduly macroscian building at the edge of the park

macrotous   (ma-KRO-tus) having large ears
a chubby and macrotous character actor whose name I forget

mactation   (mak-TAY-shun) a sacrificial killing
involving some abracadabra and the mactation of chickens

madefy   (MAD-e-fy) to moisten
a cloth to madefy the patient's skin

madescent   (ma-DES-ent) growing damp
a madescent and heavier sleeping bag

magia   (MAY-jee-a) white magic; theurgy
ordinary love as a kind of magia

magiric   (ma-JY-rik) pert. to the art of cooking
her flour-smeared magiric books on the kitchen shelf

magirology   (ma-ji-ROL-o-gee) the art of cooking
another television program on magirology

malacophonous   (mal-a-KOF-i-nus) having a soft voice
the malacophonous Peter Lorre

maladive   (MAL-a-div) delicate or sickly
Kathy's maladive gerbil

maladresse   (mal-a-DRES) awkwardness
with all the maladresse of a fish out of water

malapert (MAL-a-pert) impudent or saucy
her malapert teenage years

maleolent (mal-ee-O-lent) bad-smelling
a maleolent plastic covering

malison (MAL-i-zun) (MAL-i-sun) a curse
his secret malisons and vows of revenge

malominous (mal-OM-in-us) portending or boding evil
an ill-advised political appointment that is malominous

malposed (mal-POZD) badly placed
a malposed camera and a badly posed model

maltalent (MAL-tal-ent) ill will or malice
no question of their maltalent regarding us

mamilla (ma-MIL-a) nipple
a thick and discreet top that does not accentuate the mamilla

mancation (man-KAY-shun) mutilation or maiming
*a horror film rife with the slow-motion mancation of attractive
and frivolous teenagers*

mancinism (MAN-si-niz-um) left-handedness
*not likely that the condition of inborn mancinism can ever be
righted*

manducate (MAN-dyoo-kayt) to chew
a nostalgic longing to manducate some saltwater taffy

maniform (MAN-i-form) hand-shaped
your typical maniform oven mitt

mansuetude (MAN-swe-tood) mildness, gentleness, or
meekness
the mansuetude of a monastic order

manuary (MAN-yoo-er-ee) manual labor
something satisfying about doing a little manuary

manubiary (ma-NYOO-bee-er-ee) pert. to the spoils of
war
some violent manubiary disputes between the youth gangs

manuductory (man-yoo-DUK-to-ree) leading by or as if
by the hand
a fast learner needing no manuductory help

manurage (ma-NYOOR-aj) the cultivation or occupation
of land
the history of the manurage of the American West

manutention (man-yoo-TEN-shun) a holding or restraining with the hands
*the standard police manutention procedure against the side of
the car*

manustupration (man-yoo-stoo-PRAY-shun) masturbation
old wives' tales about the evils of manustupration

marcid (MAR-sid) withered or decayed
a revoltingly marcid navel orange

marcor (MAR-kawr) decay
the marcor of a once-great civilization

margaritaceous (mar-ga-ri-TAY-shus) pearly
his hideously ill-fitting and margaritaceous dentures

marigenous (ma-RIJ-e-nus) produced in the sea
marigenous oil deposits

maritorious (ma-ri-TO-ri-us) very fond of one's husband
a famous opera singer who is in private a quite maritorious wife

materteral (ma-ter-TER-al) pert. to an aunt
materteral advice to go with the avuncular

mathesis (ma-THEE-sis) mental discipline
a rolling stone without much mathesis

matriotism (MAY-tri-o-tiz-um) love of one's alma mater
matriotism and the old school tie

mattoid (MAT-toyd) a semi-insane person
living not with a mere neurotic but with a mattoid

maximious (mak-ZIM-ee-us) of great power
a Nobel Prize winner who makes a maximious impression

102

mechanolater (mek-a-NOL-a-ter) one who overestimates the importance of machines
an engineer who seems to be a soulless mechanolater

mediocrist (MEE-dee-o-krist) one having mediocre ability or talent
a disappointing applicant pool of eager mediocrists

megalomartyr (MEG-a-lo-mar-ter) a great or honored martyr
their dread of turning a political outlaw into a megalomartyr

megalophonic (meg-a-lo-FON-ik) having a high or loud voice
a properly megalophonic auctioneer

megalophonous (meg-a-LOF-o-nus) imposing in sound
the rocket's spectacular, megalophonous ignition

megalopsychy (meg-a-LOP-si-kee) greatness of soul
the megalopsychy of a genuine prophet

melancounterous (mel-an-KOWNT-er-us) ill-timed
a melancounterous surprise visit

melanocomous (mel-an-OK-i-mus) having black hair
a melanocomous villain

melpomenish (mel-POM-e-nish) tragic
a grand, melpomenish epic

mendaciloquent (men-da-SIL-o-kwent) telling lies
two very mendaciloquent children

mendicity (men-DI-si-tee) begging or beggary
increasing mendicity in the city's streets

mentery (MEN-te-ree) lying; mendacity
appalled at the mentery of his schoolmates

menthaceous (men-THAY-shus) minty
some kind of menthaceous cocktail

mentimutation (men-ti-myoo-TAY-shun) a change of mind
the exceedingly rare mentimutations of a major league umpire

mentulate   (MEN-tyoo-let) having a large penis
a mentulate horse

meracious   (mer-AY-shus) pure or unmixed
a meracious rather than an eclectic art form

mercation   (mer-KAY-shun) buying
the frenzy of holiday mercation

merdiverous   (mer-DI-ve-rus) dung-eating
dismissed him as a merdiverous swine

merdurinous   (mer-DYOOR-i-nus) composed of dung and
urine
described the script, to paraphrase, as merdurinous

merenda   (mer-EN-da) a light meal
just time for a merenda before the evening rehearsal

meretriculate   (mer-e-TRIK-yoo-layt) to deceive or con as
a prostitute does
a young hustler who gladly meretriculates his clients

meridiation   (me-rid-ee-AY-shun) a siesta
a brief meridiation after getting up so early

meropic   (me-ROP-ik) able to speak
a meropic infant

merotomize   (mer-OT-om-ize) to divide into parts
a legal need to merotomize the acreage

meshantery   (me-SHANT-er-ee) a wicked deed
the shocking meshantery of his betrayal

metagnostic   (met-ag-NOS-tik) unknowable
one of the great metagnostic things

metagrobolism   (met-a-GROB-o-liz-um) mystification
the ritual's silly metagrobolism

metagrobolize   (met-a-GROB-o-lyz) to bewilder or mystify; figure or puzzle out
an abstract sculpture that metagrobolized even the art critics

metaphrast   (MET-a-frast) a translator
an English prose style almost requiring a metaphrast

methysis (me-THY-sis) alcoholic addiction
a society in which teenage methysis is too prevalent

metromania (met-ro-MAY-ni-a) a mania for writing verse
a greeting-card poetaster with metromania

micropsychy (MY-kro-sy-kee) cowardice; pusillanimity
a little character test that revealed her basic micropsychy

miction (MIK-shun) urination
liquid intake to increase miction

micturate (MIK-tyoo-rayt) urinate
forced to micturate into a milk bottle while they drove

micturient (mik-TYOOR-ee-ent) wanting or needing to urinate
helplessly micturient and no place to go

millesimal (mi-LES-i-mal) a thousandth
having only a millesimal of his wife's intelligence

mimp (mimp) to purse one's lips
to wink and mimp in a conciliatory look

minacious (or minatory) (mi-NAY-shus) (MIN-a-to-ree) threatening
a minacious tone of voice

minauderie (mee-NO-dree) affected or coquettish airs
the mincing minauderies of a dandy

minimifidian (min-i-mi-FID-ee-an) enough to make one's faith minimal
the minimifidian effect of Leonard's pitiful demonstration

minitant (MIN-i-tant) threatening
a minitant atmosphere in that bar

minutissimic (mi-noo-TIS-i-mik) very minute
ridiculously proud of his minutissimic contribution

mirandous (my-RAN-dus) wondrous
the musical's large and mirandous sets

mirific (my-RIF-ik) working wonders; wonderful
an absolutely mirific physical therapist

mirligoes   (MER-li-goze) dizziness
a cliffside stroll that gave me the mirligoes

misacceptation   (mis-ak-sep-TAY-shun) the taking of a
word in a wrong sense; verbal misinterpretation
the common misacceptation of the word fulsome

misandry   (MIS-an-dree) hatred of men
desperately accused his long-suffering girlfriend of misandry

misculate   (MIS-kyoo-layt) mingled
a feeling of misculate sadness and joy

misopolemical   (mis-o-po-LEM-i-kal) (my-so-po-LEM-i-kal)
hating war
a decorated Marine veteran's misopolemical autobiography

misoxene   (mis-OK-seen) (my-SOK-seen) a hater of
strangers
a rural recluse and misoxene

mnestic (or **mnesic)**   (NES-tik) (NEE-sik) pert. to memory
the profound mnestic theme of Proust's great work

modicity   (mo-DIS-i-tee) moderateness in price
a store popular for its basic modicity and nice salespeople

modulaminous   (mod-yoo-LAM-i-nus) melodious
a large and modulaminous soprano

molimen   (mo-LY-men) a strenuous effort
the molimen of their return trek

moliminous   (mo-LIM-in-us) massive or momentous;
laborious
a moliminous task

mollescent   (mol-LES-ent) becoming soft
a sun-warmed, mollescent plastic fork

mollitude   (MOL-i-tyood) softness or effeminacy
not charmed by the salesman's coyness and mollitude

monomachy   (mo-NOM-a-kee) a duel
the classic monomachy of pugilism

106

morate (MOR-ayt) moral, respectable, or well-mannered
rebelling against the morate bourgeoisie

mordacious (mor-DAY-shus) biting or inclined to bite
assured that the dog was not mordacious

morganize (MOR-ga-nyz) to assassinate in order prevent
or punish revelations of secrets
a secret order to morganize the informer

morigerous (mo-RIJ-er-us) obedient or obsequious
a nervous part-timer who's far too morigerous

mortuous (MOR-tyoo-us) deathlike
an oppressive, mortuous silence throughout the house

moschate (MOS-kit) musky-smelling
a moschate piece of old leather

mournival (MOR-ni-val) a group or set of four
a mournival to play nine holes

mucid (MYOO-sid) musty or moldy
a mucid toolshed

muculent (MYOO-kyoo-lent) slimy
the creaky and muculent boards of the old dock

mugient (MOO-jee-ent) bellowing
the whistlings and mugient exhortations of the stadium crowd

muliebral (myoo-lee-EE-bral) pert. to women
muliebral health in tropical countries

muliebria (myoo-lee-EE-bri-a) the female genitals
a discreet pose in which the leg hid the muliebria

muliebrous (myoo-lee-EE-brus) effeminate
a theatrically muliebrous voice and bearing

mulierose (MYOO-lee-er-ose) fond of women
an employer a little too mulierose for his own good

multivious (mul-TIV-ee-us) having many ways or roads
the multivious cloverleaf where you might easily get lost

multivolent (mul-TIV-o-lent) of many minds
a woefully multivolent and ineffectual committee

mundicidious (mun-di-SID-ee-us) world-destroying
the spectre of mundicidious ecocide

mundify (MUN-di-fy) to cleanse or purify
to mundify everything in the sickroom

mundivagant (mun-DIV-a-gant) wandering over the world
the tale of a mundivagant adventurer

mundungus (mun-DUNG-us) bad-smelling tobacco
clothes reeking of mundungus

munerary (MYOO-ner-er-ee) pert. to a gift
munerary generosity

mutuation (myoo-tyoo-AY-shun) lending or borrowing
to be financially independent and eschew mutuation or risky investment

mycterism (MIK-ter-iz-um) sneering
the mycterism of critics secretly envious

mystagogue (MIS-ta-gog) one who initiates or counsels others in mystical matters
a Masonic mystagogue

N

nanoid (NAY-noyd) (NAN-oyd) abnormally small in body
a wonderfully nanoid and nimble kid to play the role of Puck

nares (NAY-reez) nostrils
the doctor's distractingly bushy nares

nasute (NAY-soot) having a good sense of smell
an expert and nasute big-game tracker

natalitial (nay-ta-LISH-al) pert. to a birthday or birthdays
natalitial remembrances

natatile (NAY-ta-tyl) able to swim
a lively and natatile pet

nates (NAY-teez) buttocks
a hard slap on the nates

natuary (NAT-yoo-er-ee) a maternity ward
a natuary waiting room filled with apprehensive men

naufrageous (naw-FRAY-jus) in danger of shipwreck
small vessels always naufrageous in the North Sea

naufragous (NAW-fra-gus) causing shipwreck
a huge, naufragous rock just below the surface

naufrague (NAW-frayg) a shipwrecked person
a magazine cartoon showing the usual male and female naufragues

nebulochaotic (neb-yoo-lo-kay-OT-ik) confused in a hazy way
if you'll forgive my nebulochaotic mind

necropsy (NEK-rop-see) an autopsy
a court-ordered necropsy after the exhumation

nectareous (nek-TAIR-ee-us) delicious
a chill and nectareous frozen daiquiri

neophilism (ne-OF-i-liz-um) a mania for novelty
the neophilism of an instant-gratification generation

nepotal (NEP-o-tal) pert. to a nephew
strong nepotal ties

nerterology (ner-ter-OL-o-jee) learning pert. to the dead
his disquietingly sudden interest in nerterology

nescient (NESH-yent) ignorant
dealings with nescient bigots

neuromimetic (noor-o-mi-MET-ik) psychosomatic
wondering whether his sister's routine bodily complaints were neuromimetic

nictitate (NIK-ti-tayt) to wink
watching an owl slowly nictitate

109

nidor (NY-dor) (NY-der) a strong odor of burning meat
a redolent nidor and wafts of smoke on the patio

niggle (NIG-ul) minute or meticulous handwriting
an orderly niggle that suggested a pedantic streak

nimbiferous (nim-BIF-er-us) bringing rain or storm clouds
a nimbiferous Tuesday

nisus (NY-sus) an effort or endeavor
the nisus of overcoming self-consciousness

nitency (NY-ten-see) an impulse
Daniel's periodic nitency to self-destruct

nitid (NIT-id) shining, bright, or lustrous
a nitid silver costume

nitigram (NIT-i-gram) a second-rate epigram
a snob whose lame nitigram fell flat

nittiness (NIT-ee-nes) being filled up with small air bubbles
the bracing nittiness of a ginger ale

niveous (NIV-ee-us) snowy
the niveous peaks of distant mountains

noctidial (nok-TID-ee-al) comprising a night and a day
a noctidial voyage to an outlying island

noctilucous (nok-ti-LOO-kus) shining at night; phosphorescent
the misty noctilucous glow of a distant marina

noctivagant (nok-TIV-a-gant) night-wandering
uneasy about the sounds of some noctivagant animal

noctuolent (NOK-too-o-lent) smelling strongest at night
the noctuolent bog on the property

nocument (NOK-yoo-ment) harm
the growing nocument to his self-confidence

nod-crafty (NOD-kraf-tee) nodding so as to appear wise
a cluster of nod-crafty, pipe-smoking professors

noddary (NOD-er-ee) a foolish act
apologizing for her occasional noddaries

nolition (no-LISH-un) unwillingness
Patty's demonstrable nolition

nolleity (no-LEE-i-tee) the state of being unwilling
confronting the nolleity of complacent students

nomic (NOM-ik) (NO-mik) customary or conventional
a rebelling against nomic values

nonage (NON-ayj) (NON-ij) the state or being underage;
minority
the shocking nonage of some of those hired

noncurantist (non-kyoo-RAN-tist) characterized by
indifference
annoyed by her perfunctory, noncurantist attitude

nosocomial (nos-o-KO-mi-al) pert. to a hospital or
hospitals
that nosocomial smell that always made his stomach queasy

nosopoetic (nos-o-po-ET-ik) producing disease
dangerously nosopoetic conditions

nostomania (nos-to-MAY-ni-a) acute homesickness
a wrenching nostomania set off by the letter from home

notionalist (NO-shun-al-ist) a theorist or speculative
thinker
admired as an observer and notionalist

novercal (no-VER-kal) pert. to or like a stepmother
declared in court to be a good novercal influence on the children

novolescence (no-vo-LES-ense) up-to-dateness
an old and traditional magazine eschewing shallow novolescence

nubilous (NOO-bi-lus) vague
nubilous but harmful rumors

nucal (NOO-kal) pert. to nuts
a nucal health-food snack

nullabicity (or **nullabiety**)   (nul-a-BIS-i-tee) (nul-a-BY-i-tee) being nowhere
a depressing feeling of nullabicity

nullibiquitous   (nul-i-BI-kwi-tus) existing nowhere
a version of an America that is nullibiquitous or at least long gone

numquid   (NUM-kwid) an inquisitive person
an aggressive journalist who was a pesty numquid even as a child

nundination   (nun-di-NAY-shun) buying and selling; trading
the heady uncertainties of nundination

nutrice   (NOO-tris) a nurse
a portly and imposing nutrice

nychthemeron   (nik-THEE-me-ron) a night and a day
over the course of a nychthemeron

nympholepsy   (NIM-fo-lep-see) a yearning for an unattainable ideal
an artist's melancholy nympholepsy even in his later years

nysot   (NY-sot) a wanton or loose girl
the ranking nysot of the junior class

O

obambulate   (ob-AM-byoo-layt) to walk about or wander
perfectly willing to go off on her own and just obambulate

oblectate   (ob-LEK-tayt) to please or delight
a liquid concoction that cannot but oblectate

oblivescence   (ob-li-VES-ens) forgetfulness
aching for a respite and at least temporary oblivescence

obmutescent   (ob-myoo-TES-ent) obstinately silent
an attentive but obmutescent lifeguard

obolary (OB-o-le-ree) poor or impecunious
obolary migrant workers

obsecrate (OB-se-krayt) to beg
too proud to obsecrate for his job

observandum (ob-zer-VAN-dum) a thing to be observed
or noted
found the whole exhibit a boring observandum

obstaculous (ob-STAK-yoo-lus) constituting or like an
obstacle
a tall, obstaculous bouncer in the doorway

obstipation (ob-sti-PAY-shun) extreme constipation
a taut, pained face that seemed to reflect two years of obstipation

obstriction (ob-STRIK-shun) an obligation
a further obstriction to write about it

obtenebrate (ob-TEN-e-brayt) to cast a shadow over
a resolve not to allow anything to obtenebrate the proceedings

obtest (ob-TEST) to beg
obtesting the indulgence of the security guard

obtrect (ob-TREKT) to decry or disparage
corruption that should be exposed and obtrected

obtruncate (ob-TRUNG-kayt) to cut the top off
washed and obtruncated the carrots

obturate (OB-tyoo-rayt) to close or stop up
whoever obturated the car's exhaust pipe

obvallate (ob-VA-layt) walled around
one of Europe's obvallate medieval cities

obvelation (ob-ve-LAY-shun) a veiling or concealing
a very artful obvelation of the damaged area

obvention (ob-VEN-shun) incidental occurrence
an obvention that could have altered history

ochlesis (ok-LEE-sis) unhealthy crowding
the oppressive ochlesis of the small ferry

ocivity (ah-SIV-i-tee) laziness
quite unapologetic about his ocivity

ocreate (OK-ree-ayt) wearing leggings or boots
a gangly, ocreate woodsman

oecodomic (ee-ko-DOM-ik) architectural
a plaster oecodomic model of the whole complex

ogganition (og-a-NISH-un) growling, grumbling, or
snarling
the general ogganition heard in a zoo

Ogygian (o-JIJ-yun) very old
an Ogygian village cemetery

oikiomiasmata (oy-kee-o-mee-AZ-ma-ta) noxious fumes
from household conditions
the deplorable shantytown oikiomiasmata

oikology (oy-KOL-o-jee) housekeeping
males who could use a crash course in basic oikology

oikotropic (oy-ko-TROP-ik) homesick
the oikotropic pangs of a frequent-flyer life

olent (O-lent) scented; fragrant
a warm and olent gift and candle shop

olid (OL-id) stinking
an olid refrigerator filled with spoiled food

oligoglottism (ol-i-go-GLOT-iz-um) a little knowledge of
languages
the clumsy oligoglottism of the typical business traveler

oligophrenic (ol-i-go-FREN-ik) feebleminded
*a wonderfully forced and oligophrenic conversation in the
elevator*

olitory (OL-i-to-ree) belonging to a kitchen garden
my neighbor's fresh olitory herbs

omnifarious (om-ni-FAIR-i-us) of all kinds
omnifarious stationery items

omnigenous   (om-NI-jen-us) of all kinds
a show of omnigenous collectibles

omniregency   (OM-ni-ree-jen-see) total or universal rule
visions of a cure-all omiregency by a wise leader

omnist   (OM-nist) one receptive to all aspects of thought
or truth
a sage judge who was a true omnist

oneiric   (o-NY-rik) pert. to dreams
a notebook by the bed to keep a careful oneiric diary

onerary   (ON-er-er-ree) suitable for carrying freight
the rickety but serviceable onerary cart

oniomania   (o-ni-o-MAY-ni-a) mania to buy things
her sister's incorrigible shopping-mall oniomania

onology   (o-NOL-o-jee) foolish talk
the vapid onology of a glitzy talk show

onym   (ON-im) a scientific or technical name
the plant's unpronounceable onym

onymatic   (on-i-MAT-ik) pert. to names
*the nice-sounding onymatic absurdities conjured up by unscru-
pulous developers*

onymous   (ON-i-mus) having a name
a phenomenon not yet onymous or adequately described

onymy   (ON-i-mee) nomenclature
the extensive and difficult onymy of botany

operiment   (o-PER-i-ment) a covering
an old blanket serving as operiment for the valuable tools

operose   (OP-er-ose) diligently busy
*the main thing being to look bright-eyed and operose while she's
around*

operosity   (o-per-OS-i-tee) painstaking effort or work;
laboriousness
the unacknowledged operosity of young campaign workers

opiparous (o-PIP-a-rus) rich or sumptuous
the palazzo's opiparous tapestries and other furnishings

opitulate (o-PIT-yoo-let) to help or aid
some old photo albums to opitulate his memory

oppilate (OP-i-layt) to obstruct or block up
old pipes oppilated by sludge

oppugnant (op-PUG-nant) antagonistic or hostile
an oppugnant business rival

opsimath (OP-si-math) one who learns late in life
a halfway house staffed by helpful opsimaths

oragious (o-RAY-jus) stormy
an oragious period

orbate (OR-bayt) parentless; childless
ailing and orbate children who are casualties of civil war

orbation (or-BAY-shun) lack of parents; lack of children
the theme of orbation in the Victorian novel

orectic (o-REK-tik) pert. to desires or appetites
a spoiled individual badly in need of some orectic curbing

orexigenic (o-reks-i-JEN-ik) (o-reks-i-GEN-ik) appetite-stimulating
good orexigenic exercise

oriency (O-ri-en-cee) brilliancy of color
the pure oriency of the reds and greens

oscitant (OS-i-tant) drowsy and yawning
oscitant but trying to keep awake at the meeting

oscitate (OS-i-tayt) to yawn
a jaw so numb and sore it was painful to oscitate

osphretic (os-FRET-ik) smellable; olfactory
air polluted with osphretic chemicals

osseous (OS-ee-us) bony
a tall and osseous farmer in overalls

ossifragous   (os-SIF-ra-gus) bone-breaking
an ossifragous fall from the ladder

otacust   (OT-a-kust) a listener; spy
a waiting room filled with closet otacusts

othergates   (UTH-er-gayts) in another way
to stop and just begin again othergates

otiant   (O-shee-ant) unemployed or idle
a town with a high percentage of otiant factory workers

outrecuidance   (oo-tre-KWEE-dans) conceit or arrogance
thoroughly unlikeable because of her smug outrecuidance

oxyphonia   (ok-si-FO-nee-a) shrillness of voice
their comical oxyphonia from inhaling helium

ozostomia   (o-zos-TO-mee-a) bad breath
their dog's ozostomia

P

pacative (or pacate)   (PAY-ka-tiv) (PAY-kayt) calming or
tranquilizing
the unbelievably pacative effect of his presence

pachydermatous   (pak-i-DER-ma-tus) thick-skinned
a job for which you'd have to be morally pachydermatous

pactitious   (pak-TISH-us) arranged or settled by agreement
not a thing to be decreed but a patient and pactitious matter

palaestrics   (pa-LES-triks) gymnastics
enough floor mats for a large palaestrics class

paletot   (PAL-e-tow) (PAL-tow) a loose overcoat
walking around in boots and an old paletot

palingenesy   (pal-in-JEN-e-see) rebirth or revival
the alarming palingenesy of extremist groups

pallescent   (pal-ES-ent) growing pale
her frightened and pallescent sister

palmary   (PAL-ma-ree) praiseworthy; preeminent
a palmary acceptance speech

paltrement   (PAWL-tre-ment) worthless things; rubbish
not worth getting upset about such paltrement

panary   (PAN-a-ree) pert. to bread
the panary secrets of bakers

pandiculation   (pan-dik-yoo-LAY-shun) stretching and
yawning
his usual eye rubbing and pandiculation late in the day

panivorous   (pa-NIV-o-rus) bread-eating
those panivorous birds

pantaraxia   (pan-ta-RAK-see-a) actions to keep people on
their toes
the imaginative methods of pantaraxia used by good employers

panurgic   (pan-ER-jik) ready to do work of all kinds
an energetic and panurgic odd-jobs man

papable   (PAY-pa-bul) qualified to become pope
respected but not papable prelates of the church

Paphian   (PAY-fe-an) a prostitute
a hotel assignation with a middle-aged Paphian

papyraceous   (pap-i-RAY-shus) papery
a messy, papyraceous desk

paracme   (par-AK-me) the beginning of decline or decay
the paracme of a baseball player's career

paradromic   (par-a-DROM-ik) running side by side
paradromic channels in the pattern

paralipophobia   (par-a-ly-po-FO-bee-a) fear of neglect of
some duty
overworked and haunted by paralipophobia

paramuthetic (par-a-myoo-THET-ik) encouraging or consoling
some paramuthetic songs

paraph (PAR-af) a flourish made at the end of a signature
signed with a bold paraph

parapherna (par-a-FER-na) a wife's belongings or property that she legally retains
a divorcee looking out for her parapherna as she remarries

paravent (PAR-a-vent) a windscreen
trying to use the open car door as a paravent

parbreak (par-BRAYK) (PAR-brayk) to vomit
a nauseated first-class passenger about to parbreak

pareunia (pa-ROO-nee-a) sexual intercourse
the contemporary risks of pareunia

parous (PAR-us) having borne a child
the many parous women on the day-school staff

parthenian (or **parthenic**) (par-THEE-nee-an) (par-THEN-ik) virgin
a parthenian Caribbean reef not yet despoiled

parvenant (par-ve-NON) one on the way up socially or professionally
a parvenant young lawyer just entering politics

parvipotent (PAR-vi-po-tent) having little power
an impressive title but a fairly parvipotent position

parviscient (par-VISH-ent) uninformed or knowing little
people who are shockingly parviscient

parvule (PAR-vool) a very small pill
a bottle of prescription parvules that cost a small fortune

pastose (pas-TOSE) covered with thick paint
a pastose white shed that had seen better days

patefy (PAT-e-fy) to reveal or disclose
a refusal to patefy the names of those charged

pathematic   (path-e-MAT-ik) pert. to emotion or the emotions
the pathematic ups and downs in the third act

patricentric   (PAT-ri-sen-trik) centered on the father
a severe, patricentric household

patulous   (PAT-yoo-lus) spreading or opening widely
a patulous entrance into the arena

paulopast   (PAW-lo-past) just completed or finished
a paulopast lecture tour

pavid   (PAV-id) afraid or timid
too pavid to take action

peccable   (PEK-a-bul) liable to sin
a sermon for all who are mortal and peccable

peccaminous   (pek-KAM-i-nus) sinful
excitingly peccaminous thoughts

pedaneous   (ped-AY-nee-us) petty
a pedaneous concern about who owed more for a taxi ride

pedetentous   (ped-e-TEN-tus) proceeding cautiously or step by step
a wisely patient and pedetentous investigation

pedestrious   (pe-DES-tri-us) going on foot
driving past some heartier, pedestrious sightseers

pedionomite   (ped-i-ON-o-myt) one who lives in or on a plain
the hard-scrabble pedionomites in the middle of the country

pegamoid   (PEG-a-moyd) artificial leather
an armchair covered with pegamoid

peirastic   (py-RAS-tik) experimental or tentative
her innovative if only peirastic curriculum

penadjacent   (peen-a-JAY-sent) next to adjacent
the penadjacent house

penelopize   (pen-EL-o-pyz) to do and undo and do and . . .
to gain time
*those who temporize and penelopize at the highest levels of
government*

penetralia   (pen-e-TRAY-lyuh) hidden things or places;
secrets
the penetralia of a very secret organization

penial   (PEE-ni-al) pert. to the penis
women amused at male penial envy

pensum   (PEN-sum) a chore as school punishment
gave both boys the pensum of washing the blackboards

peracute   (PER-a-kyoot) very acute or violent
a peracute fall that broke her hip

peradvertence   (PER-ad-ver-tense) extreme carefulness or
attention
the peradvertence of the inspection team

peraffable   (per-AF-a-bul) easy to go up to and speak to
relieved and thrilled at how peraffable the senator was

perculsion   (per-KUL-shun) shock
social perculsions from a racial crime

perduellion   (per-dyoo-EL-yon) treason
the gravity of perduellion in wartime

perflate   (per-FLAYT) to blow through or ventilate
only two small portholes to perflate the stifling compartment

perfricate   (PER-fri-kayt) to rub thoroughly
a companion who perfricated his freezing limbs

perfuncturate   (per-FUNGK-tyoo-rayt) to do halfheartedly
his tendency to delay and then perfuncturate the job

pergameneous (or **pergamentaceous**)   (per-ga-MEE-ni-us)
(per-ga-men-TAY-shus) like parchment
a pergameneous whitish fabric

perhorresce   (per-hor-RES) to have a horror of; shudder at
*could only perhorresce her husband's taste in videocassette
movies*

121

periclitate (per-IK-li-tayt) to expose to risk or danger
a dangerous route that would periclitate their parents

periculant (pe-RIK-yoo-lant) being in danger
innocent, periculant tourists in the wrong part of town

periegesis (per-ee-e-GEE-sis) a tour or description of a region
the usual VIP periegesis upon arrival

perigraph (PER-i-graf) a careless sketch or diagram
a hasty perigraph of the new house

periplus (PER-i-plus) a circuit or tour; a circumnavigation
an adventurous coastal periplus of Australia

peristerophily (per-i-ster-OF-i-lee) pigeon raising and training
rooftop peristerophily

perlegate (PER-le-gayt) to read through
the tedium of having to perlegate the entire three volumes

perpession (per-PE-shun) enduring suffering
a heroic perpession that was an example to all

perquest (per-KWEST) to search through
a guest who had sneakily perquested all his belongings

perseverate (per-SEV-e-rayt) to recur constantly or persist; keep repeating
an uneasy feeling that the problem will only perseverate

persolve (per-SOLV) to pay in toto
her determination to persolve all her school loans

perstreperous (per-STREP-er-us) noisy
a perstreperous monkey house

perstringe (per-STRINJ) to criticize
a readiness to freely perstringe his friend's faults

pervagate (PER-va-gayt) to ramble through
inviting bused-in groups to pervagate the big old mansion

pervicacious (per-vi-KAY-shus) stubborn
an aging and very pervicacious grandfather

pervulgate (per-VUL-gayt) to publish
a controversial decision to pervulgate the writer's personal letters

petitor (PET-i-ter) (pe-TY-ter) a seeker, applicant, or candidate
many petitors responding to the newspaper ad

petrescent (pe-TRES-ent) turning to stone
so frozen with embarrassment that she looked petrescent

petulcous (pe-TUL-kus) butting like a ram; wantonly aggressive
a man who behaved on their first date like a petulcous stag

Phalarism (FAL-ar-iz-um) inhuman cruelty; love of inflicting torture
the Phalarism of a monstrous serial killer

phanic (FAN-ik) visible or obvious
the phanic, omnipresent beauty of the monastery's surroundings

phasm (FAZ-um) a meteor
the lovely arc of a phasm in the night sky

phemic (FEE-mik) pert. to speech
phemic exercises to overcome her thick accent

philargyry (fil-AR-ji-ree) love of money
Andy's unapologetic philargyry

philauty (phi-LAW-tee) conceit
the leading man's insufferable philauty

philhippic (fil-HIP-ik) liking horses
an exciting coming-of-age story for philhippic young adults

philia (FIL-ee-uh) affection or love for friends or fellow human beings
a divided society crying out for basic human philia

philocalist (fi-LOK-a-list) a lover of beauty
a scholarly philocalist and collector

philodemic (fil-o-DEM-ik) liking the common people
an entertainer who has always been philodemic

philogeant (fil-o-GEE-ant) a lover of the earth
a shrinking, endangered world in which all people should be philogeants

philogynous (fi-LOJ-i-nus) very fond of women
a Texan whose short stories evince his philogynous values

philoplutary (fil-o-PLOO-ta-ree) a lover of wealth
an unregenerate philoplutary who can never have enough

philopolemic (fil-o-po-LEM-ik) loving debate or contention
a philopolemic armchair lawyer

phiz (fiz) face
an anchorperson with a pretty phiz and nothing else

phoenixity (fe-NIK-si-tee) matchless excellence or beauty; the quality of being unrivaled
the phoenixity of a classic Greek statue

phreatic (free-AT-ik) pert. to wells
the phreatic respite of a desert oasis

phrontistery (FRON-tis-te-ree) a place for thought or study
a small rear room in the library perfect as a phrontistery

phthisozoics (fthys-o-ZO-iks) the art of killing harmful animals
issues of phthisozoics with regard to the ecosystem

physagogue (FIS-a-gog) (FY-sa-gog) flatulent or passing gas
a theater filled with overfed, physagogue society people

physiophilist (fiz-ee-OF-o-list) a nature lover
a fervent hiker and physiophilist

pilgarlic (pil-GAR-lik) a hapless bald-headed man
a company owned by two brothers who are both mousy pilgarlics

pilpulistic (pil-pool-IS-tik) hairsplitting
the pilpulistic absurdities of tenure-driven pedants

124

pingle (PING-ul) to nibble or pick at food; eat with little appetite
a disappointing buffet at which they could only pingle

pinguescent (ping-GWES-ent) becoming fat
an old friend now almost unrecognizably pinguescent

pinguinitescent (ping-gwi-ni-TES-ent) shining with grease
four talented and pinguinitescent doo-woppers

piperitious (pip-er-ISH-us) peppery
a crisp and piperitious Mexican dish

piscation (pis-KAY-shun) fishing
disputes about piscation rights on the lake

pistic (PIS-tik) pert. to faith
a religion offering pistic affirmation rather than dogmatic answers

plagose (pla-GOSE) fond of flogging
a treacherous, plagose slave trader

plangorous (PLANG-er-us) lamenting loudly
the plangorous demonstrations of the slain leader's followers

planiloquent (plan-IL-o-kwent) plain-speaking
surely our most planiloquent president

plasmator (PLAZ-ma-tor) a maker or creator
an idea man, not a plasmator

plastography (plas-TOG-ra-fee) forgery
a secret workshop with all the tools of state-of-the-art plastography

plaustral (PLAW-stral) pert. to a wagon or cart
muddy, plaustral ruts along the route west

pleniloquence (ple-NIL-o-kwense) excessive talk
the sporadic pleniloquence and lack of focus of the three volunteer workers

plenilunary (plee-ni-LOO-ne-ree) pert. to a full moon
a bright, plenilunary light over the valley

pleonectic (plee-o-NEK-tik) greedy or grasping
the couple's ruthless and pleonectic new landlord

ploration (plo-RAY-shun) weeping
the huddled ploration of frightened and untested soldiers

plumbeous (PLUM-be-us) leaden
a manifestly plumbeous touch when it comes to writing verse

plumeopician (ploo-me-o-PY-si-an) consisting of tar and
feathers
deserving of a plumeopician reception

plurennial (plu-REN-i-al) lasting for several years
for once a plurennial romantic relationship

pluripresence (ploor-i-PREZ-ens) being present at more
than one place at a time
the seeming pluripresence of an incredible private investigator

pluvial (PLOO-vi-al) pert. to rain
heavy pluvial damage to the uncompleted buildings

pneumatosis (noo-ma-TO-sis) flatulence
how to avoid health foods causing formidable pneumatosis

poculation (pok-yoo-LAY-shun) to drink wine
the pleasures of leisurely poculation at a Paris cafe

poculent (POK-yoo-lent) drinkable
poculent water from a mountain stream

podex (PO-deks) the rump or posterior
described as being portly in the podex

podical (POD-i-kal) anal
podical fixations

poecilonym (PEE-si-lo-nim) a synonym
wished she had a dictionary of unusual poecilonyms

poietic (poy-ET-ik) creative, formative, productive, or
active
a colony providing a lively, poietic atmosphere

poimenic (poy-MEN-ik) pert. to pastoral care
the poimenic duties of a young priest

poisable   (POY-za-bul) weighable
so small it's not poisable

pollincture   (pol-LINGK-tyoor) the preparation of a corpse
for a funeral
a thesis on ancient Egyptian pollincture

poltophagic   (pol-to-FAJ-ik) chewing thoroughly
amazed at her aunt's poltophagic jaw movements

polychresty   (POL-i-kres-tee) a remedy or drug good for
many things
the polychresty known as witch hazel

polylogize   (po-LIL-o-jize) to talk too much
begging Peter not to polylogize at the wake

polymicrian   (pol-i-MY-kri-an) compressed into a small
space; compact
the house's wonderfully polymicrian and fragrant pantry

polyonymous   (pol-ee-ON-i-mus) having many names
a polyonymous ancient deity

polysarcia   (pol-i-SAR-shi-a) fatness, obesity, or grossness
the waddling polysarcia of a sumo wrestler

polysemant   (pol-i-SEE-mant) a word with several
meanings
the poem's use of the polysemant cleave

ponent   (PO-nent) western or occidental
the less-settled ponent parts of the state

pootly-nautch   (POOT-lee-nawch) a children's puppet show
*a simplistic play with the depth of character of a preschool
pootly-nautch*

populicide   (POP-yoo-li-cyd) the slaughter of a people or
nation
a dictator capable of populicide

pornerastic   (por-ne-RAS-tik) licentious
a slightly pornerastic class-night skit

127

porporate   (POR-po-rayt) purple-clad
a porporate high school marching band

postation   (post-AY-shun) the placing of one thing after another
a carefully measured postation of the colored streamers over the gym

post-cenal   (post-SEE-nal) after-dinner
an excellent post-cenal brandy

postern   (PO-stern) a back or side entrance
a rented room with its own private postern

postical   (POS-ti-kal) posterior
the woman's postical shapeliness

postliminous   (post-LIM-i-nus) subsequent
a few postliminous complications

postnatus   (post-NAY-tus) one born after a particular event
important to remember that he is a World War II postnatus

potvaliant   (POT-val-i-ant) drunk and feeling brave
some potvaliant and mean-spirited conventioneers

pou sto   (poo sto) (pow sto) a place to stand
a good pou sto or base of operations

praesertim   (pree-SER-tim) something insisted on
with the praesertim that they get to accompany him there

prairillon   (pra-RIL-yun) a small prairie
a forgotten area that is essentially a prairillon

precony   (pre-KO-nee) public commendation or praise
a politician with an insatiable hunger for precony

prehensible   (pre-HEN-si-bul) graspable or seizable
an easily prehensible escape latch

premiate   (PREE-mee-ayt) to reward
important to premiate struggling beginners

premorse (pree-MORSE) having the end broken or bitten off; truncated
my suspiciously premorse popsicle

prepollent (pree-POL-ent) superior in influence, power, or weight
an ultimately prepollent rival

preproperous (pree-PROP-er-us) overly hasty; precipitate
a nervous and preproperous greeting

prepunctual (pree-PUNG-tyoo-al) overly prompt; happening previous to a particular time
if anything, a prepunctual person

preterist (PRET-er-ist) (PREE-ter-ist) one who lives in the past
the mawkish reminiscences of a preterist

preterlethal (pree-ter-LEE-thal) after death or postmortem
the family's very specific preterlethal arrangements

pretervection (pree-ter-VEK-shun) a carrying past a particular place
the solemn pretervection of the holy statue past the church

prévenance (PREV-e-nans) anticipating others' needs
a host loved for his warmth and prévenance

pricker (PRIK-er) horse rider
three prickers on the bridle path

pridian (PRID-i-an) pert. to the day before yesterday
a closer look at their pridian box office receipts

primaveral (pry-ma-VEER-al) pert. to early spring
the dreamy breezes of a lovely primaveral day

pringle (PRING-ul) to feel or cause an unpleasant tingling
as vibrations from the boat's motor pringled her bare feet

proairesis (pro-AIR-e-sis) (pro-EER-e-sis) a deliberate or rational choice
his declared proairesis to give up drugs

procacious (pro-KAY-shus) forward or insolent
a successful photographer with a procacious manner

procation (pro-KAY-shun) wooing or a marriage proposal
Seth's both courtly and romantic procation

proceleusmatic (pros-e-lyoos-MAT-ik) inspiring
a proceleusmatic speech by the union leader

procellous (pro-SEL-us) stormy
an isolate and procellous promontory

procerity (pro-SER-i-tee) tallness
the proximity and procerity of numerous skyscrapers

procinct (PRO-sinkt) readiness or preparation
thinking ahead and with various different strategies in procinct

procryptic (pro-KRIP-tik) camouflaged
going hunting in procryptic clothing

proditorious (prod-i-TO-ri-us) apt to reveal secret thoughts
an innocent and proditorious associate

proficuous (pro-FIK-yoo-us) useful, advantageous, or profitable
a person who could be a proficuous connection

profluent (PROF-loo-ent) going ahead or flowing smoothly on
steady and profluent repairs

progeria (pro-JEER-ee-a) premature senility
to chalk his oddness up to regrettable progeria

projicient (pro-JISH-ent) projecting
leapt from the window onto a projicient tree limb

proletaneous (pro-le-TAY-nee-us) having many children
the proletaneous womenfolk of a very fertile family

prolocutor (pro-LOK-yoo-ter) a spokesperson
a respected and ideal prolocutor for the cause

pronken (PRONG-ken) to prance (like a goat)
carousing and pronkening halfway across the campus

propadeutic (pro-pe-DOO-tik) basic or introductory
a boring, propadeutic lecture that is unfortunately mandatory

propale (pro-PAYL) to disclose
a hesitation to propale her friendship with Arthur

proparent (PRO-payr-ent) one taking the place of a parent
fortunate to be raised by two loving proparents

propine (pro-PEEN) to drink a toast to
felt called upon to propine their top-notch managing editor

propugnator (PRO-pug-nay-tor) a defender or champion
an indefatigable propugnator of lost causes

prosodemic (pros-o-DEM-ik) pert. to something spread by
personal contact
a skin condition that happens to be prosodemic

prosopic (pro-SOP-ik) pert. to the face
the navy pilot's prosopic scars

protervity (pro-TER-vi-tee) peevishness
the protervity of an around-the-clock hypochondriac

protogenist (pro-TOJ-en-ist) an originator or inventor
a genius of a protogenist in the field of electronics

proxenete (PROK-se-neet) a matchmaker
a woman who is an indefatigable proxenete

proxysm (PROK-siz-um) a close relationship
an acquaintanceship but not exactly a heartfelt proxysm

psaphonic (sa-FON-ik) planning one's own rise to fame
and fortune
a girl who had psaphonic fantasies from an early age

pseudodox (SOO-do-doks) (PSOO-do-doks) a false
doctrine
*a cult belief considered by detractors to be a malicious pseudo-
dox*

pseudolatry (soo-DOL-a-tree) the worship of false gods
a fetishism that is a kind of throwback to pagan pseudolatry

pseudopsia   (soo-DOP-see-a) (psoo-DOP-see-a) an optical
illusion
*a harbor so beautiful to them it might have been a collective
pseudopsia*

psithurism   (SITH-er-iz-um) a whispering sound, as of
wind among leaves
a faint and scary psithurism at the edge of the dark woods

psychagogic   (sy-ka-GOJ-ik) inspiring or persuasive to the
mind or soul
a compelling recitation that was truly psychagogic

psychalgia   (sy-KAL-juh) mental distress
a poor soul carrying about some sort of unspoken psychalgia

psychiasis   (sy-KY-a-sis) spiritual healing for the soul
psychiasis by virtue of diligent meditation

psychrophobia   (sy-kro-FO-bee-a) dread of cold
the typical psychrophobia of a dyed-in-the-wool West Indian

psychurgy   (SY-kur-jee) (PSY-kur-jee) mental energy
*a scientific study of individual psychurgy during sleep
deprivation*

psyllic   (SIL-ik) pert. to snake charming
psyllic secrets of the Indian subcontinent

ptarmic   (TAR-mik) (PTAR-mik) causing sneezing
a ptarmic cloud of talcum powder

ptochocracy   (to-KOK-ra-see) (pto-KOK-ra-see) rule by
the poor
a fanciful and satiric fable of a short-lived ptochocracy

pucelage   (POO-se-lij) virginity
the new virtue of pucelage in the age of AIDS

pudendous   (pyoo-DEN-dus) shameful
a pudendous loss of face

pudibund   (PYOO-di-bund) bashful or modest; prudish
too old for that pudibund act she cultivates

puerperal (pyoo-ER-per-al) pert. to childbirth
puerperal deaths among women of the last century

pulicose (PYOO-li-kose) infested with fleas
a ratty and pulicose old tweed vest

punaise (pyoo-NAYZ) bedbug
*a rank sleeping bag that is probably a housing project for
punaises*

pundigrion (pun-DIG-ree-on) a pun
tabloid headlines that cannot resist the predictable pundigrion

purgament (PER-ga-ment) an excretion; excrement
a novelty item resembling a dog's purgament

purlicue (PER-li-kyoo) the space between the thumb and
forefinger
a deep gash in the purlicue of his left hand

purse-proud (perse prowd) vain about one's wealth
the financier's new and now purse-proud young wife

pursy (or pursive) (PER-see) (PER-siv) breathing strenuously or short-winded
a pursy, plump salesman mopping his face

pyrosis (py-RO-sis) heartburn
*a humor book on avoiding pyrosis through a bread and water
diet*

pyrrhonic (pi-RON-ik) skeptical
a pyrrhonic approach to things that disqualifies her as a mediator

pysmatic (PIZ-mat-ik) questioning or interrogatory
a largely pysmatic article offering few answers

Q

quadrimum (kwod-RY-mum) the best wine or liquor
a perfect occasion to bring out the country club's quadrimum

quaestuary   (KWES-tyoo-er-ee) profit-oriented; money-making
a good cause but in truth a quaestuary enterprise

quantulum   (KWON-tyoo-lum) a small quantity
a mere quantulum

querimonious   (kwer-i-MO-nee-us) complaining
a person far too querimonious to fit into the beach house group

querimony   (KWER-i-mo-nee) complaining or a complaint
worn out by the nagging querimony of her in-laws

quesited   (kwe-SY-ted) a thing or person inquired about
the quesiteds of the dogged private investigator

question extraordinaire   (kes-ti-OWN eks-tra-or-di-NAYR) the final or worst torture
a disastrous shared vacation with Pat and Al's conversation the question extraordinaire

quillet   (KWIL-et) a quibble
raised a ludicrous quillet that got the discussion way offtrack

quisquilian (or quisquiliary, quisquilious)   (kwis-KWIL-yun) (kwis-KWIL-ya-ree) (kwis-KWIL-ee-us) trashy
a quisquilian genre of formula fiction

quisquose (or quisquous)   (KWIS-kwoze) (KWIS-kwose) (KWIS-kus) hard to deal with or handle; ticklish
a quisquose situation requiring a creative explanation

quizzacious   (kwiz-AY-shus) bantering
my quizzacious tennis partner

quizzatorial   (kwiz-a-TO-ri-al) questioning in a mock or insincere way
that nasty, quizzatorial lawyer at the party

quomodo   (KWO-mo-do) (kwo-MO-do) means or manner
an agreed goal but no quomodo

quomodocunquize   (kwo-mo-do-KUN-kwyze) to make money in any conceivable way
a serious financial emergency and time to quomodocunquize

134

quop (kwop) to throb
a strange excitement that made one's heart quop

quotennial (kwo-TEN-i-al) annual or yearly
a quotennial check from her aunt

quoz (kwoz) a strange or absurd thing or person
a performer who in private is 100 percent quoz

R

rabulistic (or rabulous) (rab-yoo-LIS-tik) (RAB-yoo-lus) carping or quibbling
a small-minded, rabulistic theater critic

raddled (RAD-uld) highly rouged
the frail elderly woman with the raddled cheeks

ragmatical (rag-MAT-i-kal) wild or riotous
hanging out with an older and ragmatical crowd

ramage (RAM-ij) boughs or branches of a tree
climbing like a monkey through the thick ramage

ratihabition (rat-i-ha-BISH-un) approval
a step that had everybody's complete if silent ratihabition

réclame (RAY-klom) publicity or notoriety
his local réclame since he won that contest

rectigrade (REK-ti-grayd) walking in a straight line
a heavy drinker but usually rectigrade

reculade (rek-yoo-LOD) a retreat or going back
the faculty's reculade to a tried-and-true grading system

redact (re-DAKT) to put in writing
the wisdom of redacting the particulars of their agreement

redamation (red-a-MAY-shun) loving in return
could only hope for a glimmer of redamancy from her

redargue (red-AR-gyoo) to disprove
an urgent mandate to redargue the report's distorted findings

redivivous (red-i-VY-vus) liable to revive
this ever redivivous and resilient competitor

redivivus (red-i-VY-vus) reborn
the community's civic pride finally redivivus

refluent (REF-loo-ent) flowing back; ebbing
the hypnotic rhythms of the refluent tide

refocillate (ree-FOS-i-layt) to refresh or revive
a treat guaranteed to refocillate the kids

reginal (re-JY-nal) queenly
an out-of-touch executive with almost reginal pretensions

regnant (REG-nant) reigning or dominant
the regnant king of popular music

regrate (re-GRAYT) to repay or reward
insisted on regrating every one of the boys who did the shoveling

religiose (re-lij-i-OSE) excessively religious
an intolerance for religiose zealots

relume (re-LOOM) to relight or rekindle
slightly sulfurous air signaling a need to relume the oven's pilot light

remplissage (ron-plee-SAZH) artistic or literary padding
a terribly overwritten novel with big swatches of remplissage

renable (REN-a-bul) fluent or eloquent
a compellingly renable science writer

renascible (re-NAS-i-bul) capable of being reborn
assuring them that the project will always be renascible

renitent (re-NY-tent) (REN-i-tent) resistant or constantly opposed
the balking of a particularly renitent member of the board

repandous (re-PAN-dus) bent upward
a repandous red lever

reptant   (REP-tant) crawling or creeping
a bumptious careerist rather than a reptant toady

rescribe   (ree-SKRYB) to write in reply; rewrite
a desire to rescribe to his sister right away

resipiscent   (res-i-PIS-ent) brought back to one's senses
some heedless campers resipiscent after a sobering experience

respue   (re-SPYOO) to reject strongly
*somebody who first questioned, then respued the changes in the
document*

retromingent   (re-tro-MIN-jent) urinating backward
the gender that is retromingent

rhabdus   (RAB-dos) a magic wand
*protested that she could not just wave a rhabdus and make
things right*

rhadamanthine   (rad-a-MAN-thin) severely or inflexibly
just
a solid, rhadamanthine circuit court judge

rhathymia   (ra-THY-mee-a) lightheartedness
the idyllic rhathymia of a happy childhood

rhonchisonant   (ron-KIS-o-nant) snorting or snoring
barracks life with thirty rhonchisonant sleepers

rictal   (RIK-tal) agape or grimacing
a cutting caricature showing a spectral, rictal face

ridibund   (RID-i-bund) laughing easily
a soft-spoken and delightfully ridibund companion

rigescent   (ri-JES-ent) tending to be stiff or numb
legs rigescent from arthritis

rivage   (RIV-ij) a bank, shore, or coast
tall palm trees along the bay's rivage

riviation   (riv-ee-AY-shun) fishing
a district known for its good riviation

rixation   (rik-SAY-shun) quarreling or scolding
the continual turmoil and rixation of that household

roborant   (ROB-o-rant) restorative
the bracing taste of a roborant, après-ski hot toddy

Roscian   (ROSH-ee-an) pert. to acting
one of many Roscian emotive techniques

roupy   (ROOP-ee) hoarse or husky
the famously roupy voice of a legendary movie star

routous   (ROWT-us) uproarious or noisy
a routous and steamy restaurant kitchen

rubedinous   (roo-BED-in-us) reddish
her chapped, rubedinous hands

rubescent   (roo-BES-ent) blushing
*a sea of either ashen or rubescent young faces in the dancing
class*

rubigenous   (roo-BIJ-en-us) rust-colored; affected by rust
a clanky and rubigenous old pickup truck

ruderous   (ROO-der-us) filled with garbage
the city's many ruderous and desolate empty lots

rupestrian   (roo-PES-tri-an) written in stone
not to say that my comments are rupestrian

rurigenous   (roo-RIJ-en-us) born in the country
a rurigenous and unsophisticated man

rutilant   (ROO-ti-lant) glittering with golden or reddish
light
rutilant flashes from the bronze flagon

S

saccadic   (sa-KAD-ik) jerky or discontinuous
the saccadic but steady advance of the monster robot

saeculum   (SEK-yoo-lum) an age or generation
a saeculum of profound social unrest

saginate   (SAJ-i-nayt) to fatten
an administration that only saginated the ranks of venal lobbyists

salebrous   (SAL-e-brus) rough or rugged
a salebrous period of her life

saliferous   (sa-LIF-er-us) containing salt
canned goods that are usually staggeringly saliferous

salsuginous   (sal-SOO-jin-us) slightly salty; brackish
the state's salsuginous inland streams

saltatorial   (sal-ta-TOR-i-al) fond of leaping
a fearlessly saltatorial cat burglar

salutiferous   (sal-yoo-TIF-er-us) healthful
a more salutiferous working schedule

salvediction   (SAL-ve-dik-shun) a greeting upon meeting
well-dressed but always casual or sporty in his salvedictions

sanable   (SAN-a-bul) curable
a painful but sanable respiratory condition

sanguisugent (or **sanguisugous, sanguivorous**)   (sang-wi-SOO-jent) (sang-wi-SOO-gus) (sang-WIV-er-us) blood-sucking
described as a sanguisugent rack-rent landlord

sanitude   (SAN-i-tyood) a healthy condition
the economic sanitude of the firm

sapid (or saporous)   (SAP-id) (SAP-o-rus) tasty
some unusual and sapid hors d'oeuvres

saprostomous   (sa-PROS-to-mus) having bad breath
a chattery, saprostomous dentist

sarcophilous   (sar-KOF-i-lus) fond of flesh
sarcophilous white slavers

sarcous   (SAR-kus) pert. to flesh or muscle
a recommended masseur for forty minutes of sarcous ecstasy

Sardoodledum   (sar-DOO-dul-dum) contrived, stagy, or
unrealistic drama; melodrama
like the Sardoodledum and mugging of a bad soap opera

sartor   (SAR-tor) a tailor
the special skills of a bespoke sartor

satisdiction   (sat-is-DIK-shun) enough said or saying enough
concerned more about satisdiction than satisfaction

scacchic   (SKAK-ik) pert. to chess
*physical training that was part of the grandmaster's scacchic
regimen*

scaevity   (SKAY-vi-tee) unluckiness
my constitutional scaevity

scaff   (skaff) to beg for food in a contemptible way
a well-dressed youth scaffing near the cafe entrance

scantle   (SKAN-tul) a small portion
only a scantle for each person present

scaphoid   (SKAF-oyd) shaped like a boat
scaphoid pea pods

scarebabe   (SKAIR-bayb) something to scare a baby
*a closeup snapshot of him that Jim said could be a veritable
scarebabe*

scaturient   (ska-TYOOR-ee-ent) gushing
a snake's nest of scaturient sprinklers

scaurous   (SKOR-us) having large ankles
as scaurous as a hefty Clydesdale

scelerate   (SKEL-er-it) extremely wicked
the scelerate deeds of depraved and desperate outlaws

schediasm   (SKEE-dee-az-um) something done impromptu
or offhand
*an all-round entertainer capable of enchanting musical and
magical schediasms*

schemozzle   (she-MOZ-ul) a mess or confused state of affairs
*a badly organized reception that turned into a pointless
schemozzle*

schiztic (SKIZ-tik) separating or characterized by separation
the brief schiztic period of their up-and-down marriage

scialytic (sy-a-LIT-ik) dispersing or dispelling shadows
a brighter, scialytic porch light

sciapodous (sy-AP-o-dus) having large feet
a loping, sciapodous basketball player

scious (SY-us) possessing knowledge
her scious and compassionate grandmother

sciscitation (sis-i-TAY-shun) questioning or inquiry
opposed to any meddlesome sciscitation

sciture (SIT-yoor) knowledge
encyclopedia sciture

scleragogy (SKLER-a-go-jee) discipline of the body; physical self-discipline
a regimen of Spartan scleragogy

scobicular (or **scobiform**) (sko-BIK-yoo-ler) (SKOB-i-form) like sawdust
a tastelessly scobicular breakfast cereal

scopate (or **scopiferous**) (SKO-payt) (sko-PIF-er-us) like a brush
her bristling—forgive the pun—at his scopate mustache

scopic (SKOP-ik) visual
a huge motion picture screen that is an unforgettable scopic treat

scortation (skor-TAY-shun) fornication
a case for abstinence over scortation

scortatory (SKOR-ta-to-ree) pert. to lewdness or fornication
his telltale scortatory preoccupations

scrannel (SKRAN-el) grating and unmelodious
a particularly scrannel jingle

141

screation   (skree-AY-shun) hawking or spitting
the sounds of screation by players along the sidelines

scribaceous   (skry-BAY-shus) fond of writing
the record of a scribaceous soldier

secundate   (se-KUN-dayt) to make prosperous
a promise to restore and secundate the nation

segnity   (SEG-ni-tee) laziness or sluggishness; slothfulness
the creeping segnity of people living in an automobile culture

seity   (SEE-i-tee) individuality or selfhood
the preciousness of seity under totalitarianism

sejunction   (see-JUNGK-shun) separation
the sejunction of the locomotive from the other cars

selcouth   (sel-KOOTH) unusual or strange
a selcouth way to behave at an office party

semese   (se-MEESE) half-eaten
a visibly half-eaten but very inviting-looking ham sandwich

semisomnous   (sem-i-SOM-nus) half-asleep
a long bus ride that soon had her slumping and semisomnous

sempervirent   (sem-per-VY-rent) evergreen
a sempervirent Scandinavian wilderness

sennight   (SEN-nyt) (SEN-it) a week
a package tour for a rather hectic sennight

septentrional   (sep-TEN-tri-on-al) northern
adjusting the instrument for a more septentrional orientation

septimanal   (sep-ti-MAY-nal) weekly
the security of receiving a fat septimanal check

sequacious   (see-KWAY-shus) subservient or sycophantic
the evangelist's markedly sequacious aides

serotinal   (se-ROT-i-nal) pert. to late summer
a feeling of serotinal melancholy

sesquialteral   (ses-kwi-AL-ter-al) one and a half times as
large
an entrance building and a sesquialteral main building

sevocation   (sev-o-KAY-shun) a calling aside
a discreet sevocation of the four girls in trouble

sexdigitism   (seks-DIG-i-tiz-um) six-fingeredness
stood out like a case of sexdigitism

sialogogic   (sy-a-lo-GOJ-ik) causing one to salivate
those full-color, sialogogic food advertisements

sialoquent   (sy-AL-o-kwent) spitting while one is speaking
a loud and sialoquent panel member

siccaneous   (si-KAY-ne-us) dry
that stark and siccaneous terrain

siffilate   (SIF-i-layt) to whisper
schoolboys told not to siffilate during the service

sightsome   (SYT-sum) delightful to behold
her sightsome appearance in the doorway

sigillate   (SIJ-i-layt) to seal or seal up
to gather together and sigillate a packet of confidential papers

sigla   (SIG-la) signs or abbreviations representing words
a native wall hanging bearing bizarre and undecipherable sigla

signate   (SIG-nayt) marked, designated, or distinguished
the signate objectionable parts of the text

silentious   (sy-LEN-shus) taciturn
a silentious but certainly not shy person

similia   (si-MIL-i-a) things that are alike or similar
sorting and categorizing the similia

similitudinize   (si-mil-i-TOO-di-nyz) to draw comparisons
not meaning to similitudinize invidiously

simity   (SIM-i-tee) being flat-nosed
a face with the gnarled simity of an old prizefighter

simultation   (sim-ul-TAY-shun) quarreling
their heated simultation in the conference room

singult   (SING-ult) a sob
the theatrical singult of a hammy opera singer

143

singultus (sing-GUL-tus) hiccups
the embarrassment of singultus during an important vocal audition

sinistral (SIN-is-tral) left-handed
a new support group for sinistral mendicants

siquis (SY-kwis) a public notice
to post the petition as a siquis

siriasis (si-RY-a-sis) sunstroke
the danger of siriasis along the baking, exposed route

siserary (sis-e-RARE-ree) a tongue-lashing
a sizzling siserary from the angry coordinator

sitient (SISH-i-ent) thirsty
less sitient during the winter

sizzard (SIZ-erd) unbearably humid heat
a preference for the desert over the sweltering sizzard of the coast

skillagalee (skil-a-ga-LEE) (SKIL-a-ga-lee) a worthless coin
the common U.S. penny that is nowadays considered a skillagalee

slatch (slatch) an interval of fair weather
a few pleasant slatches amid the inclemency of April

slimpsey (SLIMP-see) hanging limp or drooping
a soaked and slimpsey wool shawl

slipslop (slip-slop) a malapropism
the priceless slipslops of her piano teacher

slurvian (SLUR-vee-an) slurred speech
the mushy slurvian of some witless teenagers

smectic (SMEK-tik) purifying or detergent
a disgraceful sink needing smectic attention

smockfaced (SMOK-fayst) pale-facedly maidenly or effeminate
an overprotected, smockfaced nephew

soliloquacious (so-lil-o-KWAY-shus) prone to holding
forth
a soliloquacious man but an interesting one

somnifery (som-NIF-er-ee) a place of sleep
a corner bunk for a warm and cozy somnifery

sophrosyne (so-FROS-i-nee) self-control or moderation
the virtue of sophrosyne in many Eastern religions

sorbile (SOR-bil) liquid (and hence drinkable)
a popsickle now sorbile

soterial (so-TEER-ee-al) pert. to salvation
the preacher's frequent soterial theme

spadish (SPAY-dish) blunt-spoken
a frowzy, spadish woman from the trailer park

spatiate (SPAY-she-ayt) to rove, ramble, or stroll
to spatiate down the boardwalk

spectabundal (spek-ta-BUN-dal) eager to see
a gaggle of spectabundal passersby

specular (SPEK-yoo-ler) pert. to a mirror or mirrors
the specular splendors of the palace at Versailles

spelaean (or spelean) (spe-LEE-an) living or occurring in
a cave
a fire to dispel the spelaean chill

speratory (SPER-a-to-ree) expected or hoped for
the speratory promotion that never came

sphairistic (sfair-IST-ik) tennis-playing
sphairistic retirees

sphalm (sfom) an erroneous or mistaken belief or doctrine
*a memoir that confesses all the sphalms of her wild and radical
days*

spheterize (SFET-er-aiz) to appropriate
unclaimed lots spheterized by the state

sphingine (SFIN-jyn) (SFIN-jin) sphinxlike
the professor's annoyingly quizzical and sphingine manner

spiflicate (SPIF-li-kayt) to destroy or crush utterly
a vow to spiflicate their crosstown rival

spintry (SPIN-tree) a male prostitute
the autobiography of a onetime spintry

spirituel (spi-ri-too-EL) mentally refined or graceful
an excellent private tutor both learned and spirituel

spissitude (SPIS-i-tood) density or thickness
fog patches of surprising spissitude

splanchnic (SPLANGK-nik) visceral
a splanchnic queasiness

spodogenous (spo-DOJ-e-nus) pert. to waste matter
the problem of spodogenous removal

sponsional (SPON-shun-al) pert. to a promise or an agreement
just a sponsional obligation to a good friend

sportulary (SPOR-tyoo-le-ree) living on handouts
the ignominy of the sportulary life

spuddy (SPUD-ee) (SPOOD-ee) thickset
a spuddy but agile shooting guard

spumescent (spyoo-MES-ent) like foam or froth
a wonderfully spumescent brandy Alexander

spurcidical (sper-SID-i-kal) foulmouthed or scurrilous
the captain's spurcidical tirade

sputative (SPYOO-ta-tiv) apt to spit
an ugly and sputative lizard

squage (skwayj) to dirty with handling
Betty's request not to squage the photograph in the slightest way

squassation (skwos-AY-shun) a severe shaking
uneasy at the sudden squassation of the elevator

squiss (skwiss) to squeeze and crush
his compulsion to squiss empty beer cans

staffage (sta-FAZH) (STA-fazh) details added to a
painting
the intricate staffage of a large canvas

stagiary (STAY-gee-er-ee) a law student
an older but just as idealistic stagiary

staurolatry (stawr-OL-a-tree) worship of the Cross or
Crucifix
the staurolatry of a mystical sect

steatopygous (stee-at-o-PY-gus) having lardy buttocks
a little too steatopygous for a bikini

steganography (steg-a-NOG-ra-fee) cryptography; a code
or cipher
a master of modern steganography

stegmonth (STEG-month) the recovery period after childbirth
back at work during her supposed stegmonth

stegnotic (steg-NOT-ik) stopping diarrhea
needing something stegnotic to combat Montezuma's revenge

stentorophonic (sten-to-ro-FON-ik) speaking loudly
a product demonstrator too stentorophonic for his taste

stercoraceous (or stercoral) (ster-ko-RAY-shus) (STER-
ko-rul) excremental
a stercoraceous chicken coop

sternutation (ster-nyoo-TAY-shun) sneezing
*a magazine perfume ad that must have been the cause of her
shrill sternutation*

stertorous (STER-to-rus) snoring
stertorous rumbles from bed in the loft

stillatitious (stil-a-TISH-us) falling in drops
a steady trickle reduced to a stillatitious flow

stirious (STIR-ee-us) like an icicle
stirious chandelier pendants

147

stochastic   (sto-KAS-tik) conjectural
a purely stochastic happenstance

stoicheiotical   (stoy-kee-OT-i-kal) pert. to magic
an old trunk of stoicheiotical props

stomatic   (sto-MAT-ik) pert. to the mouth
a disease with no stomatic symptoms

storge   (STAWR-jee) instinctive parental love
the lack of storge and the price that some children pay

stound   (stound) (stoond) a short time or moment
a stound's time out

stoundmeal   (STOUND-meel) now and then or at
intervals
glanced over at them stoundmeal

stramash   (stra-MASH) (STRAM-ash) a disturbance or
uproar
a nasty stramash at their family reunion

stramineous   (stra-MIN-ee-us) straw-colored
a stramineous wall hanging

stratonic   (stra-TON-ik) pert. to an army
secret stratonic funding

stratumen   (STRAT-yoo-men) pavement
the glistening rainy stratumen

strepitous   (STREP-i-tus) noisy or boisterous
a gratingly strepitous upstairs party

stupex   (STOO-peks) a stupid person
*a symposium at which two of the panel members were clearly
stupexes*

stupor mundi   (STOO-per MUN-dee) a marvelous or
wondrous object
a legendary stupor mundi such as the Holy Grail or Excalibur

stupration   (stoo-PRAY-shun) rape
the primal human crime of stupration

suaveolent (swa-VEE-o-lent) smelling sweet
both suaveolent and spicy soap bars

suaviation (swov-ee-AY-shun) kissing
a scene of very romantic suaviation

subagitate (sub-AJ-i-tayt) to copulate
encouraged in the 1960s both to agitate and to subagitate

subagitatory (sub-AJ-i-ta-to-ree) pert. to copulation
gross pornography's numbing subagitatory descriptions

subcontiguous (sub-kon-TIG-yoo-us) nearly touching
dangerously subcontiguous lips

subderisorious (sub-de-ris-OR-ee-us) gently scoffing
Ollie's avuncular, subderisorious air

subdititious (sub-di-TISH-us) placed secretly in lieu of
something else
the embarrassed host's last-minute subdititious gift

subdolous (SUB-do-lus) sly or crafty
the coach's brilliantly subdolous game plan

subfocal (sub-FO-kal) not entirely conscious
woozy and subfocal after the hard tackle

subfusc (or subfuscous) (SUB-FUSK) (sub-FUS-kus)
dingy or somber
a subfusc November day

subingression (sub-in-GRESH-un) a subtle or unseen
entrance
the diva's subingression through a side door

subitaneous (sub-i-TAY-ne-us) sudden, hasty, or
unexpected
a side trip to a winery that was quite subitaneous

subitary (SOOB-i-ter-ee) suddenly or hastily done or made
a meal that was obviously subitary but nonetheless appetizing

sublate (sub-LAYT) to take away or cancel
an order to sublate all weekend passes

subpedital (sub-PED-i-tal) a shoe
a locker filled with expensive athletic subpeditals

subrident (or **subrisive**) (sub-RY-dent) (sub-RY-siv)
smiling
the fresco's subrident cherubs

subsannation (sub-san-NAY-shun) derision
her withering subsannation

subsicive (SUB-si-siv) left over or for leisure
subsicive fireworks for a few of the older children

sub silentio (sub si-LEN-shi-o) without a particular point
being made of
to assume sub silentio that that detail will be taken care of

subtegulaneous (sub-teg-yoo-LAY-nee-us) indoor
the jarring subtegulaneous decor

subtrist (sub-TRIST) a little sad
her face lookling a little subtrist at her award ceremony

subvention (sub-VEN-shun) aid and succor
the country's requested subvention from the United Nations

subvocal (sub-VO-kal) "articulated" in thought only
his subvocal but intense revenge scenarios

succedaneum (suk-se-DAY-nee-um) a substitute (esp. as a
remedy)
chicken soup as the classic succedaneum

succus (SUK-us) juice
longing for the succoring succus of a simple coconut

succussion (suk-KUSH-un) violent shaking
the worrisome succussion of the cargo in the hold

sufflaminate (suf-LAM-i-nayt) to obstruct or balk
an uncooperative superior guaranteed to sufflaminate

suggilate (SUG-ji-layt) to beat black-and-blue
not only thwarted but suggilated the mugger

suggilation (sug-ji-LAY-shun) a black-and-blue mark
a handsome and skilled light-heavyweight who seemed immune
to suggilation

superbiate (soo-PER-bee-ayt) to make arrogant or haughty;
to be proud
flattery and toadying that will only superbiate the governor

superincumbent (soo-per-in-KUM-bent) lying or pressing
on
a toppled, superincumbent gravestone

superlation (soo-per-LAY-shun) aggrandizing hype
commercial television's banality and strident superlation

supermundane (soo-per-MUN-dayn) unearthly or
transcendent
portraying a supermundane, futuristic world

supernaculum (soo-per-NAK-yoo-lum) (to drink) to the
last drop; a first-rate liquor
drank the double shot supernaculum

supersalient (soo-per-SAY-li-ent) leaping upon
avoiding their tenants' filthy and supersalient dog

suppalpation (sup-al-PAY-shun) coaxing or wheedling
a little heart-to-heart suppalpation to persuade him

suppeditor (sup-PED-i-tor) a support
used two sawhorses as suppeditors for the large poster

suppelectile (soop-e-LEK-til) pert. to household furniture
very questionable suppelectile taste

supplosion (sup-PLO-zhun) stamping the feet in
disapproval
one of her most endearing traits being her petulant supplosions
when frustrated

supraliminal (soo-pra-LIM-i-nal) conscious
a child whose awareness of good and evil is quite supraliminal

sural (SOO-ral) pert. to the calf of the leg
men's sural vanity in the eighteenth century

151

surbate (SER-bayt) to make one's feet tired
a shopping expedition that surbated my mother

surculation (ser-kyoo-LAY-shun) pruning
surculation expertise for tending English gardens

suresby (SHORZ-bee) one who can be relied upon
a solid friend and suresby

surreption (su-REP-shun) fraudulent suppression of the truth; deliberate misrepresentation
that columnist's flagrant surreption

suspirious (sus-PIR-i-us) breathing heavily or sighing
suspirious tourists at the summit overlook

susurrant (soo-SER-ant) whispering
the lulling sound of the more distant, susurrant surf

sutile (SOO-til) sewn
a mummy with sutile lips

suum cuique (SOO-um KY-kwee) (SOO-um KWY-kwee) to each his own
the question of caveat emptor versus suum cuique

swasivious (swa-SIV-ee-us) agreeably persuasive
such a swasivious way about him

sybotism (SY-bo-tiz-um) pig raising
an apparently innocuous paragraph about Albanian sybotism

symphoric (sim-FOR-ik) accident-prone
elderly and increasingly symphoric

symphronistic (sim-fro-NIS-tik) "intellectually identical" (Carlyle)
that the co-authors of Romance were hardly symphronistic

symposiarch (sim-PO-zi-ark) a master of ceremonies or toastmaster
the smoothness of a practiced symposiarch

symposiast (sim-PO-zi-ast) one who is part of a drinking party; banqueter
the witness who was not a symposiast

synallagmatic (sin-a-lag-MAT-ik) involving a mutual obligation or contract
whether divorce should be viewed as similarly synallagmatic

synchysis (SING-ky-sis) confused sentence arrangement
the synchysis of one of the freshman essays

syncrasy (SING-kra-see) a combining of different things
the imaginative syncrasy of her collages

synodite (SIN-o-dyte) a traveling companion
a synodite for their mutual destination

synomosy (si-NOM-o-see) an oath-bound brotherhood or conspiracy
a grand connivance rather than an actual synomosy

syntomy (SIN-to-mee) brevity or conciseness
editorial lucidity and syntomy

syrtis (or syrt) (SER-tis) (sert) quicksand
Richard's recurrent dream about skiing over syrtis

syssition (si-SIT-i-on) a meal shared with others; mess
a shelter encouraging syssition but not cohabitation

systatic (sis-TAT-ik) synthetic
a screamingly systatic theme park

T

tabellarious (tab-e-LAIR-ee-us) pert. to a letter carrier
a secret liaison carried on with tabellarious intermediaries

tabescent (ta-BES-ent) wasting away
the tabescent victims of a famine

tacenda (ta-SEN-da) things that shouldn't be mentioned
those Victorian tacenda

tachydidaxy (TAK-i-dy-dak-see) fast teaching
a compressed course that proved the potential of tachydidaxy

taction   (TAK-shun) touching or contact
tactless taction as a form of sexual harassment

talionic   (tal-i-ON-ik) pert. to revenge in kind or an eye
for an eye
the syndicate's harsh talionic code

tanquam   (TAN-kwam) something that only seems to exist
one of those blurry extraterrestrial tanquams

tantivy   (tan-TIV-ee) (rushing or riding) headlong
barging tantivy into the horde around the sale table

taphephobia   (taf-e-FO-bee-a) fear of being buried alive
a stupid horror movie parody about a truffle's taphephobia

tapster   (TAP-ster) a bartender
earning good tips as a roadhouse tapster

tarassis   (ta-RAS-is) male hysteria
a strange thesis on monastic tarassis

tardigrade   (TAR-di-grayd) slow-stepping or sluggish
tardigrade troops beyond weariness

tauromachy   (tawr-OM-a-kee) bullfighting or a bullfight
Hemingway's famous introduction to tauromachy

tedesco   (te-DES-ko) Germanic
an ornate drinking vessel from a tedesco university

telepheme   (TEL-ee-feem) (TEL-e-feem) a telephone
message
three telephemes on her answering machine

telesis   (TEL-ee-sis) progress through wise and conscious
planning
an administration bent on continual telesis

telestic   (te-LES-tik) mystical
a telestic experience that remained unexplained

tenebrific   (ten-e-BRIF-ik) gloomy or producing darkness
the tenebrific volcanic ash in the atmosphere

tenellous   (ten-EL-us) somewhat tender
a tenellous piece of veal

tentamen (ten-TAY-men) an experiment or attempt
a justification for a second tentamen

tentiginous (ten-TIJ-e-nus) provoking lust
her breathy and tentigenous voice

tentigo (ten-TY-go) insatiable male lust; satyriasis
his quite grabby and unromantic tentigo

tenue (ten-YOO) general appearance, bearing, or manner
a wary and almost cringing tenue

tenuity (ten-OO-i-tee) a little
asking a tenuity, not an annuity

tephrosis (tee-FRO-sis) incineration
the general tephrosis of all office waste paper for security reasons

teratism (TER-a-tiz-um) the worship of monsters
the pop-culture fad of teratism in America

terdiurnal (ter-dy-ER-nal) three times a day
his claim of practicing terdiurnal abstinence

terebrate (TER-ee-brayt) to be a bore
to drone on tediously and relentlessly terebrate

terremotive (ter-ee-MO-tiv) seismic
slight terremotive tremors just off the coast

terriculament (ter-RIK-yoo-la-ment) a bugbear
childhood terriculaments

tessarian (tess-AR-ee-an) pert. to dice or gambling
the colorful tessarian world of Guys and Dolls

thalian (tha-LY-an) comic
a honeymoon with its thalian moments

thanatoid (THAN-a-toyd) apparently dead
a painting with prone, thanatoid figures in the foreground

theic (THEE-ik) one who drinks too much tea
nor all habitual theics being English

theoktony (thee-OK-to-nee) the death of gods
the drama of Wagnerian theoktony

theomania   (thee-o-MAY-nee-a) religious insanity; the delusion that one is God
megalomania verging on theomania

theopathy   (thee-OP-a-thee) religious emotion from meditating on God
contemplatives attaining a state of theopathy

theopneust (or **theopneustic**)   (THEE-op-noost) (thee-op-NYOO-stik) divinely inspired
oratory that has been called theopneust

thereoid   (THEER-e-oid) beastlike or savage
the fraternity's old thereoid hazing rituals

theriacal   (thee-RY-a-kal) antidotal
to offer some kind of countering, theriacal explanation

theriodic   (theer-i-OD-ik) malignant
a struggle against theriodic powers

thersitical   (ther-SIT-i-kal) foulmouthedly abusive
a thersitical but cowardly old bartender

thetic   (THET-ik) prescribed or dogmatic
a narrow and thetic party line

theurgy   (THEE-er-jee) white magic; magia
a guru whose very presence seemed to work a kind of theurgy

thigging   (THIG-ing) begging or borrowing
a musician who's annoying because of his constant thigging

thob   (thob) to rationalize one's opinions or beliefs
a fool with an infinite capacity to thob

thrasonical   (thray-SON-i-kal) boastful
nothing here to be thrasonical about

thymopsyche   (THY-mo-sy-kee) (THY-mo-psy-kee) emotion and desire
the confused thymopsyche of adolescence

tintamarre   (tin-ta-MAR) a confused din or uproar
a tintamarre audible from outside the theater

tirret (TER-et) an outburst of temper
her husband's rare and brief tirrets

titivate (TIT-i-vayt) to dress up or adorn
to titivate the gym for a prom

tittupy (TIT-up-ee) merrily gay or dancing
a tittupy band of revelers

titubate (TIT-yoo-bayt) to stagger or stumble
the driver incoherent and titubating

togated (or togate) (TO-gayt-ed) (TO-gayt) stately and
Latinate in literary style
the sonorous, togated clauses of Gibbon's history

tohubohu (to-hoo-BO-hoo) chaos or confusion
a scene of utter tohubohu

tongueshot (TUNG-shot) vocal range
the trick of eavesdropping out of tongueshot

tootlish (TOOT-lish) muttering in a childish way
the tootlish complaints of an old geezer

toparchy (TO-par-kee) (TOP-ar-kee) a petty state or
country
banana republics and Far East toparchies

topesthesia (top-es-THEE-zhi-a) (top-es-THEE-zha)
using touch to determine where one is
nocturnal topesthesia

topolatry (to-POL-a-tree) reverence for a place
the topolatry of some fans for his birthplace

torminal (TOR-mi-nal) pert. to colic pain
chronic torminal discomforts

torvous (TOR-vus) stern or severe
a pirate of torvous mien

tournure (toor-NYER) grace in one's bearing; poise
an elegant lady with regal tournure

tracasserie (tra-kas-REE) a fretting, bother, quarrel, or squabble
the foolish tracasseries of the rival merchants

traduction (tra-DUK-shun) slander
the resorting to very ad hominem traduction in the campaign

traject (TRAJ-ekt) to cross over
to traject the stream after a long portage

trangam (TRAN-gam) an odd trinket or puzzle
a wonderful novelty store with all kinds of trangams

tranont (tra-NONT) to sneakily change position
always tranonting during hide-and-seek

transpicuous (tran-SPIK-yoo-us) easily seen through; easily understood
a transpicuous public relations announcement

transumption (tran-SUMP-shun) a copying or copy
the age of electronic transumption

trantles (TRAN-tuls) things of little value
a house of many trantles and few memories

traulism (TRAW-liz-um) stammering
the traulism of several famous statesmen

treen (TREE-en) made of wood; wooden
antique treen toys

tregetour (TREJ-e-ter) (TREJ-i-ter) a magician or juggler
a young tregetour who does children's shows

tremellose (TREM-e-lose) jellylike; gelatinous
a liquid that had turned into something disgustingly tremellose

tressilate (TRES-i-layt) to quiver
to feel an attractive woman tressilate in his arms

tretis (tre-TIS) well-proportioned and graceful
a modest but tretis Italian villa

trichobezoar (trik-o-BE-zo-er) a hair ball
as tasty as a mildewed trichobezoar

trieteric   (try-ee-TER-ik) occurring every other year
making the commemoration a trieteric one

trilapse   (TRY-laps) a third downfall or "slip"
an unforgivable trilapse at the academy

trillibub   (TRIL-i-bub) a trifle
trillibubs for prizes at the small fair

triplasian   (try-PLAY-zhan) threefold
a triplasian strategy

tripudiary   (tri-PYOO-dee-er-ee) pert. to dancing
the choreographer's tripudiary hieroglyphics

troche   (TRO-ke) a tablet (pill)
troches from the dispensary

troke   (troke) a bargain or business deal
great little trokes at garage sales

trophonian   (tro-FO-nee-an) making forever sad
this immemorial and trophonian tragedy

truandise   (TROO-an-dyz) fraudulent begging
streetcorner truandise and three-card monte games

trucidation   (troo-si-DAY-shun) slaughter
internecine warfare and civilian trucidation

trullization   (trul-i-ZAY-shun) laying on plaster with a
trowel
the trullization of one more room

trusatile   (TROO-sa-til) (TROO-sa-tyl) worked by
pushing
a trusatile door bar

trutinate   (troo-ti-NAYT) to consider, balance, or weigh
well-advised to trutinate all factors before deciding

tucket   (TUK-et) a (cavalry) trumpet flourish or signal
the canned fan-rallying tuckets of modern baseball stadiums

Tudesque   (tyoo-DESK) German (language)
that dark Tudesque script called fraktur

turgescent   (ter-JES-ent) swelling
a turgescent and palpitating membrane

tursable   (TER-sa-bul) portable
a kind of tursable reading lamp

tussiculation   (tus-ik-yoo-LAY-shun) a hacking cough
kept awake by his brother's tussiculations

tutament   (TYOO-ta-ment) a defensive safeguard
an alarm system as a home tutament

tutmouthed   (TUT-mowthd) (TUT-mowtht) having protruding lips
a tutmouthed but softspoken women

tuzzymuzzy   (TUZ-ee-muz-ee) a bunch of flowers; nosegay
*presented to her with a pretty tuzzymuzzy and a tendered
apology*

tyrology   (ty-ROL-o-jee) a set of instructions for beginners
a real tyrology instead of amorphous, on-the-job training

tyronic   (ty-RON-ik) amateurish
tyronic methods of detection

U

ubiety   (yoo-BY-e-tee) one's being in a particular place;
whereness
an American city they say has no real ubiety

ubity   (YOO-bi-tee) a place or locality
escaping to some unknown and hidden ubity

ughten   (UT-en) morning twilight
from the ughten to the gloaming

uliginose (or **uliginous)**   (yoo-LIJ-i-nose) (yoo-LIJ-i-nus)
slimy
the uliginose bark of a strange tree

uloid (OO-loid) scarlike
a crosshatched and uloid design

ulotrichous (yoo-LOT-ri-kus) having woolly hair
a sallow-complexioned and ulotrichous people

ultion (UL-shun) revenge
fixated on his personal ultion

ultrafidian (ul-tra-FID-ee-an) blindly gullible or credulous
a bogus evangelist preying on ultrafidian believers

ultroneous (ul-TRO-nee-us) spontaneous
death by ultroneous combustion

umbratile (UM-bra-til) (UM-bra-tyle) done or carried on
indoors or in seclusion; private rather than public
an umbratile regimen of videotape aerobics

unasinous (yoo-NAS-i-nus) equally stupid
debaters who were unasinous

unguicule (UNG-wi-kool) a fingernail
the chilling unguicules of a vampire

unguinous (UNG-wi-nus) oily or greasy
grasped the man's tattered and unguinous overcoat sleeve

unplausive (un-PLAW-siv) not approving
your eternally unplausive parents

uranic (yoo-RAN-ik) heavenly or celestial
evocatively uranic music

urbacity (er-BAS-i-tee) city or metropolitan insularity
a mayor with more urbacity than urbanity

urbicolous (er-BIK-o-lus) city-dwelling
the plight of urbicolous immigrants

uvate (YOO-vayt) grape jam
aspic the color of uvate

uvid (YOO-vid) moist or wet
the uvid and slippery windowsill

uxorious   (uks-O-ree-us) overly devoted to one's wife
a husband once liberated and now fully uxorious

V

vaccary   (VAK-a-ree) pasture; dairy farm
the muck and mire of a rain-soaked vaccary

vaccimulgence   (vas-i-MUL-jense) cow milking
things that go together like a city kid and vaccimulgence

vacivity   (vas-IV-i-tee) emptiness
the chill vacivity of outer space

vadelect   (VAY-de-lekt) a servant
the king's retinue of vadelects and flatterers

vagarious   (va-GAIR-ee-us) whimsical or capricious;
erratic
a vagarious but always engaging story

vagient   (VAY-gee-ent) crying like an infant
a frail and vagient old woman

vastate   (VAS-tayt) to make unsusceptible or immune
an insipid apology that will not vastate him from further criticism

vectitation   (vek-ti-TAY-shun) carrying or being carried
their sleeplike vectitation across the desert by camels

vegete   (VEJ-eet) alive and flourishing
*a medium who described the house's ghosts as vegete and
articulate*

velitation   (vel-i-TAY-shun) a minor argument or contest;
skirmish
the two women's audible velitation in the ladies' room

vellicate   (VEL-i-kayt) to pinch or tickle
a sign saying "Thank You for Not Vellicating the Waitress"

vendemiate   (ven-DEM-ee-ayt) to harvest the vintage
to visit France when the vintnors are vendemiating

venditate   (VEN-di-tayt) to display ostentatiously
seeking a larger office to venditate his phony diplomas

venenate   (VEN-e-nayt) to poison
if industry should continue to venenate our air

venene (or venenose)   (vee-NEEN) (VEN-e-nose)
poisonous
this archcritic's severe judgments and venene vocabulary

ventanna (or ventana)   (ven-TA-na) a window
an airless little structure lacking a single ventanna

ventifact   (VEN-ti-fakt) a stone rounded off by the wind
combing for seashells and ventifacts

ventose   (VEN-tose) (ven-TOSE) given to windy talk
an overpaid and ventose television weatherman

ventripotent   (ven-TRIP-o-tent) having a large belly
not a properly ventripotent Santa Claus

verecund   (VER-ee-kund) shy or bashful
a surprisingly verecund policeman

veridical   (ve-RID-i-kal) truthful
the burden of having to be impeccably veridical

veriloquous   (ve-RIL-o-kwus) speaking the truth
as rare as a veriloquous used-car salesman

verjuice   (VER-joos) sour juice
the greenish verjuice of an unripe melon

verrucose   (VER-uh-kose) warty
a wonderful teacher with the sharp and verrucose features of a witch

vertumnal   (ver-TUM-nal) pert. to spring; vernal
the coming of the vertumnal rains

vesania   (ve-SAY-ni-a) mental derangement
overwork that brought on an unfortunate vesania

vespertilionize   (ves-per-TIL-yun-aiz) to turn into a bat
my strange escort who I thought might vespertilionize any moment

163

vespertine (VES-per-tin) (VES-per-tyn) during the evening
a pleasant vespertine stroll down to the waterfront

vespiary (VES-pi-ar-ee) wasp's nest
two small vespiaries over the garage door

vestiary (VES-ti-er-ee) pert. to clothing
vestiary donations for the homeless

vetanda (ve-TAN-da) forbidden things
children tempted by no-matter-what vetanda

vetusty (VET-us-tee) antiquity
the fascinations of Mediterranean vetusty

viaggiatory (vi-AJ-a-to-ree) (vi-AJ-a-ter-ee) traveling about
from summer stock to viaggiatory road companies

viands (VY-ands) food or provisions
a small cache of viands

vicinage (VIS-i-nij) neighborhood
the immediate vicinage

vicinal (VIS-i-nal) neighboring
the encroachments of vicinal shopping malls and supermarts

videnda (vy-DEN-da) things that ought to be seen
the various videnda of Europe's classic Grand Tour

viduate (VID-yoo-ayt) widowed
a membership mostly of viduate pensioners

vilipensive (vil-i-PEN-sive) abusive
some vilipensive and disorderly fans in the grandstand

villatic (vi-LAT-ik) rural or rustic
an isolated cabin offering a perfect villatic escape

vinculum (VING-kyoo-lum) a link, tie, or bond
the issue of a vincula between reading pornography and violence

viraginity (vir-a-JIN-i-tee) masculinity in a woman
the presumed viraginity of many Russian peasant women

virason (vee-ra-SON) a sea breeze
with feet up and taking in the balmy virason

viridity (vi-RID-i-tee) youth, inexperience, or greenness
the viridity of raw recruits

viripotent (vi-RIP-o-tent) (vy-RIP-o-tent) fit to marry a
man; nubile
his awkward daughters whom he considered not yet viripotent

viscid (VIS-id) wet and sticky
a viscid, drippy opened can of paint

vitative (VY-ta-tiv) loving life
vibrant and vitative young people

vitellus (vi-TEL-us) (vy-TEL-us) egg yolk
a special dessert baked sans vitellus

vitilitigate (vit-i-LIT-i-gayt) to be particularly
quarrelsome
no need to vitilitigate

vivisepulture (viv-i-SEP-ul-tyoor) (viv-i-see-PUL-tyoor)
burial alive
a horror tale about vividly imagined vivisepulture

voidee (VOY-dee) a last-minute or parting dish
the chef's excellent voidee

volage (vo-LAZH) giddy or flighty
a volage ingenue

volitorial (vol-it-O-ri-al) pert. to flying; able to fly
a volitorial insect

volupty (VOL-up-tee) sexual pleasure
pipe dreams of utter sloth and volupty

volutation (vol-yoo-TAY-shun) wallowing
the second-guess volutations of spectator sports fanatics

voraginous (vo-RAJ-i-nus) gulflike or devouring
the nation's voraginous federal deficit

vulnific (or **vulnifical)**   (vul-NIF-ik) (vul-NIF-i-kal)
   wounding
   her cruelly vulnific aspersions

W

wanion   (WON-yun) a plague or vengeance
   the contemporary wanion of drug-related crime

wantonize   (WON-tun-aiz) to come on to or flirt with;
   solicit
   his bar-stool wantonizing

wepmankin   (WEP-man-kin) the male sex
   a side effect seemingly limited to wepmankin

witzelsucht   (VITZ-el-zookt) strained or futile humor
   the salesman's oppressive witzelsucht

would-have-been   (wood-hav-ben) one who wanted or
   would have liked to be (something)
   *that if she hadn't been successful, she could have been a would-
   have-been*

X

xanthodontous   (zan-tho-DON-tus) having yellow teeth
   encountering a band of xanthodontous nomads

xanthous   (ZAN-thus) yellow-skinned
   an old xanthous rubber doll

xenagogy   (ZEN-a-go-jee) (ZEN-a-goj-ee) a guidebook for
   visitors or strangers
   the serendipity of exploring the town without a pocket xenagogy

xenelasia (or **xenelasy)**   (zen-a-LAY-zhee-a) (ze-NEL-a-
   see) generally forbidding residence to foreigners
   a country's not so subtle policy of xenelasia

xenial (ZEE-ni-al) pert. to hospitality
a xenial snack or two for the visitors

xenodocheionology (zen-o-do-KY-on-ol-o-jee) the lore or
love of hotels and inns
a well-read adept in New England xenodocheionology

xenodochial (zen-o-DOKE-ee-al) hospitable
depending on the kindness of xenodochial strangers

xeres (ZER-es) sherry
his grandmother's late-afternoon spot of xeres

xerophagy (ze-ROF-a-jee) eating dry food
the continual xerophagy of health-food addicts

xilinous (ZIL-i-nus) pert. to cotton
their preference for xilinous sportswear

xiph (or xiphias) (zif) (ZIF-i-as) the swordfish
a soupçon of herbs in the xiph

Z

zelotypia (zel-o-TIP-ee-a) fanatical zeal
the unbridled zelotypia of the nationalist factions

zoetic (zo-ET-ik) pert. to life; living; vital
renouncing morbidness for more zoetic preoccupations

Reverse
GLOSSARY

A

abilities for work, enhancing: ERGOGENIC
ability: DACITY
able or skillful: HABILE
abnormality or disorder: DEORDINATION
abortion: AMBLOSIS
absence, pupil's excused: ABSIT
absentminded or preoccupied, worriedly: DISTRAIT
abstinent or self-controlled: ENCRATIC
absurdity: ALOGY
absurd or strange thing or person: QUOZ
abundant source: ABUNDARY
abusive: VILIPENSIVE
abusive, foulmouthedly: THERSITICAL
accident-prone: SYMPHORIC
accumulation: ACERVATION

accusation or charge: IMPETITION
accuse or blame, to: INCULPATE
acknowledgment or recognition: AGNITION
act, an earlier or previous: ANTEFACT
act, catching in the: DEPRENSION
act, the desire or impulse to: ACTURIENCE
acting, pert. to: ROSCIAN
action that is thoughtless: ETOURDERIE
active, creative, formative, or productive: POIETIC
activity: DACITY
act that is foolish: NODDARY
acute or violent, very: PERACUTE
addiction to alcohol: METHYSIS

addition: ADJECTAMENT

additional: ADSCITITIOUS

addressing or calling upon somebody, a way of: COMPELLATION

adjacent, next to: PENADJACENT

administration, good: EUNOMY

adorn or dress up, to: TITIVATE

advance, a gradual: ILLAPSE

advance, to: INCEDE

advantageous, useful, or profitable: PROFICUOUS

advice, giving: CONSILIARY

advise against or dissuade, to loudly or strongly: DEHORT

adviser or initiator to others in mystical matters: MYSTAGOGUE

affected or coquettish airs: MINAUDERIE

affection or love for friends or fellow human beings: PHILIA

affecting or moving: FLEXANIMOUS

affection, a show of: EMPRESSEMENT

affection, lack of natural: ASTORGY

affect or influence, to: ATTINGE

affirmative: CATAPHATIC

afraid or timid: PAVID

after-dinner: POST-CENAL

agape or grimacing: RICTAL

age, equality of: COEVALITY

age, great or old: GRANDEVITY

aged, pert. to the medical treatment of the: GEROCOMICAL

age or generation: SAECULUM

aggressive, wantonly: PETULCOUS

aging, not: INSENESCIBLE

agreeably persuasive: SWASIVIOUS

agreement, arranged or settled by: PACTITIOUS

agreement, rote or insincere: ASSENTATION

agreement-breaking: FEDIFRAGOUS

agreement or promise, pert. to an: SPONSIONAL

aid and succor: SUBVENTION

aid or help, to: OPITULATE

ailment or pain that is imaginary: HUMDUDGEON

aimless or clumsy way, to move in a: FLOB

air, to remove or purify of foulness: DEMEPHITIZE

airs, coquettish or affected: MINAUDERIE

alcoholic addiction: METH-
YSIS
alike, things that are similar
or: SIMILIA
alike in kind: CONGENEROUS
alive and flourishing: VE-
GETE
allegiance: LIGIAMENT
allied in friendship: CONTES-
SERATE
all kinds, of: OMNIFARIOUS
all kinds, of: OMNIGENOUS
all-powerful: CUNCTIPOTENT
all things, possessing or
holding: CUNCTITENANT
alluring: ILLECEBROUS
alma mater, love of one's:
MATRIOTISM
alms or handouts, to give:
ELEEMOSYNATE
amateurish: TYRONIC
amazing object: STUPOR
MUNDI
ambush for a victim, waiting in: LOCHETIC
amends or satisfaction:
ASSETH
amusing or witty, not: INFI-
CETE
anal: PODICAL
anatomy, human: ANTHRO-
POTOMY
anemic or bloodless: EXSAN-
GUINE

angel, an apparition (on
earth) of: ANGELOPHANY
angered, easily: IRACUND
angry, growing: IRASCENT
anguish, causing: DOLORIFIC
animal, smelling like an: CA-
PRYLIC
animal fat: ADEPS
animals, the art of killing
harmful: PHTHISOZOICS
ankles, having large: SCAUR-
OUS
annual or yearly:
QUOTENNIAL
another as a sexual object,
loving: ALLOEROTICISM
another's happiness, joy or
pleasure in: CONFELICITY
another's happiness, joy or
pleasure in: MACARISM
another source, from: ALI-
UNDE
another thing: ALIUD
another type or sort, of: AN-
OTHER-GUESS
another way, in: OTH-
ERGATES
ant: CALICRAT
antagonistic or hostile: OP-
PUGNANT
anticipating other's needs:
PREVENANCE
antidotal: BEZOARDIC
antidotal: THERIACAL

antidote for poison: ALEXI-
PHARMIC
anti-Gentile: ANTIETHNIC
antiquity: VETUSTY
anti-Semitism: JUDOPHOB-
ISM
anus or buttocks: FUNDA-
MENT
anxiety, tension, or excitement, a state of: FAN-
TIGUE
anxious or dejected, mor-
bidly: DYSTHYMIC
anxious to see: SPECTABUN-
DAL
apart, causing to separate or
come: DIVELLENT
apathy, characterized by:
NONCURANTIST
appearance, bearing, or
manner: TENUE
appetite, taking away one's:
APOSITIC
appetites or desires, pert. to
human: EPITHUMETIC
appetites or desires, pert.
to: ORECTIC
appetite-stimulating: OREXI-
GENIC
applicant, seeker, or candidate: PETITOR
apply oneself (as to a task),
to: ACCINGE
approachable to speak to:
PERAFFABLE

approach indirectly, to: CIR-
CUMAMBULATE
approaching, an: APPULSE
appropriate, to: SPHETERIZE
appropriate, fit, or becoming: CONDECENT
approval: RATIHABITION
approving, not: UNPLAUSIVE
apt or suitable: IDONEOUS
archaic, worship of any-
thing: ARCHAEOLATRY
architectural: OECODOMIC
arguing in a circle: DIAL-
LELOUS
argument, debate, or quarrel: DEMELE
argument or contest, a minor: VELITATION
aristocrat: EUPATRID
arms, a stretch or span of
the outstretched: ENVERG-
URE
army, pert. to an: STRA-
TONIC
arouse, to: ABRAID
arrangement or order,
good or established: EU-
TAXY
array or deck out, to: BE-
DIGHT
arrogance or conceit: OUT-
RECUIDANCE
arrogant or haughty, to
make: SUPERBIATE
artificial leather: PEGAMOID

artistically conventional,
  bourgeois, or vulgar: BIE-
  DERMEIER
ashamed or shameful: HON-
  TOUS
ashes, like: FAVILLOUS
aside, a calling: SEVOCA-
  TION
asked-about thing or person:
  QUESITED
asleep, half: SEMISOMNOUS
assassinate in order to prevent or punish revela-
  tions, to: MORGANIZE
assistance, mutual: COADJU-
  MENT
assistant: ADJUTATOR
astonishing: EXTONIOUS
astrology: ESTELLATION
attachment: ALLIGATION
attempt or experiment: TEN-
  TAMEN
attention, the inability to
  sustain: APROSEXIA
attention or carefulness, extreme: PERADVERTENCE

attention-paying or lis-
  tening: AUDIENT
attracted sexually to either
  sex: AMPHIEROTIC
attractive: ALLICIENT
attractive girl: BELLIBONE
attractiveness or entice-
  ment: ALLICIENCY
attractive or magnetic: AT-
  TRAHENT
aunt, pert. to an: MATERTE-
  RAL
authority, pert. to: EXOUSI-
  ASTIC
autopsy: NECROPSY
auxiliary: ADJUVANT
avert or ward off, to: AVER-
  RUNCATE
awaken, causing to: HYPNO-
  POMPIC
awaken, to: ABRAID
awakening: EXPERGEFACIENT
awakening: EXPERRECTION
away, to move: ABSCEDE
awkwardness: MALADRESSE

B

babble or prattle, tending
  to: BABBLATIVE
babbler or chatterer: CLAT-
  TERFART

baboon: BAVIAN
baby, something to scare a:
  SCAREBABE
bachelor: CELIBATARIAN

back, a retreat or a going: RECULADE

back or side entrance: POSTERN

bad (wicked), extremely: SCELERATE

bad breath: OZOSTOMIA

bad breath, having: SAPROSTOMOUS

badly constructed: INCONDITE

badly or clumsily made: BLUNDERLY

bad outlook or way of thinking, a chronically: CACHEXIA

baking or roasting: ASSATION

balance, consider, or weigh, to: TRUTINATE

bald: ACOMOUS

bald: CALVOUS

bald: GLABROUS

bald-headed man, a hapless: PILGARLIC

baldness: ATRICHIA

balk or obstruct, to: SUFFLAMINATE

band or choir leader: CHORAGUS

bank, shore, or coast: RIVAGE

banqueter: SYMPOSIAST

bantering: QUIZZACIOUS

barbarity: FERITY

barbarous: ALABANDICAL

barbecue: BUCCAN

barefoot: DISCALCED

bargain-binding money: ARLES

bargain or business deal: TROKE

barking: LATRANT

barking, like: HYLACTIC

bark like a dog, to: ALLATRATE

bartender: TAPSTER

bashful or modest: PUDIBUND

bashful or shy: DAPHNEAN

bashful or shy: VERECUND

basic or introductory: PROPADEUTIC

bask in the sun, to: APRICATE

bat, to turn into a: VERPERTILIONIZE

bath, mud: ILLUTATION

baths, pert. to warm: BALNEAL

battle-ready or warlike: BATTAILOUS

bauble or trinket: FLAMFEW

beacon or lighthouse: FANAL

beard, having a small: BARBATULOUS

bearded: BARBATE

bearded or hairy: BARBIGEROUS

beardless: IMBERBE
bearing, grace in one's:
TOURNURE
bearing, appearance, or
manner: TENUE
beast, like a wild: FERINE
beastlike or savage: THER-
EOID
beat around the bush, to:
CIRCUMAMBULATE
beat black-and-blue, to: SUG-
GILATE
beautify, to: ADONIZE
beauty: BELLITUDE
beauty, a lover of: PHILOCAL-
IST
beauty more than skin deep:
KALON
beauty or excellence, matchless: PHOENIXITY
beauty prizes: CALLISTEIA
becoming, fit, or appro-
priate: CONDECENT
bed, confining to a bed: LEC-
TUAL
bedbug: CHINCH
bedbug: PUNAISE
bedroom, pert. to the: CU-
BICULAR
beer, pert. to: CERVISIAL
before a particular time: PRE-
PUNCTUAL
beg or importune, to: FLAGI-
TATE
beg, to: OBSECRATE

beg, to: OBTEST
beg for food in a contemptible way, to: SCAFF
begging, fraudulent: TRUAN-
DISE
begging or beggary: MENDIC-
ITY
begging or borrowing: THIG-
GING
beginners, a set of instructions for: TYROLOGY
beginning, without: INNAS-
CIBLE
behave or talk foolishly, to:
FOOTLE
behavior: ABEARANCE
behavior that is improperly
licentious: GRIVOISERIE
beheading: DECOLLATION
behold, delightful to:
SIGHTSOME
belief or trust, worthy of:
FAITHWORTHY
belief that things tend to
work out for the better:
AGATHISM
believed, things to be:
CREDENDA
bell, a small: CODON
bellowing: MUGIENT
bellowing or roaring: BOA-
TION
belly, having a large: AB-
DOMINOUS

belly, having a large: VEN-
TRIPOTENT
below and in front: IN-
FEROANTERIOR
bent upward: REPANDOUS
between, to run or come: IN-
TERCUR
between others, shining: IN-
TERLUCENT
beware, let the doer: CA-
VEAT ACTOR
bewilder or mystify, to: MET-
AGROBILIZE
bias or inclination: CLINA-
MEN
big toe, pert. to the: HALLU-
CAL
birth, nobleness of: EUGENY
birthday or birthdays, pert.
to a: NATALITIAL
bisexuality: AMPHIEROTICISM
bistro: ESTAMINET
bite, biting or inclined to:
MORDACIOUS
bitten off or broken, having
the end: PREMORSE
bittersweet, something that
is: GLYCIPRICON
bizarreness: BIZARRERIE
black-and-blue: ECCHYMOTIC
black-and-blue, to beat: SUG-
GILATE
black-and-blue mark: SUGGI-
LATION

black hair, having: MELANO-
COMOUS
black magic: GOETY
blackmail: CHANTAGE
blame or accuse, to: INCUL-
PATE
blather or prate, to: DEBLAT-
ERATE
bleach, to: DEALBATE
blend, unite, or grow to-
gether, to: INOSCULATE
bless or congratulate, to:
MACARIZE
blindness: CECITY
block up or obstruct, to: OP-
PILATE
blood, aversion to the sight
of: HEMOPHOBIA
bloodless: INCRUENT
bloodless or anemic: EXSAN-
GUINE
blood pressure that is high:
HYPERPIESIS
bloodshed, a scene of: ACEL-
DAMA
blood-sucking: SANGUI-
SUGENT
blood vengeance: GOELISM
bloody: CRUENTOUS
blossoming: INFLORESCENT
blowing-sound-like, like
that across the mouth of
a bottle: AMPHORIC
blowing the nose, pert. to:
EMUNCTORY

blow or breathe upon, to: INSUFFLATE

blow through or ventilate, to: PERFLATE

blue, steel: CHALYBEUS

blueprint: CYANOTYPE

bluntness or brusqueness: BRUSQUERIE

blunt-spoken: SPADISH

blushing: ERUBESCENT

blushing: RUBESCENT

boards, to use for flooring: CONTABULATE

boastful: THRASONICAL

boasting: JACTATION

boasting, triumphant exultation or: GLORIATION

body, abnormally small in: NANOID

body, discipline of the: SCLERAGOGY

boil, to: ESTUATE

boil down, to: DECOCT

boisterous and noisy: CALLITHUMPIAN

boisterous or noisy: STREPITOUS

bombast: AMPOLLOSITY

bombastic or pretentious in speech: LEXIPHANIC

bond, link, or tie: VINCULUM

bone-breaking: OSSIFRAGOUS

bonfire: FEU DE JOIE

bony: OSSEOUS

book as a guide for visitors or strangers: XENAGOGY

book's pages, a label or memo slip projecting from a: LEDGIT

boots or leggings, wearing: OCREATE

borderland or frontier, on the: LIMITROPHE

bore, to be a: TEREBRATE

born after a particular event, one: POSTNATUS

born again: REDIVIVUS

born amid chaos: CHAOGENOUS

born in heaven: COELIGENOUS

borrowing or begging: THIGGING

borrowing or lending: MUTATION

bosom or lap, pert. to the: GREMIAL

bother, fretting, quarrel, or squabble: TRACASSERIE

bottle, like the sound of blowing across the mouth of: AMPHORIC

boughs or branches of a tree: RAMAGE

bought, corruptible or capable of being: EMPTITIOUS

bought provisions: ACATES

boundary, having a natural

one as a defensive fron-
tier: ARCIFINIOUS
bowels, a rumbling in the:
GURGULATION
bracelet: ARMILLA
brackish: SALSUGINOUS
branches or boughs of a
tree: RAMAGE
brassy: AEROSE
bread, pert. to: PANARY
bread-eating: PANIVOROUS
breakfast: JENTATION
breakfast, pert. to: JENTACU-
LAR
break-in or burglary: EFFRAC-
TION
breast, to wean from the:
ABLACTATE
breast cleavage, having
deep: BATHYCOLPIAN
breath, bad: OZOSTOMIA
breath, having bad: SAP-
ROSTOMOUS
breath, short of: ANHELOUS
breathable, not: IRRESPI-
RABLE
breathe or blow upon, to:
INSUFFLATE
breathing heavily or sighing: SUSPIRIOUS
breathing strenuously or
short-winded: PURSY
breeze, a sea: VIRASON
brevity or conciseness: SYN-
TOMY

brick, like: LATERITIOUS
brief time or moment:
STOUND
brightness, a splendid or dazzling: FULGOR
bright, shining, or lustrous:
NITID
brilliancy of color: ORIENCY
bringing (carrying) back: RE-
VEHENT
broad-minded: LATITUDI-
NARIAN
broken or bitten off, having
the end: PREMORSE
broken or violated: INFRACT
broker: MACKELER
brothel, pert. to a: LUPAN-
ARIAN
brotherhood or conspiracy
bound by oath: SYNOMOSY
brush, like a: SCOPATE
brusqueness or bluntness:
BRUSQUERIE
brutal: BELLUINE
bubbles, being filled up with
small: NITTINESS
buck-toothed: GUBBER-
TUSHED
buffoon, a contemptible:
BALATRON
buffoonish: BALATRONIC
bugbear: TERRICULAMENT
bullfighting or a bullfight:
TAUROMACHY

bunch of flowers: TUZZY-
MUZZY
burglary or a breaking into:
EFFRACTION
burial alive: DEFOSSION
burial alive: VIVISEPULTURE
buried alive, fear of being:
TAPHEPHOBIA
burnt smell: EMPYREUMA
burrowing or digging: FO-
DIENT
bursting open or apart: ERUP-
MENT
bury, to: INHUME
business deal or bargain:
TROKE
busy, diligently: OPEROSE
butting like a ram: PETUL-
COUS
butting like a ram, a: ARIE-
TATION

buttocks: CURPLE
buttocks: NATES
buttocks, having beautiful:
CALLIPYGIAN
buttocks, having hairy: DA-
SYPYGAL
buttocks, having lardy: STE-
ATOPYGOUS
buttocks, pert. to the: GLU-
TEAL
buttocks or anus: FUNDA-
MENT
buy, an itch to: EMACITY
buyable: EMPTIONAL
buying: MERCATION
buying and selling: NUNDI-
NATION
buying things, a mania for:
ONIOMANIA
buzzing in the ears or stomach: BOMBUS
buzz or hum, to: BOMBILATE

C

calendar: HEMEROLOGY
calf of the leg, pert. to the:
SURAL
calling aside: SEVOCATION
calming or soothing: HESY-
CHASTIC
calming or tranquilizing:
PACATIVE

camouflaged: PROCRYPTIC
camp or campsite, pert. to
a: CASTRENSIAN
cancel or take away, to: SUB-
LATE
candidate, seeker, or applicant: PETITOR
candy, sugar: ALPHENIC

cannibal: LESTRIGON

capricious or whimsical: VA-
GARIOUS

carefulness or attention, extreme: PERADVERTENCE

carelessness, negligence, or
slackness: LACHES

caring, an absence of: DIS-
SYMPATHY

caring for or solicitude: AC-
CURANCE

carping or quibbling: RABUL-
ISTIC

carrying freight, suitable for:
ONERARY

carrying or being carried:
VECTITATION

carrying past a particular
place: PRETERVECTION

cart or wagon, pert. to a:
PLAUSTRAL

cashews, pert. to: ANACAR-
DIC

castrate or emasculate, to:
EVIRATE

casual or easygoing: DÉGAGÉ

catching in the act: DEPREN-
SION

cautionary rule or reminder:
CAUTELA

cautiously or step by step,
proceeding: PEDETENTOUS

cavalry trumpet flourish or
signal: TUCKET

cave, living or occurring in
a: SPELAEAN

caviar: IKARY

celebrating a victory: EPINI-
CIAN

celebrating or rejoicing together: CONGAUDENCE

celebration of a holiday:
FERIATION

celestial or heavenly: URA-
NIC

cement together, to: FER-
RUMINATE

censure: EPITIMESIS

censure or upbraid, to: EX-
PROBATE

center of attention: CLOU

certain, utterly: APODICTIC

certainable, not: ACATALEP-
TIC

champion or defender: PRO-
PUGNATOR

chance occurrences, a series
of: CHAPTER OF ACCI-
DENTS

change of mind: MENTIMU-
TATION

change others' minds, able
to: FLEXANIMOUS

change position, to sneakily: TRANONT

changing from one foolish
doctrine or theory to an-
other: ISMY

180

changing into human form,
a: ANTHROPOMORPHOSIS
chaos, born amid: CHAOGE-
NOUS
chaos or confusion: TOHU-
BOHU
character, personal nobility
of: KALOGATHIA
characteristic, an individual: APPROPRIAMENT
character or disposition,
one's natural or innate:
INDOLES
charge or accusation: IMPETI-
TION
charity, living on: SPORTU-
LARY
charm or ornament, a foolish: BRIMBORION
chatterer or babbler: CLAT-
TERFART
cheap and gaudy: BRUMMA-
GEM
cheesecake (the edible
kind): JUNCATE
chess, pert. to: SCACCHIC
chew, to: MANDUCATE
chewing thoroughly: POLTO-
PHAGIC
chiding, rebuke, or reproof:
INCREPATION
child, having borne a: PAR-
OUS
childbirth, pert. to: PUER-
PERAL

childbirth, the recovery period after: STEGMONTH
childbirth or pregnancy, the
concealing of: CELATION
childless: ORBATE
childlessness: ATEKNIA
children, having many: PRO-
LETANEOUS
children's puppet show:
POOTLY-NAUTCH
child that's illegitimate:
ADULTERINE
chin, double: BUCCULA
chin, double: CHOLLER
chin, having a projecting:
GASH-GABBIT
chinks, having: FATISCENT
chitchat or small talk: BA-
VARDAGE
choice, a deliberate or rational: PROAIRESIS
choirmaster or bandleader:
CHORAGUS
chore as school punishment:
PENSUM
chosen, worthy to be: DELIG-
IBLE
cipher or code: STEGANOGRA-
PHY
circle, arguing in a: DIALLEL-
OUS
circuit or tour: PERIPLUS
circumcised: APELLOUS
circumlocutory: AMBAGIOUS
circumnavigation: PERIPLUS

181

city-dwelling: URBICOLOUS
city or metropolitan insularity: URBACITY
cleanse or purify, to: MUN-
DIFY
cleansing or washing: CLYS-
MIC
cleavage, having deep:
BATHYCOLPIAN
cloak, wearing a cowled:
BARDOCUCULLATED
close or stop up, to: OBTU-
RATE
close relationship, a:
PROXYSM
closing or terminal: DESI-
NENT
clothe or enwrap, to: CIR-
CUMVEST
clothing, a woman's article
of: BILIMENT
clothing, pert. to: VESTIARY
clothing or a garment: INDU-
MENT
clotted or thick: GRUMOUS
clouds, bringing rain or
storm: NIMBIFEROUS
clumsily or badly made:
BLUNDERLY
clumsy: AMBILEVOUS
clumsy or aimless way, to
move in a: FLOB
clumsy with both hands: AM-
BISINISTER

cluster, grouped together in
a: AGMINATE
coast, bank, or shore: RI-
VAGE
coaxing or wheedling: SUP-
PALPATION
code or cipher: STEGANOGRA-
PHY
cohabitation of the unmarried: CONCUBINAGE
coin, a worthless: SKILLA-
GALEE
cold, dread of: PSYCHROPHO-
BIA
cold, easily affected by: FRI-
GOLABILE
cold, head: GRAVEDO
cold, making: ALGIFIC
cold-blooded: HAEMATOC-
RYAL
colic pain, pert. to: TORMI-
NAL
collapsing in the middle or
sunken: COLLABENT
collected or piled up: COAC-
ERVATE
collectible into one mass:
AGGREGABLE
collision, an intentional
ship: ALLISION
color, brilliancy of: ORIENCY
color, having (throughout)
the same: ISOCHROOUS
color photography: HELIO-
CHROMY

combined enterprise or management, pert. to: COINONOMIC

combining of different things: SYNCRASY

comfort or refresh, to: FOCILLATE

comic: THALIAN

come on to or flirt with: WANTONIZE

commendation or praise, public: PRECONY

common, not: SELCOUTH

common people, liking the: PHILODEMIC

communism: ASPHETERISM

compact: POLYMICRIAN

company, honoring another with one's: COHONESTATION

comparison: COLLIBRATION

comparisons, to draw: SIMILITUDINIZE

competent, legally: CAPAX

complaining: QUERIMONIOUS

complaining or a complaint: QUERIMONY

complementary and polar: CONTRAPLETAL

complete and rich: LOCUPLETE

completed or finished, just: PAULOPAST

complimentary or praising, not: ILLAUDATORY

compliments or respects, one's: BAISEMAINS

comprehensible to most people, readily: EXOTERIC

compressed into a small space: POLYMICRIAN

compress or squeeze, to: CONSTRINGE

compulsory or obligatory: COACTIVE

concave: INVEX

concealing or vealing: OBVELATION

concealment, adapted for: CELATIVE

conceit: PHILAUTY

conceit or arrogance: OUTRECUIDANCE

conciseness or brevity: SYNTOMY

condemn or reject, to: ASPERNATE

confinement or imprisonment: DURANCE

confused din or uproar: TINTAMARRE

confused in a hazy way: NEBULOCHAOTIC

confused sentence arrangement: SYNCHYSIS

confused state of affairs or a mess: SCHEMOZZLE

confusion or chaos: TOHUBOHU

congratulate or bless, to:
MACARIZE

conjectural: STOCHASTIC

conquerable, not: INVICTIVE

conqueror or subduer: DEBEL-
LATOR

conscience: INWIT

conscience, against one's:
CONTRACONSCIENTIOUS

conscience, lacking: DISCON-
SCIENT

conscious: SUPRALIMINAL

conscious, not entirely: SUB-
FOCAL

conscious but passive and
unthinking: ANOETIC

consequentially following or
resulting: CONSECTARY

considerateness or kindliness in speech: BENEDI-
CENCE

consider, balance, or weigh,
to: TRUTINATE

consoling or encouraging:
PARAMUTHETIC

conspiracy or brotherhood
bound by oath: SYNOMOSY

constipated: COSTIVE

constipation, extreme: OB-
STIPATION

constructed, badly: INCON-
DITE

constructed, made, or created, something: FACTURE

constructive: CATASKEUAS-
TIC

contact, pert. to something
spread by personal: PROSO-
DEMIC

contact, to lose: ABSCEDE

contact or touching: TAC-
TION

contact with or touching,
in: ATTINGENT

contempt: DESPICIENCY

contemptuous or insolent:
HUBRISTIC

contention or trouble, wanting: DIVERSIVOLENT

contention, struggling, or
wrangling: COLLUCTATION

contest or argument, a minor: VELITATION

continuing ahead or flowing
smoothly on: PROFLUENT

contracted or narrowed: AN-
GUSTATE

contract or mutual obligation, involving a: SYNAL-
LAGMATIC

contributory: ADJUVANT

control, out of: EMPORTE

conventional or customary:
NOMIC

convention or social cus-
tom: CONSUETUDE

conversation: CONFARIATION

cooking, pert. to the art of:
MAGIRIC

cooking, the art of: MAGI-
ROLOGY
cool, losing one's: EMPORTÉ
cooling: ALGEFACIENT
cooling: FRIGORIFIC
cooling down: DEFERVES-
CENCE
cool walkway or a shady
place: FRESCADE
coppery: AEROSE
copulate, to: SUBAGITATE
copulation, pert. to: SUBAGI-
TATORY
coquetry: AGACERIE
coquettish or affected airs:
MINAUDERIE
corpse, the preparation of
for a funeral: POLLINC-
TURE
corroborative: ADMINICULAR
corrupted or defiled: CON-
SPURCATED
corrupted or defiled: INQUI-
NATED
corruptible or capable of being bought: EMPTITIOUS
cottage that is thatched:
CHAUMIERE
cotton, pert. to: XILINOUS
cough, a hacking: TUSSICU-
LATION
cough remedy: BECHIC
cough syrup: LINCTUS
cough up or spit out, to: EX-
CREATE

counsel, giving: CONSILIARY
country, born in the: RU-
RIGENOUS
country, to renounce residence in one's: DEPATRI-
ATE
country or state, a petty: TO-
PARCHY
covering: OPERIMENT
covering private parts: ANTI-
PUDIC
cover or enclose protec-
tively, to: LORICATE
cowardice: MICROPSYCHY
cow milking: VACCIMUL-
GENCE
cracks or clefts, having: FAT-
ISCENT
crafty or cunning: CALLID
crafty or sly: SUBDOLOUS
crawling: REPTANT
crazy, a person who is
partly: MATTOID
crazy, to drive: LYMPHATE
crazy person: DÉTRAQUÉ
created, made, or con-
structed, something: FAC-
TURE
creative, formative, productive, or active: POIETIC
creator or maker: PLAS-
MATOR
creatures, the effect of the
environment on: HEXIOL-
OGY

credit, honor, or reputation: IZZAT

credulous or gullible, blindly: ULTRAFIDIAN

creeping: REPTANT

creeping or insinuated into: IRREPTITIOUS

crisis, pert. to a: CRISIC

criticism: INCREPATION

criticism or scolding, tedious: JOBATION

criticize, to: PERSTRINGE

Cross or Crucifix, worship of the: STAUROLATRY

cross over, to: TRAJECT

crossroads, pert. to a: COMPITAL

crowd, obvious playing to the: CABOTINAGE

crowding, unhealthy: OCHLESIS

crowd or jam together, to: CONTRUDE

Crucifix or Cross, worship of the: STAUROLATRY

cruel or inhuman deed: ABHOMINALITY

cruel or violent: HARAGEOUS

cruelty, inhuman: PHALARISM

crush by squeezing: SQUISS

cry, not able to: ILLACHRYMABLE

crying (weeping): PLORATION

crying like an infant: VAGIENT

crying or weeping, swollen of face because of: BEGRUTTEN

cryptography: STEGANOGRAPHY

cuckold, to make a ~ of: ADHORN

cuckolded: CORNUTED

cunning or crafty: CALLID

curable: SANABLE

curl of hair, a dangling: FEAK

currying favor: CAPTATION

curse: MALISON

customary or conventional: NOMIC

cut the top off, to: OBTRUNCATE

cutting both ways or two-edged: ANSAL

D

dainty, a: FRIAND
dairy farm: VACCARY
damp, growing: MADESCENT
dance, a frenzied: CORYBAN-
TIC
dancing, pert. to: TRIPUDI-
ARY
dandify, to: ADONIZE
dandruff, covered with: FUR-
FURACEOUS
dandyish or foppish: BEAU-
ISH
danger, being in: PERICU-
LANT
danger or risk, to expose to:
PERICLITATE
daring, willful recklessness
or foolish: HARDYDARDY
darkness, gloomy or producing: TENEBRIFIC
dark or late, to get: ADVES-
PERATE
dark or obscure: CALIGINOUS
dawn, before: ANTELUCAN
dawn or the east, pert. to:
EOAN
day after or the morrow,
the: CRASTIN
day and a night, a: NYCH-
THEMERON

day and a night, comprising
a: NOCTIDIAL
day before yesterday, pert.
to the: PRIDIAN
day, lucky: DIES FAUSTUS
day, pert. to this: HODIER-
NAL
day's work: DARG
daytime sleeping: DIURNA-
TION
dazzling or stunning: FOU-
DROYANT
dead: EXANIMATE
dead, apparently: THANA-
TOID
dead, learning pert. to the:
NERTEROLOGY
deadly: LETHIFEROUS
dead person: DEFUNCT
dead person, the prepara-
tion of for a funeral: POL-
LINCTURE
death: DEFUNCTION
death, after: PRETERLETHAL
death, pert. to: DEFUNCTIVE
death-bringing planet: IN-
TERFECTOR
deathlike: MORTUOUS
death of gods: THEOKTONY
debate, argument, or quarrel: DEMELE

debate or disputation: DIS-
CEPTATION
decay: MARCOR
decay, beginning or tending
to: DECADESCENT
decayed: CARIOUS
decayed or withered: MAR-
CID
decay or decline, the beginning of: PARACME
deceitfully, speaking: FAL-
LACILOQUENT
deceitful or fraudulent: COVI-
NOUS
deceiving or pretending by
a show of excellence: CA-
LOPHANTIC
deception as an art or
make-believe: FACRERE
deception or fraud, a: IN-
GANNATION
decisions, difficulty in making: HYPOBULIA
decisiveness: ARBITRAMENT
deck out or array, to: BE-
DIGHT
declare or proclaim, to: IN-
DIGITATE
decline or decay, the beginning of: PARACME
decline or deterioration, a
speedy: DEGRINGOLADE
decry or disparage, to: OB-
TRECT

deduction or inference: ILLA-
TION
deem of little value or as being worthless: FLOCCIFY
deep-sea: BATHYAL
defeatable, not: INVICTIVE
defecate, to: EJEST
defender or champion: PRO-
PUGNATOR
defense of something that
prevented something else:
ANTISTASIS
defensive frontier, having a
natural boundary as a: AR-
CIFINIOUS
defensive safeguard: TUTA-
MENT
defiled or corrupted: CON-
SPURCATED
defiled or corrupted: INQUI-
NATED
defining, distinguishing, or
distinctive: DIORISTIC
deflower or violate, to: CON-
STUPRATE
dejected or anxious, mor-
bidly: DYSTHYMIC
delicate or sickly: MALADIVE
delicious: NECTARIOUS
delight or please, to: OBLEC-
TATE
delusion that one is a famous person: APPERSONA-
TION

delusion that one is God:
THEOMANIA

demand or desire eagerly,
to: EFFLAGITATE

demon, a little: DEMONETTE

density or thickness: SPISSI-
TUDE

deny or refuse, to: DENE-
GATE

dependent, overly: ANA-
CLITIC

depict, represent, or portray
artistically, to: EXICONIZE

depressed or in low spirits,
somewhat: HYPPISH

deranged person: DÉTRAQUÉ

derangement, mental: VESA-
NIA

derision: SUBSANNATION

description, vivid: HYPOTY-
POSIS

description of the sea: HALI-
OGRAPHY

description or tour of a region: PERIEGESIS

deserving trust or belief:
FAITHWORTHY

designated, marked, or distinguished: SIGNATE

desirable or to be lusted
after: CONCUPISCIBLE

desire, a fervent: APPRECA-
TION

desire and emotion: THYMO-
PSYCHE

desire or demand eagerly,
to: EFFLAGITATE

desire or yearning: APPE-
TITION

desire or appetites, pert. to:
ORECTIC

desires or appetites, pert. to
human: EPITHUMETIC

destroyable or losable, not:
IMPERDIBLE

destroy or crush utterly, to:
SPIFLICATE

destruction or killing: INTER-
EMPTION

destruction or fatal: EXI-
TIOUS

detachment, intellectual:
ATARAXY

detergent or purifying: SMEC-
TIC

deterioration, physical: EM-
PERIMENT

deterioration or decline, a
speedy: DEGRINGOLADE

devouring or gulflike: VO-
RAGINOUS

diagram or sketch, a careless: PERIGRAPH

diarrhea, stopping: STEG-
NOTIC

dice or gambling, pert. to:
TESSARIAN

diction or pronunciation,
bad: CACOLOGY

didactive: DIDASCALIC

dietary therapy for disease:
ALIMENTOTHERAPY
different, being: ALTERITY
different, being: ALIETY
different in kind: ALLOGE-
NEOUS
different things, a combining of: SYNCRASY
different ways, speaking in:
DIVERSILOQUENT
differ or be out of keeping
with, to: ABLUDE
difficult to deal with or handle: QUISQUOSE
difficulty, persevering
through: LABORIFEROUS
difficulty in making decisions: HYPOBULIA
dig out, to: EXFODIATE
dig up, to: EXTER
digesting slowly: BRADYPEP-
TIC
digestion, having bad: CA-
COGASTRIC
digestion, having good: EU-
PEPTIC
digestive: CONCOQUENT
digging or burrowing: FO-
DIENT
digression: EVAGATION
dilemma: DULCARNON
diminishing, lessening, or
subtractive: ABLATITIOUS
dimple in a smile: GELASIN
dingy or somber: SUBFUSC

dining, the science of: ARIS-
TOLOGY
dinner, following: POST-
CENAL
dinner (supper)-loving: COE-
NACULOUS
din or uproar, a confused:
TINTAMARRE
directions, leading in two:
BIVIOUS
directive or guiding: DIRI-
GENT
dirt or mud, to spatter with:
BELUTE
dirty or obscene literature:
COPROLOGY
dirty speech: COPROLALIA
dirty with handling, to:
SQUAGE
dirty with rain or mud, to:
BEDRABBLE
disapproval, stamping the
feet in: SUPPLOSION
discerning or insightful: IN-
SCIENT
discipline, mental: METH-
ASIS
discipline of the body: SCLE-
RAGOGY
disclose, to: PROPALE
disclose or reveal, to: PA-
TEFY
disconnected: ABJUNCTIVE
disconnected or severed: AB-
JUNCT

190

discontinuous or jerky: SAC-
CADIC
discordant: ABSONANT
disease, dietary therapy for:
ALIMENTOTHERAPY
disease, producing: NOSO-
POETIC
dishes, side: ENTREMETS
dismay or terrify, to: CON-
STERNATE
dismiss or fire, to: EXAUC-
TORATE
disorder or abnormality:
DEORDINATION
disparage or decry, to: OB-
TRECT
display ostentatiously, to:
VENDITATE
disposition or character,
one's natural or innate:
INDOLES
disprove, to: REDARGUE
disseminate or divulge, to:
FAMIGERATE
dissuade or advise against
loudly or strongly, to: DE-
HORT
distance, to remove (one-
self) to a: ELOIN
distant, the most: EXTIMATE
distinctive, distinguishing,
or defining: DIORISTIC
distinguished, marked, or
designated: SIGNATE

distinguishing, distinctive,
or defining: DIORISTIC
distinguish or set off, to: DIS-
PUNCT
distress, mental: PSYCHALGIA
disturb by interrupting, to:
INTERTURB
disturbance: BRUSLERY
disturbance or uproar:
STRAMASH
divide in half, to: DIMIDIATE
divide into parts, to: MERO-
TOMIZE
divine and human, both:
DEIVIRILE
divinely inspired: THEOP-
NEUST
divine or unworldly: SUPER-
MUNDANE
divine power, having: DEIPO-
TENT
divorce: DIFFAREATION
divulge or disseminate, to:
FAMIGERATE
dizziness: MIRLIGOES
do and undo to gain time,
to: PENELOPIZE
doctrine, false: PSEUDODOX
dog, to bark like a: ALLA-
TRATE
dog days, pert. to the: CA-
NICULAR
dog-faced or -headed: CYNO-
CEPHALOUS

dogmatic or prescribed:
THETIC

dogs, raising: CANICULTURE

doll-pricking as witchcraft:
INVULTUATION

domesticate, to: AMENAGE

dominant or reigning: REG-
NANT

domination or rule, under:
DITIONARY

donation that is not voluntary: DATION

done, something to be: GE-
RENDUM

donkey: CARDOPHAGUS

door: JANUA

double chin: BUCCULA

double chin: CHOLLER

doubt, the suggestion of a:
ADDUBITATION

doubtful: ANCIPITOUS

doubting or skeptical: APO-
RETIC

downfall: DEGRINGOLADE

drama that is contrived,
stagy, or unrealistic: SAR-
DOODLEDUM

drawing, a careless: PERI-
GRAPH

dreams, pert. to: ONEIROTIC

dreamy and peaceful state:
KEF

dregs or sediment: FAEX

dress, a woman's ornamen-
tal: BILIMENT

dressed, partly or loosely:
DISCINCT

dressed, partly or loosely:
DISHABILLE

dressed up in one's Sunday
clothes: ENDIMANCHE

dress up or adorn, to: TITI-
VATE

drinkable: POCULENT

drink and food, lavish
spending on: ABLIGURI-
TION

drinker of water: AQUABIB

drinking party, one who is
part of a: SYMPOSIAST

drinking together: COMPOTA-
TION

drinking vessel, a large: JO-
RUM

driving or running toward,
a: APPULSE

drooping or hanging limp:
SLIMPSEY

drop by drop: GUTTATIM

drops, falling in: STILLATI-
TIOUS

drops, in the form of small:
GUTTULOUS

drowsy: GRAVEDINOUS

drowsy or yawning: OSCI-
TANT

drunk and feeling brave:
POTVALIANT

dry: SICCANEOUS

dry food, eating: XEROPHAGY

drying up, incapable of: IN-
TARRISABLE
dry up, to: AREFY
duel: MONOMACHY
duel to the death: HOLM-
GANG
dulled or made gross: IN-
CRASSATE
dull or obtuse: HEBETUDI-
NOUS

dull or obtuse, to become or
make: HEBETATE
dung and urine, composed
of: MERDURINOUS
dung-eating: MERDIVOROUS
duration, comparatively
short in: CURTATE
dwarf tree: ARBUSCLE
dwelling place: HABITACLE
dwell or live, a place to:
COMMORATORY

E

each his own, to: SUUM
CUIQUE
eager to see: SPECTABUNDAL
earlier: ANTECEDANEOUS
earlier: ANTEVENIENT
earlier example or proto-
type: ANTETYPE
earlier or previous act: ANTE-
FACT
early stage of growth, pert.
to: BREPHIC
earnest money: ARLES
earn money in any conceivable way, to: QUOMO-
DOUNCIZE
ears, between the: IN-
TERAURAL
ears, having large: MAC-
ROTOUS

ears or stomach, a buzzing
in the: BOMBUS
earth, a lover of the: PHILO-
GEANT
earthen vessel: CAPRUNCLE
east (the) or dawn, pert. to:
EOAN
easygoing or casual: DÉGAGÉ
easy to go up to and speak
to: PERAFFABLE
eatable: ESCULENT
eatable, not: INESCULENT
eaten, half: SEMESE
eater, an expert or refined:
GASTROSOPH
eating: CIBATION
eating: COMESTION
eating, pert. to: EDACIOUS
eating dry food: XEROPHAGY

eating to the point of a
feast: EPULATION

eating too much: GAS-
TRIMARGY

ebbing: REFLUENT

ecology: BIONOMICS

ecology: HEXICOLOGY

economic management or
economy, bad: CACO-
ECONOMY

economic misery or poverty:
ILLTH

economy or economic man-
agement, bad: CACO-
ECONOMY

edge, having a knifelike:
CULTELLATED

edible: ESCULENT

edible, not: INESCULENT

editor: DIASKEUAST

education, good: EUPSY-
CHICS

effect or result: CAUSATUM

effeminacy or softness: MOL-
LITUDE

effeminate: MULIEBROUS

effort, a strenuous: MOLIMEN

effort, painstaking work or:
OPEROSITY

effort or endeavor: NISUS

egg yolk: DEUTOPLASM

egg yolk: VITELLUS

ejected or spit out: EX-
SPUTORY

elegant or graceful: LEG-
GIADROUS

elegiac or funereal: EPI-
CEDIAL

elephant, to make the
sound of an: BARR

eloquent: CHRYSOSTOMATIC

eloquent: FACUND

eloquent or fluent: RENABLE

else, something: ALIUD

elsewhere, from: ALIUNDE

emasculate or castrate, to:
EVIRATE

embraceable, nicely:
CLIPSOME

embracing: AMPLEXATION

emotion, showing outwardly
and naturally: ESSENTIC

emotion and desire: THYMO-
PSYCHE

emotion from meditating on
God: THEOPATHY

emotion or emotions, pert.
to: PATHEMATIC

emptiness: VACIVITY

enable, to: ABILITATE

enclose or cover protec-
tively, to: LORICATE

encouraging or consoling:
PARAMUTHETIC

end broken or bitten off,
having the: PREMORSE

endeavor or effort: NISUS

enduring suffering: PERPES-
SION

enema: CLYSTER
energy: DACITY
energy, mental: PSYCHURGY
English or plain English, in:
    ANGLICE
enjoyment or use: JOUIS-
    SANCE
enough said or saying
    enough: SATISDICTION
enrich, to: DIVITIATE
enroll or inscribe (on a
    list), to: INTABULATE
enroll or register, to: IM-
    BREVIATE
ensnare or trap, to: IL-
    LAQUEATE
entangled and twisted: CON-
    TORTUPLICATE
entertainment: HARBERGAGE
enticement or attrac-
    tiveness: ALLICIENCY
enticing or tempting to evil:
    LENOCINANT
entrance, a subtle or un-
    seen: SUBINGRESSION
environment, the effect of
    on creatures: HEXIOLOGY
epigram, a second-rate: NITI-
    GRAM
equal age or the same pe-
    riod, of: EQUAEVAL
equal in power or validity:
    EQUIPOLLENT
equal in weight: EQUIPON-
    DERATE

equality of age: COEVALITY
equal level, to treat as be-
    ing on an: EQUIPARATE
equally stupid: UNASINOUS
equal political rights: ISON-
    OMY
erasing or erasure, pert. to:
    DELETITIOUS
erasure, to mark for: DIS-
    PUNCT
erratic: VAGARIOUS
erroneous or mistaken be-
    lief, opinion, or doctrine:
    SPHALM
error, an inadvertent:
    BEVUE
ethical indifference, a mat-
    ter of: ADIAPHORON
evening, during the: VESPER-
    TINE
event, one born after a par-
    ticular: POSTNATUS
evergreen: SEMPERVIRENT
everlasting and perfect: IN-
    DEFECTIBLE
every other year, occurring:
    TRIETERIC
evil, extremely: SCELERATE
evil, portending or boding:
    MALOMINOUS
evil, tempting or enticing
    to: LENOCINANT
evil deed: MESHANTERY
excellence or beauty, match-
    less: PHOENIXITY

excellence, pretending or deceiving by a show of: CALOPHANTIC

excellent or select: EXHIMIOUS

excepting: BATING

exceptional: ABJUNCTIVE

excitement, anxiety, or tension, a state of: FANTIGUE

exciting: AGACANT

excrement: ALVINE DEJECTIONS

excrement: DEJECTA

excrement: PURGAMENT

excremental: STERCORACEOUS

excrement and urine, composed of: MERDURINOUS

excrement-eating: MERDIVOROUS

excretion, an: PURGAMENT

excused absence, pupil's: ABSIT

executioner: CARNIFEX

exemplary, gentlemanly, or heroic: GRANDISONIAN

exile, living in: EXULANT

exist, something that only seems to: TANQUAM

existence, in actual: IN ESSE

existing always: INNASCIBLE

existing nowhere: NULLIBIQUITOUS

expatriate (oneself): DEPATRIATE

expected or hoped for: SPERATORY

expensive: DISPENDIOUS

experimental or tentative: PEIRASTIC

experiment or attempt: TENTAMEN

explanatory: EXEGEMATIC

expose to risk or danger, to: PERICLITATE

expression, overly subtle or refined in: ALEMBICATED

extensive: AMPLIVAGANT

exterior, external, or outside: ECTAL

external, exterior, or outside: ECTAL

extirpate, to: ABERUNCATE

extravagance or impropriety: EVAGATION

extravagant spending on food and drink: ABLIGURITION

exultation or boasting, triumphant: GLORIATION

eye-corner gook: GOUND

eye for an eye or revenge in kind, pert. to: TALIONIC

eyesore: DISSIGHT

eye squint upward: ANOOPSIA

F

fabricated or untruthful:
COMMENTITIOUS
face: PHIZ
face, pert. to the: PROSOPIC
face, swollen of because of
weeping: BEGRUTTEN
faint or swoon, tending to:
LIPOTHYMIC
faint or tire, becoming: LAN-
GUESCENT
fair weather, an interval of:
SLATCH
faith, enough to minimize
one's: MINIMIFIDIAN
faith, having implicit: FIDIM-
PLICITARY
faith, pert. to: PISTIC
faithful and true, a solemn
vow to be: AFFIDATION
false: COMMENTITIOUS
false, to reject as: ATHETIZE
false doctrine: PSEUDODOX
falsely suggesting what is
true: FALSIDICAL
false reasoning: CROCODILITY
fame and fortune, planning
one's own rise to: PSAPHO-
NIC
famous person, delusion
that one is a: APPERSONA-
TION

fanatical zeal: ZELOTYPIA
fanfare, to proclaim like a:
ABUCCINATE
fanning: FLABELLATION
fashionableness: ALAMODAL-
ITY
fasting: JEJUNATION
fast teaching: TACHYDIDAXY
fat, animal: ADEPS
fat, becoming: PINGUESCENT
fatal or destructive: EXI-
TIOUS
fat and squat: FUBSY
father, centered on the: PA-
TRICENTRIC
fatigue or weariness: DELAS-
SATION
fatness: ALETUDE
fatness, obesity, or grossness: POLYSARCIA
fatten, to: SAGINATE
fauna and flora: BIOTA
favor, currying: CAPTATION
fazability, lack of: ATARAXY
fearless: IMPAVID
fear of supernatural powers:
DEISIDAIMONIA
feasting: EPULATION
feebleminded: HYPOPHRENIC
feebleminded: OLI-
GOPHRENIC

feeding: CIBATION
feel, ability to: ESTHESIA
feeling, shared: COMPATHY
feeling bad generally: DYS-
PHORIA
feelings, having surging or
agitated: ESTUOUS
feet, having large: SCIAPO-
DOUS
feet, having long: DOLICHO-
PODOUS
feet tired, to make one's:
SURBATE
fellable as a tree: CEDUOUS
fellow human beings or
friends, affection or love
for: PHILIA
fellow student: CONDISCIPLE
female masculinity: VIRAGIN-
ITY
fever, a slight: FEBRICULA
fever, producing: FEBRIFA-
CIENT
fever, producing: FEBRIFER-
OUS
fighting or strife: DIMICA-
TION
figure or puzzle out, to:
METAGROBILIZE
filling up or making full: IM-
PLETION
filth: ACATHARSIA
filth, covered with: FECU-
LENT

filth, cultish worship of:
AISCHROLATREIA
filth or garbage, collected:
COLLUVIES
filth that is sticky, slimy, or
greasy: GLEET
filthy or obscene literature:
COPROLOGY
filthy talk: BORBOROLOGY
financial enrichment: DITA-
TION
financially needy: INOPIOUS
find out or fish out, to: EX-
PISCATE
finery or frippery: FALBALAS
finger (the obscene gesture),
the: FICO
fingering or touching: CON-
TRECTATION
fingerlike: DACTYLOID
finger next to the little finger: LEECH-FINGER
fingerprint: DACTYLOGRAM
finished or completed, just:
PAULOPAST
fire or dismiss, to: EXAUC-
TORATE
fiscal: AERARIAN
fishing: PISCATION
fishing: RIVIATION
fishing, pert. to: HALIEUTIC
fish out or find out, to: EX-
PISCATE
fit, appropriate, or becoming: CONDECENT

flat-nosed, being: SIMITY
flat surface: AEQUOR
flattering for favor: CAPTA-
TION
flattery, open to: ELOZABLE
flatulence: PNEUMATOSIS
flatulence, relieving: CARMI-
NATIVE
flatulent or passing gas:
PHYSAGOGUE
flavor, having a pleasant:
GEUSIOLEPTIC
flavor, similar in taste or:
CONGUSTABLE
fleas, infested with: PULI-
COSE
flesh, fond of: SARCOPHI-
LOUS
flesh, pert. to: CREATIC
flesh creep, to make the:
HORRIPILATE
flesh or muscle, pert. to:
SARCOUS
fleshy: CARNOUS
flighty or giddy: VOLAGE
flirtatiousness: AGACERIE
flirt with or come on to:
WANTONIZE
flit, to: CURSITATE
flogging, fond of: PLAGOSE
flood or overflow: ALLUVIUM
flooring, to use boards for:
CONTABULATE
flora and fauna: BIOTA

flowers, a bunch of: TUZZY-
MUZZY
flowing back: REFLUENT
flow or run together, to
cause to: CORRIVATE
fluent or eloquent: RENABLE
fluorescent: EPIPOLIC
fly, able to: VOLITORIAL
fly away, to: ABVOLATE
flying, pert. to: VOLITORIAL
flying high: ALTIVOLANT
foam or froth, like: SPUMES-
CENT
foggy: BRUMOUS
following as a consequence:
CONSECTARY
food and drink, lavish
spending on: ABLIGURI-
TION
food, stuffed with: FARC-
TATE
food, to beg for in a contemptible way: SCAFF
food, to nibble or pick at:
PINGLE
food or provisions: VIANDS
foolish act: NODDARY
foolish daring or willful recklessness: HARDYDARDY
foolish or unwise: INSIPIENT
foolish, silly, or trifling: DE-
SIPIENT
foolish talk: ONOLOGY
foot, going on: PEDESTRIOUS
foppish or dandyish: BEAUISH

forbidden things: VETANDA

forefinger and thumb, the
space between the: PUR-
LICUE

foreign-born: ALIENIGENATE

foreigners, generally forbidding residence to: XENELASY

foretell or prophesy, to: ARI-
OLATE

forgery: PLASTOGRAPHY

forgetfulness: OBLIVESCENCE

fork-tongued: FISSILINGUAL

formative, creative, productive, or active: POIETIC

formed or proportioned
well: FEATOUS

former or erstwhile: CI-
DEVANT

fornication: SCORTATION

fornication or lewdness,
pert. to: SCORTATORY

fortune and fame, planning
one's own rise to: PSAPHO-
NIC

forward or insolent: PROCA-
CIOUS

foulmouthedly abusive:
THERSITICAL

foulmouthed or scurrilous:
SPURCIDICAL

foulmouthed speech: COPRO-
LALIA

fountainhead: ABUNDARY

four, a group or set of:
MOURNIVAL

fragment or a part: FRUS-
TRUM

fragrant: OLENT

fraud or deception, a: IN-
GANNATION

fraudulent or deceitful: COVI-
NOUS

fraudulent suppression of
the truth: SURREPTION

freckled, extremely: FERN-
TICLED

freckled, extremely: LENTIGI-
NOUS

free will or free choice: AR-
BITRAMENT

freight, suitable for carrying:
ONERARY

French, in: GALLICE

frequent: CREBOUS

fretting, bother, quarrel, or
squabble: TRACASSERIE

Freudian slip, making a:
HETEROPHEMY

friendship: AMITURE

friendship, allied in: CON-
TESSERATE

friends or one's fellow human beings, affection or
love for: PHILIA

frippery or finery: FALBALAS

frontier defensive boundary,
having a natural: ARCI-
FINIOUS

frontier or borderland, on
the: LIMITROPHE

front of, to walk in: ANTE-AMBULATE

froth or foam, like: SPUMESCENT

fruit, to pack placing the best on top: DEACON

fruitful or prolific: FERACIOUS

frying pan: FRIXORY

full moon, pert. to a: PLENILUNARY

fully stocked: LOCUPLETE

fumes that are noxious from household conditions: OIKIOMIASMATA

functional, practical, or utilitarian: BANAUSIC

funereal or elegiac: EPICEDIAL

funny: GELOGENIC

furious or raging: FURABUND

furniture, pert. to household: SUPPELECTILE

G

gaiety or lightheartedness: ALLEGRESSE

gain time by doing and undoing, to: PENELOPIZE

gambling or dice, pert. to: TESSARIAN

gaping or yawning: HIANT

garbage, filled with: RUDEROUS

garbage or filth, collected: COLLUVIES

garden, belonging to a kitchen: OLITORY

gardening, pert. to: HORTULAN

garlic- or onion-smelling: ALLIACEOUS

garment, a woman's: BILIMENT

garment or clothing: INDUMENT

gas, relieving stomach: CARMINATIVE

gas, flatulent or passing: PNEUMATOSIS

gas-causing drug: PHYSAGOGUE

gatherable into one mass: AGGREGABLE

gaudy and cheap: BRUMMAGEM

gelatinous: TREMELLOSE

general or overall view, an ability to take a: ENSYNOPTICITY

generation or age: SAECULUM

genitals, the external: EDEA

genitals, the female: MULI-
EBRIA
gentlemanly, exemplary, or
heroic: GRANDISONIAN
gentleness, mildness, or
meekness: MANSUETUDE
genuine or straightforward:
JANNOCK
German (language):
TUDESQUE
Germanic: TEDESCO
ghastly and grim: ALLAGRU-
GOUS
ghosts, belief in: EIDOLISM
gibberish: BARAGOUIN
giddy or flighty: VOLAGE
gift, pert. to a: MUNERARY
girl, an attractive: BELLI-
BONE
girl, a wanton or loose: NY-
SOT
girlfriend, jilted by one's:
LASSLORN
girl or young woman: JUVEN-
CLE
give up residence in one's
country, to: DEPATRIATE
giving that is not voluntary:
DATION
glance of love: BELAMOUR
glassy or glasslike: HYALINE
gloom or sorrow, bringing:
LUCTIFEROUS
gloomy or producing dark-
ness: TENEBRIFIC

glowing white: CANDENT
glow of passion: ESTUS
gluttonous or piggish: IN-
GLUVIOUS
gluttony: GASTRIMARGY
gnashing one's teeth: FREN-
DENT
goatishness or lewdness: HIR-
COSITY
goat-smelling: HIRCINOUS
God, the delusion that one
is: THEOMANIA
gods, the death of: THE-
OKTONY
gods, worship of false: PSEU-
DOLATRY
going ahead or flowing
smoothly on: PROFLUENT
gold, producing: AURIFIC
gold and ivory, of: CHRYSELE-
PHANTINE
golden: AURULENT
golden-haired: AURICOMOUS
golden mean: JUSTE-MILIEU
golden or reddish light, glittering with: RUTILANT
golden-tongued (eloquent):
CHRYSOSTOMATIC
good and evil, comprising
or showing both: AGATHO-
KAKOLOGICAL
good and innocent, lucky in
being happily: EUMOIROUS
good health: EUCRASIA

good qualities, a lack of: IM-
BONITY
good spirit: CALODEMON
goose bumps, to give one:
HORRIPILATE
gossiping woman: COMMERE
gourd or watermelon: ANGU-
RIA
government by the worst element: KAKISTOCRACY
graceful and well-propor-
tioned: TRETIS
graceful or elegant: LEG-
GIADROUS
graceful or refined, men-
tally: SPIRITUEL
gradually or step by step:
GRADATIM
grammarian: ARTIGRAPHER
grandparental: AVAL
grape jam: UVATE
graspable or seizable: PRE-
HENSIBLE
grasping or greedy: PLEONEC-
TIC
grating and unmelodious:
SCRANNEL
grating sound, to make a:
GRIDE
greasy or oily: UNGUINOUS
greedy: INGORDIGIOUS
greedy or grasping: PLEONEC-
TIC
greenness, youth, or inexperience: VIRIDITY

greeting on meeting:
SALVEDICTION
grief, something that dispels: DOLORIFUGE
grief, causing: DOLORIFIC
grimacing or agape: RIC-
TAL
grim and ghastly: ALLAGRU-
GOUS
gross, dulled or made: IN-
CRASSATE
grossness, fatness, or obesity: POLYSARCIA
ground plan: ICHNOGRAPHY
ground, lying on the: HU-
MICUBATION
grouped together in a cluster: AGMINATE
growing around: CIRCUM-
CRESCENT
growing continuously: AC-
CRESCENT
growing old together: CONSE-
NESCENCE
growling, grumbling, or
snarling: OGGANITION
growling in the stomach:
BORBORYGM
grow together, blend, or
unite, to: INOSCULATE
G-string (skimpy garment):
CACHE-SEX
guard, keeping watch or on
one's: EXCUBANT

guess or conjecture, involving: STOCHASTIC

guest, to welcome as a: GESTEN

guidebook for visitors or strangers: XENAGOGY

guiding or directive: DIRIGENT

guilt, incapable of: DOLI INCAPAX

gulflike or devouring: VORAGINOUS

gullible or credulous, blindly: ULTRAFIDIAN

gulp down or swallow up, to: INGURGITATE

gushing: SCATURIENT

gymnastics: PALAESTRICS

gymnastics or physical training, pert. to: ALEIPTIC

H

hag, old: MACKABROIN

hail, pert. to: GRANDINOUS

hair, a dangling curl of: FEAK

hair, having black: MELANOCOMOUS

hair, having gold-colored: AURICOMOUS

hair, having straight: EUTHYCOMIC

hair, having wavy: CYMOTRICHOUS

hair, having woolly: ULOTRICHOUS

hair ball: HETEROLITH

hair ball: TRICHOBEZOAR

hair care or growth, pert. to: CRINICULTURAL

hairless: DEPILOUS

hair or a mane, having long: JUBATE

hair or head of hair: CRINE

hairsplitting: PILPULISTIC

hairy or bearded: BARBIGEROUS

half, to divide in: DIMIDIATE

half-asleep: SEMISOMNOUS

half-eaten: SEMESE

halfheartedly, to do: PERFUNCTURATE

hand, leading by or as if by the: MANUDUCTORY

handle and make dirty, to: SQUAGE

handouts, living on: SPORTULARY

handouts or alms, to give: ELEEMOSYNATE

hand (palm) outstretched, with the: APPAUME

hands, clumsy with both: AMBISINISTER

hands, having no: AMANOUS

hands, holding or restraining with the: MANUTENTION

hands, voting by a show of: CHIROTONY

handsome: FEATOUS

hand space between the thumb and the forefinger: PURLICUE

handwriting, minute or meticulous: NIGGLE

handwriting flourish made at the end of a signature: PARAPH

handwriting or penmanship: CHIROGRAPHY

hanging limp or drooping: SLIMPSEY

happening every other year: TRIETERIC

happiness, joy or pleasure in another's: CONFELICITY

happiness, joy or pleasure in another's: MACARISM

happy, the inability to be: ANHEDONIA

haranguer or preacher: CONCIONATOR

hardened: INDURATE

hard to deal with or handle: QUISQUOSE

harem: ANDERUN

harm: NOCUMENT

harmonious, not: ABSONANT

harmonious proportions in a building: EURYTHMY

harsh, somewhat: AUSTERULOUS

harvest the vintage, to: VENDEMIATE

hastily or suddenly done or made: SUBITARY

hasty: FESTINATE

hasty, overly: PREPROPEROUS

hasty, sudden, or unexpected: SUBITANEOUS

hat, pert. to a: CASTORIAL

haughty or arrogant, to make: SUPERBIATE

hawking or spitting: SCREATION

hazily confused: NEBULOCHAOTIC

head (skull), having a high: HYPISICEPHALIC

head, having a large: CAPITOSE

head, having a monkeylike: CEBOCEPHALIC

head of hair: CRINE

head cold: GRAVEDO

headlong: TANTIVY

head to foot, from: CAP-A-
  PIE
healing for the soul, spiritual: PSYCHIASIS
healthful: SALUTIFEROUS
health or health matters, an
  obsession about: HYGEI-
  OLATRY
healthy condition: SANI-
  TUDE
heaping up, a: ACERVATION
heaps, in: AGEROSE
heartbreak: CREVE-COEUR
heartburn: CARDIALGIA
heartburn: PYROSIS
heaven-born: COELIGENOUS
heavenly or celestial: URA-
  NIC
height: ALTURE
heights, fear of: HYPSIPHO-
  BIA
hellish: ACHERONTIC
hellish: CHTHONIAN
help: SUBVENTION
helper: ADJUTATOR
helpful: ADJUTORIOUS
helplul: ADJUVANT
help or aid, to: OPITULATE
hemorrhoids, afflicted with:
  CRESTY
here and there, to run: CUR-
  SITATE
heroic, gentlemanly, or exemplary: GRANDISONIAN
hiccups: SINGULTUS

hidden meaning or significance: HYPONOIA
hidden or latent, lying: DELI-
  TESCENT
hidden or lurking: LATITANT
hidden power, pert. to or
  having: CRYPTODYNAMIC
hidden things or places: PEN-
  ETRALIA
hidden: ABDITIVE
hiding: ABDITIVE
hiding, adapted for: CELA-
  TIVE
hiding place: LATIBULE
hiding place for goods: ABDI-
  TORY
high blood pressure: HYPER-
  PIESIS
high-flying: ALTIVOLANT
highway robbery: LATROCI-
  NATION
hilly or steep: CLIVOSE
hirable or hired: CONDUCTI-
  TIOUS
hiss (someone) off the
  stage, to: EXSIBILATE
hither and thither, to run:
  CURSITATE
hoarse or husky: ROUPY
holding forth, prone to: SO-
  LILOQUACIOUS
holding or restraining with
  the hands: MANUTENTION
holiday, celebrating a: FERIA-
  TION

hollow-sounding: AM-
PHOROUS
home: HABITACLE
homesick: OIKOTROPIC
homesickness, acute: NOSTO-
MANIA
honor, credit, or reputation:
IZZAT
hoped for or expected:
SPERATORY
horizon: FINITOR
horizontal: ACLINAL
horizontal or level position,
to place in a: COMPLA-
NATE
hormnal: AUTACOIDAL
horoscopes, the casting of:
APOTELISM
horror of, to have a: PER-
HORRESCE
horseback, a fight on: HIP-
POMACHY
horse doctor: HIPPIATER
horse racing or horses, pert.
to: HIPPIC
horse rider: PRICKER
horses, liking: PHILHIPPIC
horses or horce racing, pert.
to: HIPPIC
hospitable: XENODOCHIAL
hospitality, pert. to: XENIAL
hospitality, to extend: HOS-
PITIZE
hospital or hospitals, pert.
to a: NOSOCOMIAL

hostile or antagonistic: OP-
PUGNANT
hot and muggy: BULDERING
hotels and inns, the lore or
love of: XENODOCHEIONOL-
OGY
hourly: HORAL
housekeeping: OIKOLOGY
human: INFRA-ANGELIC
human anatomy: ANTHRO-
POTOMY
human and divine, both:
DEIVIRILE
human appetites and de-
sires, pert. to: EPITHU-
METIC
human form, a changing
into:
ANTHROPOMORPHOSIS
human ignorance, the study
of: AGNOIOLOGY
human in shape: HOMINI-
FORM
humbug or hypocrisy: CAFAR-
DISE
humid, heat that is unbearably: SIZZARD
humor, strained or futile:
WITZELSUCHT
hum or buzz, to: BOMBILATE
hundred-eyed: CENTOCU-
LATED
hundred (one) feet square:
HECATOMPED
hundredfold: CENTUPLE

hundred times, by a: CENTU-
PLY
hungry, voraciously: ADE-
PHAGAOUS
husband, very fond of one's:
MARITORIOUS
husky or hoarse: ROUPY

hype, aggrandizing: SUPERLA-
TION
hypnotism, suggestability to:
IDEOPLASTIA
hypocrisy or humbug: CAFAR-
DISE
hysteria, male: TARASSIS

I

ice skating rink: GLACIARIUM
icicle, like an: STIRIOUS
ideal, a yearning for an unattainable: NYMPHOLEPSY
idea that is influential: IDEE-
FORCE
identical, intellectually:
SYMPHRONISTIC
idiosyncrasy or peculiarity:
IDIASM
idleness or sloth: IGNAVIA
idle or unemployed: OTIANT
idolatry: BAALISM
ignorance: AGNOSY
ignorance, a mistake due to:
IGNOTISM
ignorance, the study of human: AGNOIOLOGY
ignorance or stupidity: CRAS-
SITUDE
ignorant: NESCIENT
ignorant, one who is: INGRAM
illegible handwriting: GRIF-
FONAGE

illegitimate child: ADULTER-
INE
illiterate person: ANALPHABET
ill-timed: MELANCOUNTER-
OUS
ill will or malice: MAL-
TALENT
image maker: ICONOPLAST
imaginary ailment or pain:
HUMDUDGEON
immature: IMPUBIC
immortality: ATHANASIA
immune, to make unsuscep-
tible or: VASTATE
impair or weaken, to: LA-
BEFY
impecunious or poor: OBO-
LARY
imported: ADVECTITIOUS
importune or beg, to: FLAGI-
TATE
impotence: AGENNESIS
impotent: ANANDROUS
impotent: IMPROCREANT

impregnate, to: GRAVIDATE
impressive or striking: FRAP-
PANT
imprisonment or confine-
ment: DURANCE
impromptu or offhand,
something done: SCHEDI-
ASM
improperly licentious behavior: GRIVOISERIE
impropriety or extrava-
gance: EVAGATION
improvise, to: AUTOSCHEDI-
AZE
impudent or saucy: MAL-
APERT
impulse: NITENCY
inadvertent error: BEVUE
inanimate things, pert. to
the study of: ABIOLOGICAL
incidental occurrence: OB-
VENTION
incineration: TEPHROSIS
inclination or bias: CLINA-
MEN
incorrigible: ACOLASTIC
incorruptible: IMPRAVABLE
increasing, ever: ACCRES-
CENT
independent activity: AUT-
URGY
indescribable or unrelatable:
INENNARABLE
indestructible or imperishable: IMMARCESIBLE

India, the state of being a
white person newly ar-
rived in: GRIFFINAGE
indifference: DISSYMPATHY
indifference, a matter of ethical: ADIAPHORON
indifference, characterized
by: NONCURANTIST
indirectly, to approach: CIR-
CUMAMBULATE
individual characteristic: AP-
PROPRIAMENT
individuality or selfhood:
SEITY
indoor: SUBTEGULANEOUS
indoors or in seclusion,
done or carried on: UM-
BRATILE
inexcusable: ANAPOLOGET-
ICAL
inexhaustible: INTARRISABLE
inexperience, youth, or
greenness: VIRIDITY
infallible: INDEFECTIBLE
infant, crying like an: VA-
GIENT
inference or deduction: ILLA-
TION
infernal: ACHERONTIC
infernal: CHTHONIAN
infidelity, made a male victim of: CORNUTED
inflammation: PHLOGOSIS
inflexibly or severely just:
RHADAMANTHINE

influence or affect, to: AT-
TINGE
informed or knowing, not:
PARVISCIENT
in front and below: IN-
FEROANTERIOR
infuriate, to: ENFELON
ingrowing of a fingernail or
toenail: ONYXIS
inherent or innate: INGENIT
inheritance hunting: HERE-
DIPETY
inhuman cruelty: PHALARISM
inhuman or cruel deed: AB-
HOMINALITY
initiator or counselor to others in mystical matters:
MYSTAGOGUE
ink: ATRAMENT
innate or inherent: INGENIT
inner, interior, or inside: EN-
TAL
innocent and good, lucky in
being happily: EUMOIROUS
inn or lodging house: DEVER-
SARY
inns and hotels, the lore or
love of: XENODOCHEIONOL-
OGY
inquired-about thing or person: QUESITED
inquiry: INQUIRENDO
inquiry or questioning: SCIS-
CITATION
inquisitive person: NUMQUID

insane, a person who is
partly: MATTOID
insanity, religious: THEOMA-
NIA
inscribe or enroll (on a
list), to: INTABULATE
insensitive or unfeeling: IM-
PASSIBLE
inside, inner, or interior: EN-
TAL
inside-out, turned or folded:
INVAGINATED
insightful or discerning: IN-
SCIENT
insincere or mock way, questioning in a: QUIZZA-
TORIAL
insincere or rote agreement:
ASSENTATION
insinuated or creeping into:
IRREPTITIOUS
insisted on, something:
PRAESERTIM
insolent or contemptuous:
HUBRISTIC
insolent or forward: PROCA-
CIOUS
inspiration, a source of poetic: AGANIPPE
inspiration or actuating
power: ENTHEOS
inspired: AFFLATED
inspired, divinely: THEOP-
NEUST
inspiring: PROCELEUSMATIC

inspiring or persuasive to the mind or soul: PSYCHAGOGIC

installments, to arrange payment in: ESTALL

instructions for beginners, a set of: TYROLOGY

instruments, pert. to stringed: FIDICINAL

insularity, city or metropolitan: URBACITY

insult, an artfully veiled: CHARIENTISM

insulted person: AFFRONTEE

insulting: AFFRONTIVE

insult that is cleverly polite: ASTEISM

intellectually identical: SYMPHRONISTIC

intellectuals, literati, or scholars: CLERISY

intercourse, sexual: CONCUBITUS

intercourse, social: ENTREGENT

interior, inner, or inside: ENTAL

interrogatory: EROTETIC

interrogatory or questioning: PYSMATIC

interrupt and thereby disturb, to: INTERTURB

intervals, now and then or at: STOUNDMEAL

intrigue, to gain by: BRIGUE

introduce (people), to: CONSOCIATE

invaluable or priceless: IMPRETIABLE

inventive: EXCOGITOUS

inventor or originator: PROTOGENIST

investigate or search into, to: INDAGATE

inviolable: IRREFRANGIBLE

irritated beyond self-possession: EMPORTÉ

irritating: AMYCTIC

isolated: ABJUNCTIVE

itching or stinging: URTICANT

ivory and gold, of: CHRYSELEPHANTINE

ivorylike: EBURNEAN

J

jam, grape: UVATE

jam or crowd together, to: CONTRUDE

jaw, having a wide: EURYGNATHIC

jellylike: TREMELLOSE

jerky or discontinuous: SACCADIC

Jew's-harp: CREMBALUM

Jew's-harp: GUIMBARD

jilted by one's girlfriend:
LASSLORN
job or task: GERENDUM
job or task that is unpleasant
and unavoidable: CORVEE
joy or pleasure in another's
happiness: CONFELICITY
joy or pleasure in another's
happiness: MACARISM

judgment, penalty, or sentence: JUISE
juggler: HICCIUS DOCCIUS
juggler or magician: TREGE-
TOUR
juice: SUCCUS
juice, sour: VERJUICE
just, severely or inflexibly:
RHADAMANTHINE

K

kale: BORECOLE
keep repeating, to: PERSEV-
ERATE
kerchief, a spotted: BELCHER
keyboard, a piano or organ:
CLAVIATURE
kick aside or away, to: APO-
LACTIZE
killing, sacrificial: MACTA-
TION
killing harmful animals, the
art of: PHTHISOZOICS
killing (slaughter) of a people or nation: POPULICIDE
killing or destruction: INTER-
EMPTION
kindliness or consider-
ateness in speech: BENEDI-
CENCE

kinds, of all: OMNIGENOUS
kinds, of all: OMNIFARIOUS
kingly or royal: BASILIC
kiss, to: BASIATE
kiss affectionately, to: DEOS-
CULATE
kissing: SUAVIATION
kissing with the tongue:
CATAGLOTTISM
kitchen garden, belonging
to a: OLITORY
knee or knees, on one's:
AKNEE
knifelike edge, having a:
CULTELLATED
knowable, for certain, not:
ACATALEPTIC
knowable, not: METAGNOS-
TIC

knowing little or unin-
  formed: PARVISCIENT
knowledge: SCITURE
knowledge, possessing:
  SCIOUS

knowledge of women:
  GYNICS
knowledge or taste (of something) that is slight: DELI-
  BATION

L

label or memo slip pro-
  jecting from a book's
  pages: LEDGIT
laborious: MOLIMINOUS
laboriousness: OPEROSITY
lacking life or spirit: AMORT
lacking sexual desire: AN-
  APHRODITOUS
laden or pregnant: GESTANT
ladies' man: AGAPET
lame: CLAUDICANT
lamenting loudly: PLAN-
  GOROUS
lament or wail, to: EJULATE
land, the cultivation or occupation of: MANURAGE
landing of a staircase, a
  small: HALFPACE
language, of the same: HO-
  MOGLOT
languages, a little knowledge of: OLIGOGLOTTISM
language, mastery of: LIN-
  GUIPOTENCE

languages, skilled in: LIN-
  GUISHED
languor: KEF
lap or bosom, pert. to the:
  GREMIAL
large-headed: CAPITOSE
large or wide in scope: AM-
  PLIVAGANT
lasciviousness: ASELGEIA
last drop, (to drink) to the:
  SUPERNACULUM
lasting: DIUTURNAL
last-minute or parting dish:
  VOIDEE
late in life, one who learns:
  OPSIMATH
latent or hidden, lying: DELI-
  TESCENT
late or dark, to get: ADVES-
  PERATE
late or slow: LATREDE
late summer, pert. to: SEROT-
  INAL
Latinate and stately in literary style: TOGATE

213

laughable: GELASTIC
laughing easily: RIDIBUNDAL
laugh violently, to: CHECKLE
lavish spending on food and
    drink: ABLIGURITION
lawful or within the law: EN-
    NOMIC
lawless: EXLEGAL
law or rule that is good and
    promotes civil order: EU-
    NOMY
law student: STAGIARY
lawyer: LEGULEIAN
laxative: ALVIDUCOUS
laxative: CHALASTIC
laxative: LAPACTIC
laxative, a: APERIENT
lay bare or strip, to: DENU-
    DATE
laying on plaster with a
    trowel: TRULLIZATION
laziness: IGNAVIA
laziness: OCIVITY
laziness and stupidity, an op-
    ponent of: ANTISOCORDIST
laziness or sluggishness: SEG-
    NITY
leaden: PLUMBEOUS
leading by or as if by the
    hand: MANUDUCTORY
lean or thin: MACILENT
leap day, pert. to: BISSEX-
    TILE
leaping, fond of: SALTATO-
    RIAL

leaping upon: SUPERSALIENT
learnedly, speaking: DOC-
    TILOQUENT
learner late in life: OPSI-
    MATH
leather, artificial: PEGAMOID
leathery or leatherlike: CORI-
    ACEOUS
leaving or departing, pert.
    to: APOPEMPTIC
left from right, able to dis-
    tinguish: CHIROGNOSTIC
left-handed: SINISTRAL
left-handedness: MANCISM
leg's calf, pert. to the: SU-
    RAL
legacy hunting: HEREDIPETY
legally competent: CAPAX
legal or within the law: EN-
    NOMIC
legal system or legislation,
    bad: DYSNOMY
leggings or boots, wearing:
    OCREATE
legislation or legal system,
    bad: DYSNOMY
legs, having short:
    BRACHYSKELIC
lending or borrowing: MUTU-
    ATION
leniency or mercy: LENITY
length of life: ANNOSITY
lessening, diminishing, or
    subtractive: ABLATITIOUS
lethal: LETHIFEROUS

letter carrier, pert. to a: TA-
BELLARIOUS
let the doer beware: CAVEAT
ACTOR
level or horizontal position,
to place in a: COMPLA-
NATE
lewdness or goatishness: HIR-
COSITY
lewdness or fornication,
pert. to: SCORTATORY
liar: BUGIARD
liar, a female: LEIGHSTER
license or privilege, a special: INDULT
licentious: PORNERASTIC
lick, to: LAMBITATE
licked, meant to be: LIN-
GIBLE
lies, telling: MENDACILO-
QUENT
life, length of: ANNOSITY
life, loving: VITATIVE
life, pert. to: ZOETIC
lifeless: EXANIMATE
lifeless or spiritless: AMORT
light, glittering with golden
or reddish: RUTILANT
light, showing at night: NOC-
TILUCOUS
light (reddish) around mountaintops: ALPENGLOW
lightheartedness: RHA-
THYMIA

lightheartedness or gaiety:
ALLEGRESSE
lighthouse or beacon: FA-
NAL
lightless: APHOTIC
lightning: LEVINING
like in kind: CONGENEROUS
limp, drooping or hanging:
SLIMPSEY
limping: CLAUDICANT
link, the missing: ANTHRO-
PITHECUS
link, tie, or bond: VINCU-
LUM
lips, having protruding: TUT-
MOUTHED
lips, having thick: LABROSE
lips, pursing one's: COMPUR-
SION
lips, to purse one's: MIMP
liquid (and hence drink-
able): SORBILE
liquor, a first-rate: SUPER-
NACULUM
liquor, strong: ARDENT SPIR-
ITS
liquor or wine, the best:
QUADRIMUM
listener: OTACUST
listening or paying attention: AUDIENT
litany, pert. to a: LITANEUTI-
CAL
literary, pretentiously or
self-consciously: LITEROSE

literati, intellectuals, or
  scholars: CLERISY
literature, filthy or obscene:
  COPROLOGY
little, a: TENUITY
little by little: LITTLEMEAL
liver, pert. to: JECORAL
live or dwell, a place to:
  COMMORATORY
living: ZOETIC
living long: LONGEVOUS
living-long person: MAC-
  ROBIAN
living things (of a region):
  BIOTA
living together unmarried:
  CONCUBINAGE
loaning or borrowing: MUTU-
  ATION
locality or place: UBITY
lodging: HARBERGAGE
lodging house or inn: DEVER-
  SARY
loincloth, a skimpy: CACHE-
  SEXE
longing for an unattainable
  ideal: NYMPHOLEPSY
long-lived: LONGEVOUS
long-living person: MAC-
  ROBIAN
longsuffering: LONGANIMITY
long-winded: AEOLISTIC
look of love: BELGARD
look upon, fair or fit to: AS-
  PECTABLE

loosely dressed: DISCINCT
loosening: ABSTRICTION
loose or wanton girl: NYSOT
losable or destroyable, not:
  IMPERDIBLE
losing one's cool: EMPORTÉ
loss or yearning, a feeling
  of: DESIDERIUM
loudly, speaking: STENTORO-
  PHONIC
love, a glance of: BELAMOUR
love, instinctive parental:
  STORGE
love or affection for friends
  or one's fellow human beings: PHILIA
lovemaking, addicted to:
  LOVERTINE
loving in return: REDAMA-
  TION
loving look: BELGARD
loving tenderness: CHERTE
low-spirited or depressed,
  somewhat: HYPPISH
luck, lack of: SCAEVITY
lucky day: DIES FAUSTUS
lucky in being happily innocent and good: EUMOIR-
  OUS
lull to sleep or stupefy, to:
  CONSOPITE
lurking or hidden: LATITANT
lust: CONCUPISCENCE
lust: HIRCOSITY

lust, insatiable male: TEN-
  TIGO
lust, provoking: TENTIGI-
  NOUS
lustable after or desirable:
  CONCUPISCIBLE
lustrous, bright, or shining:
  NITID

luxurious or sensual living:
  EPICURITY
lying: MENTERY
lying down: DECUBATION
lying on the ground: HUMIC-
  UBATION
lying or pressing on: SUPER-
  INCUMBENT

M

machines, one who overestimates the importance of:
  MECHANOLATER
mad, to drive: LYMPHATE
made badly or clumsily:
  BLUNDERLY
made, constructed, or created something: FACTURE
mad or possessed: ARREPTI-
  TIOUS
magic, pert. to: STOICHEIOTI-
  CAL
magic, white: MAGIA
magic, white: THEURGY
magician or juggler: TREGE-
  TOUR
magic wand: RHABDUS
magnetic or attractive: AT-
  TRAHENT
mail carrier, pert. to a: TA-
  BELLARIOUS
maiming or mutilation: MAN-
  CATION

majority, rule of the numerical: ARITHMOCRACY
make-believe or deception
  as an art: FACRERE
make different or transform,
  to: HETERIZE
maker of images: ICONO-
  PLAST
maker or creator: PLAS-
  MATOR
make smooth or polish, to:
  LEVIGATE
making love, addicted to:
  LOVERTINE
malapropism: SLIPSLOP
male hysteria: TARASSIS
male lust, insatiable: TEN-
  TIGO
male prostitute: SPINTRY
males, dominated by: AN-
  DROCENTRIC
males, pert. to: ANDIC
male sex: WEPMANKIN

malice or ill will: MAL-
TALENT
malignant: THERIODIC
man, done or acted upon
by: ANTHROPURGIC
man-eating: ANDROPHAGOUS
mane or long hair, having
a: JUBATE
manhood, entering: EPHEBIC
manner, bearing, or appearance: TENUE
manner or means: QUO-
MODO
manners, moral, respect-
able, or having good:
MORATE
manual labor: MANUARY
manuring or manure: LAETA-
TION
many minds, of: MULTIVO-
LANT
many ways or roads, having:
MULTIVIOUS
margin, to note in the: AD-
MARGINATE
marginal note: APOSTIL
marine: AEQUORIAL
marine: HALIMOUS
marked, designated, or distinguished: SIGNATE
market to market, wander-
ing from: CIRCUMFORA-
NEOUS
marriage, absence of:
AGAMY

marriage, before: ANTENUP-
TIAL
marriage, related by: AFFI-
NAL
marriage, second: DEUTEROG-
AMY
marriage or a wedding: CON-
FARREATION
marriage proposal or woo-
ing: PROCATION
married: DESPONSATE
marry a man, fit to: VIRIPO-
TENT
martyr, a great or honored:
MEGALOMARTYR
marvelous or wondrous ob-
ject: STUPOR MUNDI
masculinity in a woman: VI-
RAGINITY
massacre or slaughter: BAT-
TUE
massive or momentous: MO-
LIMINOUS
master, pert. to a: HERILE
master of ceremonies or
toastmaster: SYMPOSIARCH
mastery of languages: LIN-
GUIPOTENCE
masturbation: MANUSTUPRA-
TION
matchmaker: PROXENETE
maternity ward: NATUARY
mazy winding, a: ANFRAC-
TURE
meal, a light: MERENDA

meal shared with others: SYS-
SITION
meaning or significance that
is hidden: HYPONOIA
meanings, a word having
several: POLYSEMANT
means or manner: QUO-
MODO
meanwhile, for the: AD IN-
TERIM
meat, sumptuous regarding:
LAUTITIOUS
meat, a strong odor of burning: NIDOR
medicine (remedy) or drug
good for many things:
POLYCHRESTY
mediocre ability or talents,
a person of: MEDIOCRIST
meditating on God, reli-
gious emotion from: THE-
OPATHY
meditation: HIGGAION
medley: BARIOLAGE
meekness, mildness, or gentleness: MANSUETUDE
meet, to cause to run or
flow and: CORRIVATE
melodious: MODULAMINOUS
melodious, grating and not:
SCRANNEL
melodrama: SARDOODLEDUM
memoranda or notes, con-
sisting of: HYPOMNEMATIC
memory, pert. to: MNESTIC

memo slip or label pro-
jecting from a book's
pages: LEDGIT
men, hatred of: MISANDRY
mendacity: MENTERY
menstrual: CATAMENIAL
mental derangement: VESA-
NIA
mental discipline: MATHESIS
mental distress: PSYCHALGIA
mental energy: PSYCHURGY
mentally deficient person:
AMENT
mentally refined or graceful:
SPIRITUEL
mental wandering: EVAGA-
TION
mentionable things, not: TA-
CENDA
merchandise, pert. to: EM-
POREUTIC
mercy or leniency: LENITY
merrily gay or dancing: TIT-
TUPY
mess or confused state of affairs: SCHEMOZZLE
meteor: PHASM
metropolitan or city insularity: URBACITY
middle, collapsing in the:
COLLABENT
mighty in war: BELLIPOTENT
mildness, gentleness, or
meekness: MANSUETUDE

military service, one trying to get out of: EMBUSQUE

milking, cow: VACCIMULGENCE

mind, a change of: MENTIMUTATION

minds, able to change others': FLEXANIMOUS

minds, of many: MULTIVOLANT

mingled: MISCULATE

minor subject, good writing on a: ADOXOGRAPHY

minty: LAMIACEOUS

minty: MENTHACEOUS

minute, very: MINUTISSIMIC

mirror or mirrors, pert. to a: SPECULAR

miserable, the making (one): IMMISERIZATION

misinterpretation, verbal: MISACCEPTATION

misrepresentation, deliberate: SURREPTION

missing link: ANTHROPOPITHECUS

mistake, an inadvertent: BEVUE

mistake due to ignorance: IGNOTISM

mistaken or erroneous belief, opinion, or doctrine: SPHALM

mockable: DERISABLE

mock or insincere way, questioning in a: QUIZZATORIAL

mock or ridicule: ILLUDE

moderateness in price: MODICITY

moderation or self-control: SOPHROSYNE

modest or bashful: PUDIBUND

moisten, to: MADEFY

moist or wet: UVID

moisture: AQUOSITY

molded object: FICTILE

molding into a unified whole: ESEMPLASTIC

moldy or musty: MUCID

moment or short time: STOUND

momentous or massive: MOLIMINOUS

money, love of: PHILARGYRY

money, to make in any conceivable way: QUOMODOUNCIZE

money-hungry: LUCRIPETOUS

money-making: QUAESTUARY

money up front: ARLES

monkey-headed: CEBOCEPHALIC

moon, pert. to a full: PLENILUNARY

moral of a story: EPIMYTH

moral, respectable, or well-mannered: MORATE

morbid overactivity: ERETHISM

morning twilight: UGHTEN

morrow or the day after, the: CRASTIN

mother's side, related on the: ENATIC

mountaintop reddish light: ALPENGLOW

mournful or sorrowful: LUCTUAL

mourning or sorrow, mutual: COLLUGENCY

mouth, pert. to the: STOMATIC

mouthwash: COLLUTORY

move away, to: ABSCEDE

move in a clumsy or aimless way, to: FLOB

moving or affecting: FLEXANIMOUS

mud, covered with: LUTOSE

mud bath: ILLUTATION

mud or dirt, to spatter with: BELUTE

mud or rain, to befoul with: BEDRABBLE

muddy: LUTACEOUS

muggy and hot: BULDERING

murmurous or noisy, becoming: FREMESCENT

muscle or flesh, pert. to: SARCOUS

music that is resounding: HIGGAION

musky-smelling: MOSCHATE

musty or moldy: MUCID

mutilation or maiming: MANCATION

muttering in a childish way: TOOTLISH

mutual assistance: COADJUMENT

mutual obligation or contract, involving a: SYNALLAGMATIC

mystical: TELESTIC

mystical matters, an initiator or counselor to others in: MYSTAGOGUE

mystification: METAGROBOLISM

mystify or bewilder, to: METAGROBILIZE

N

name, a pet: HYPOKORISTIKON

name, a scientific or technical: ONYM

name, having a: ONYMOUS

name, one's (addressed): COMPELLATIVE

name, without a: INNOMINATE

named aptly: EUONYMOUS

name for somebody: COMPEL-
LATION

nameplate for a storefront:
FACIA

names, having many: POLY-
ONYMOUS

names, pert. to: ONYMATIC

narcissism or self-love:
AUTOPHILIA

narrowed or contracted: AN-
GUSTATE

narrowing or becoming slender: GRACILESCENT

narrowmindedly provincial
or hidebound: BORNE

nation or people, the slaughter of a: POPULICIDE

natural affection, lack of:
ASTORGY

nature, living or growing in:
AGRESTAL

nature, one's innate: IN-
DOLES

nature lover: PHYSIOPHILIST

nearby, living: ACCOLENT

nearness: APPROPINQUITY

neck, having a long: DOLI-
CHODEROUS

neck, having a strong: CER-
VICOSE

necklace, a gold or jeweled:
CARCANET

necromancy: GOETY

needy, financially: INOPIOUS

needy and poor, very:
EGESTUOUS

negligence, carelessness, or
slackness: LACHES

neighborhood: VICINAGE

neighboring: ACCOLENT

neighboring: VICINAL

nephew, pert. to a: NEPO-
TAL

next to adjacent: PENADJA-
CENT

night, shining at: NOCTILU-
COUS

night, smelling strongest at:
NOCTUOLUCENT

night and a day: NYCH-
THEMERON

night and a day, comprising
a: NOCTIDIAL

night-wandering: NOCTIVA-
GANT

nipple: MAMMILLA

nobility of character, personal: KALOKAGATHIA

nobleness of birth: EUGENY

nodding so as to appear
wise: NOD-CRAFTY

noise or uproar, a confused:
TINTAMARRE

noisy: PERSTREPEROUS

noisy and boisterous: CALLI-
THUMPIAN

noisy or boisterous: STREPI-
TOUS
noisy or murmurous, becoming: FREMESCENT
noisy or uproarious: ROUT-
OUS
nomenclature: ONYMY
noose, armed with a: LAQUE-
ARIAN
northern: BOREAL
northern: SEPTENTRIONAL
nose, having a flat: SIMITY
nose-blowing, pert. to:
EMUNCTORY
nose that's runny: DEFLUX-
ION
nose-wiping: EMUNCTION
note, a marginal: APOSTIL
noted or observed, a thing
to be: OBSERVANDUM
notes or memoranda, con-
sisting of: HYPOMNEMATIC

notice, public: SIQUIS
notoriety or publicity: RÉ-
CLAME
nourishing: ALIMONIOUS
novelty, a mania for: NEO-
PHILISM
now and then or at inter-
vals: STOUNDMEAL
nowhere, being: NULLA-
BICITY
nowhere, existing: NULLI-
BIQUITOUS
nudism: GYMNOSOPHY
numb or stiff, tending to
be: RIGESCENT
numerical majority, rule of
the: ARITHMOCRACY
nurse: NUTRICE
nutrition, deficient: CA-
COTROPHY
nutrition, good: EUTROPHY
nutritional: EUTROPHIC
nuts, pert. to: NUCAL

O

oath: JURAMENT
oath-bound brotherhood or
conspiracy: SYNOMOSY
obedient or obsequious: MO-
RIGEROUS
obesity: ALETUDE
obesity, fatness, or grossness: POLYSARCIA

object that is molded: FIC-
TILE
obligatory or compulsory:
COACTIVE
obscene or filthy literature:
COPROLOGY
obscene or scurrilous: FES-
CINNINE

obscenity, cultish worship of: AISCHROLATREIA

obscure or dark: CALIGINOUS

obsequious or obedient: MORIGEROUS

observation, based on personal: AUTOPTIC

observed or noted, a thing to be: OBSERVANDUM

obstacle, constituting or like an: OBSTACULOUS

obstacles or obstruction, to free of: DEOPPILATE

obstruction or obstacles, to free of: DEOPPILATE

obstruct or balk, to: SUFFLAMINATE

obstruct or block up, to: OPPILATE

obtuse or dull: HEBETUDINOUS

obtuse or dull, to become or make: HEBETATE

obvious: CONSPECTABLE

obvious or visible: PHANIC

occidental or western: HESPERIAN

occidental or western: PONENT

occurrence that is incidental: OBVENTION

occurring every other year: TRIETERIC

oceanic: AEQUORIAL

odor, lacking an: INODOROUS

odorless: AOSMIC

odor of burning meat: NIDOR

odors that are noxious from household conditions: OIKIOMIASMATA

odor that is strong and offensive: GRAVEOLENCE

offhand or impromptu, something done: SCHEDIASM

office (public), a craving for holding: EMPLEOMANIA

oily or greasy: UNGUINOUS

ointment, rubbing in: INFRICTION

old, one year: ANNOTINOUS

old, that will not grow: INSENESCIBLE

old, very: OGYGIAN

old or great age: GRANDEVITY

old people, pert. to the medical treatment of: GEROCOMICAL

old together, a growing: CONSENESCENCE

old-womanish: ANICULAR

Old Worldish: GERONTOGEOUS

on, lying or pressing: SUPERINCUMBENT

one, a making into: ADUNA-
TION
one and a half times as
large: SESQUIALTERAL
one hundred feet square:
HECATOMPED
one mass, collectible into:
AGGREGABLE
oneself, activity by: AUT-
URGY
oneself, fear of referring to:
AUTOPHOBY
oneself, patterned after:
AUTOMORPHIC
one thing after another, the
placing of: POSTATION
onetime or former: CI-
DEVANT
one year old: ANNOTINOUS
onion-eating: CEPIVOROUS
onionlike: CEPACEOUS
onion- or garlic-smelling: AL-
LIACEOUS
opening widely or spread-
ing: PATULOUS
open-mouthed or grimacing:
RICTAL
open to all aspects of
thought or truth, one
who is: OMNIST
opinion, having the same:
HOMODOX
opponent of laziness and stupidity: ANTISOCORDIST

opposed constantly or resistant: RENITENT
opposition, struggling in:
CONTRANITENT
optical illusion: PSEUDOPSIA
orange peel: AURANTICOR-
TEX
orderliness (civil) under
good rule or good laws:
EUNOMY
order or arrangement, good
or established: EUTAXY
originate or produce, to:
GIGNATE
originator or inventor: PRO-
TOGENIST
ornament on a table, cen-
tral: EPERGNE
ornament or charm, a foolish: BRIMBORION
otherness: ALTERITY
others' happiness, joy in:
CONFELICITY
others' needs, anticipating:
PREVENANCE
outburst of temper: TIRRET
outermost or uttermost: EXTI-
MATE
out of keeping with or differ, to be: ABLUDE
out of one's element: DÉ-
PAYSÉ
out of one's senses: EX-
SENSED

outside, exterior, or external: ECTAL
outstretched arms, a stretch
or span of the: EN-
VERGURE
outwardly and naturally
showing emotion: ESSEN-
TIC
overactivity, morbid: ERE-
THISM
overall or general view, an
ability to take a: ENSYNOP-
TICITY

overdeveloped or over-
grown: HYPERTROPHIC
overflow, to: DEBORD
overflow or flood: ALLUVIUM
overgrown or overdevel-
oped: HYPERTROPHIC
overshadowed: ADUMBERED
overstrained: EPITONIC
owl: HOBHOUCHIN
ownership, pert. to: DO-
MINIAL
own sake, for its: AUTO-
TELIC

P

pack fruit placing the best
on top, to: DEACON
padding, artistic or literary:
REMPLISSAGE
pain, free of: APONIC
pain, pert. to or causing: AL-
GETIC
pain, causing: DOLORIFIC
pain or ailment that is imaginary: HUMDUDGEON
pain or suffering, incapable
of: IMPASSIBLE
painstaking: LABORIFEROUS
painstaking effort or work:
OPEROSITY
paint, covered with thick:
PASTOSE

painting, details added to a:
STAFFAGE
paired or twin: JUMELLE
pale, growing: PALLESCENT
palm outstretched, with
the: APPAUME
pan, frying: FRIXORY
panacea: CATHOLICON
panting: ANHELOUS
papery: CHARTACEOUS
papery: PAPYRACEOUS
parasitic or sycophantic:
GNATHONIC
parchment, like: PERGA-
MENEOUS
parent, one taking the place
of a: PROPARENT

226

parental love, instinctive:
STORGE
parentless: ORBATE
Parisian: LUTETIAN
parting or last-minute dish:
VOIDEE
part or a fragment: FRUS-
TRUM
parts, having separable:
CLASTIC
parts, to divide into: MERO-
TOMIZE
passion: CALENTURE
passion, a glow of: ESTUS
passion, welling with: ESTU-
OUS
passive and unthinking: AN-
OETIC
past, one who lives in the:
PRETERIST
past a particular place, a carrying: PRETERVECTION
pastoral care, pert. to:
POIMENIC
pasture: VACCARY
patched together, a thing:
COMPATCHMENT
pathless or trackless: INVI-
OUS
patient forbearance or suffering: LONGANIMITY
pavement: STRATUMEN
paying attention or lis-
tening: AUDIENT

paying in installments, to arrange: ESTALL
pay in toto, to: PERSOLVE
peace pipe: CALUMET
peaceful and dreamy state:
KEF
peaceful relations, a severing of: DIFFIDATION
pearly: MARGARITACEOUS
peculiarity or idiosyncrasy:
IDIASM
pedant, a dull-witted: DOR-
BEL
peevishness: PROTERVITY
penalty, judgment, or sentence: JUISE
penetration, resistance of
matter to: ANTITYPY
peninsula: CHERSONESE
penis, having a large: MEN-
TULATE
penis, pert. to the: PENIAL
penmanship or handwriting:
CHIROGRAPHY
people, liking the common:
PHILODEMIC
people or nation, the slaughter of a: POPULICIDE
peppery: PIPERITIOUS
perfect and everlasting: IN-
DEFECTIBLE
permission to go, giving:
DIMISSORY
persist or recur constantly,
to: PERSEVERATE

personal contact, pert. to
something spread by:
PROSODEMIC
personality, one's innate: IN-
DOLES
person or thing inquired
about: QUESITED
perspiring, causing or accom-
panied by: INSUDATE
persuasive, agreeably: SWA-
SIVIOUS
persuasive or inspiring to
the mind or soul: PSYCHA-
GOGIC
pet name: HYPOKORISTIKON
petty: PEDANEOUS
phenomenon that is secondary and resultant: EPIPHE-
NOMENON
photography, color: HELI-
OCHROMY
physical deterioration: EM-
PERIMENT
physical discipline: SCLE-
RAGOGY
physically weak: HY-
POSTHENIC
physical training or gymnastics, pert. to: ALEIPTIC
picture or sculpture of, to
make a: EFFIGIATE
pigeon raising and training:
PERISTEROPHILY
piggish or gluttonous: IN-
GLUVIOUS

pig raising: SYBOTISM
piled up or collected: COAC-
ERVATE
pill (tablet): TROCHE
pill, a very small: PARVULE
pipe of peace: CALUMET
pitted or pockmarked: FOVE-
ATE
placard: AFFICHE
place, a carrying past a particular: PRETERVECTION
place, having no spatial location or: ILLOCAL
place, one's being in a particular: UBIETY
place, reverence for a: TOPO-
LATRY
placed, badly: MALPOSED
placed secretly in lieu of
something else: SUBDI-
TITIOUS
place or locality: UBITY
place to live or dwell: COM-
MORATORY
place to stand: POU STO
placing of one thing after
another: POSTATION
plague, pert. to a: LOIMIC
plague or vengeance: WAN-
ION
plain, one who lives in or
on a: PEDIONOMITE
plain-speaking: PLANILO-
QUENT

plan, a ground: ICHNOGRA-PHY

planet bringing death: IN-TERFECTOR

planning (wise and conscious) that leads to progress: TELESIS

plaster, laying on with a trowel: TRULLIZATION

playing to the crowd or theatricality: CABOTINAGE

pleased or satisfied: BENE-PLACIT

please or delight, to: OBLEC-TATE

pleasure-loving or self-indulgent: APOLAUSTIC

pleasure or joy in another's happiness: CONFELICITY

pleasure or joy in another's happiness: MARCARISM

pluck or tear away, to: AVULSE

pockmarked or pitted: FOVE-ATE

poetaster, a malicious: BAV-IAN

poetic inspiration, a source of: AGANIPPE

poetry, a mania for writing: METROMANIA

point, without making (of) a particular: SUB SILENTIO

poise: TOURNURE

poison, an antidote for: ALEXIPHARMIC

poison, to: VENENATE

poisonous: VENENE

poke or prick (with a pin or needle), to: ACUPUNCTU-ATE

polar and complementary: CONTRAPLETAL

polish or make smooth, to: LEVIGATE

political boss: CACIQUE

pools, pert. to small: LACUS-CULAR

poor: OBOLARY

poor, rule by the: PTOCH-OCRACY

poor and needy, very: EGESTUOUS

poor or impecunious: OBO-LARY

poor or impoverished: DE-PAUPERATE

pope, qualified to become: PAPABLE

portable: TURSABLE

portion, a small: SCANTLE

portray, to: EFFIGIATE

portray, represent, or depict artistically, to: EXICONIZE

position, to sneakily change: TRANONT

position or rank, high: CELSI-TUDE

possessed or mad: ARREPTI-
TIOUS
poster: AFFICHE
posterior: POSTICAL
posterior or rump: PODEX
postmortem: PRETERLETHAL
potentially but not actually:
IN POSSE
poverty, in: DEPAUPERATE
poverty or economic misery:
ILLTH
powder, fragrant: EMPASM
power, having little: PARVI-
POTENT
power, of great: MAXIMIOUS
powerful, supremely: CUNC-
TIPOTENT
powerful in war: BELLIPO-
TENT
power (actuating) or inspiration: ENTHEOS
power that is hidden, pert.
to or having: CRYPTODY-
NAMIC
practical (useful) arts, the
science of the:
CHREOTECHNICS
practical, functional, or utilitarian: BANAUSIC
practical judgment, lack of
good: APHRONIA
prairie, a small: PRAIRILLON
praise or commendation,
public: PRECONY
praiseworthy: PALMARY

praising or complimentary,
not: ILLAUDATORY
prance (like a goat), to:
PRONKEN
prate or blather, to: DEBLAT-
ERATE
prattle or babble, tending
to: BABBLATIVE
praying together, a: COMPRE-
CATION
preacher or haranguer: CON-
CIONATOR
preaching, pert. to: KERYG-
MATIC
preceding in time: ANTE-
CEDANEOUS
preceding in time: ANTE-
VENIENT
precipitate: PREPROPEROUS
preeminent: PALMARY
pregnancy or childbirth, the
concealing of: CELATION
pregnant: ENCEINTE
pregnant: GRAVID
pregnant or laden: GESTANT
premarital: ANTENUPTIAL
preoccupied or absent-
minded, worriedly: DIS-
TRAIT
preparation or readiness:
PROCINCT
prepared or ready, not: IM-
PROMPT
prescribed or dogmatic:
THETIC

present, the quality of being: ECCEITY

present in more than one place at a time, being: PLURIPRESENCE

pressing or lying on: SUPERINCUMBENT

pretended refusal of something one wants: ACCISMUS

pretending or deceiving by a show of excellence: CALOPHANTIC

pretentious or bombastic in speech: LEXIPHANIC

previous or earlier act: ANTEFACT

previous to a particular time: PREPUNCTUAL

price, moderateness in: MODICITY

priceless or invaluable: IPRETIABLE

prick or poke (with a pin or needle), to: ACUPUNCTUATE

prison: BRIDEWELL

prison, pert. to: CARCERAL

private parts, covering: ANTIPUDIC

private rather than public: UMBRATILE

private, secret, or underhand: CLANCULAR

privilege or license, a special: INDULT

prizes for beauty: CALLISTEIA

proclaim like a fanfare, to: ABUCCINATE

proclaim or declare, to: INDIGITATE

procrastinate: COMPERENDINATE

produce or originate, to: GIGNATE

productive, creative, formative, or active: POIETIC

profit, to traffic or trade in for: CAUPONATE

profitable, useful, or advantageous: PROFICUOUS

profit-oriented: QUAESTUARY

prognosticate, to: HARIOLATE

progress through wise and conscious planning: TELESIS

projecting: PROJICIENT

prolific or fruitful: FERACIOUS

promise or agreement, pert. to a: SPONSIONAL

prompt, excessively: PREPUNCTUAL

pronounced letter or letter combination, not: APHTHONG

pronunciation: AESTHESICS

pronunciation or diction,
   bad: CACOLOGY
prophesy or foretell, to: ARI-
   OLATE
prophetic: FATIDIC
prophetic: FATILOQUENT
propitiatory: HILASMIC
prosperous, to make: SECUN-
   DATE
prostitute: CYPRIAN
prostitute: PAPHIAN
prostitute, male: SPINTRY
prostitute, to deceive or con
   in the manner of a: MERE-
   TRICULATE
prostitution, pert. to a
   house of: LUPANARIAN
prostrating oneself on the
   ground: HUMICUBATION
protectively enclose or
   cover, to: LORICATE
prototype or earlier example: ANTETYPE
protrude, to: EXSERT
protruding: EXSERTILE
proud, to be: SUPERBIATE
provincialism, urban: UR-
   BACITY
provincial or hidebound:
   BORNE
provisions, bought: ACATES
provisions, pert. to: ANNO-
   NARY
provisions or food: VIANDS
provocative: AGACANT

prudish: PUDIBUND
pruning: SURCULATION
psychosomatic: NEUROMI-
   METIC
publication: EVULGATION
public commendation or
   praise: PRECONY
publicity or notoriety: RÉ-
   CLAME
public notice: SIQUIS
public office, a craving for
   holding: EMPLEOMANIA
publish, to: PERVULGATE
published: DIVULGATE
pull up by the roots, to: AB-
   ERUNCATE
pulpit: ANABARATHRUM
pun: PUNDIGRION
punishment by whipping,
   pert. to: BACULINE
punishment in the form of a
   school chore: PENSUM
punning: ANNOMINATION
pupil, unteachable as a: IN-
   DOCIBLE
pupil's brief leave of absence: ABSIT
puppet show, a children's:
   POOTLY-NAUTCH
purchasing: MERCATION
purchasing things, a mania
   for: ONIOMANIA
pure or unmixed: MERA-
   CIOUS
purgative: ALVIDUCOUS

purification, spiritual or moral: LUSTRATION
purifying or detergent: SMECTIC
purify or cleanse, to: MUNDIFY
puritan, a: CATHARAN
purple-clad: PORPORATE
purse one's lips, to: MIMP
pursing (one's lips): COMPURSION

pushing, working by: TRUSATILE
pusillanimity: MICROPSYCHY
put off from day to day, to: COMPERENDINATE
put together, badly: INCONDITE
puzzle or figure out, to: METAGROBILIZE
puzzle or trinket, an odd: TRANGAM

Q

quantity, a small: QUANTULUM
quarrel, debate, or argument: DEMELE
quarreling: SIMULTATION
quarreling or scolding: RIXATION
quarrelsome, to be particularly: VITILITIGATE
quarrel, squabble, fretting, or bother: TRACASSERIE
queenly: REGINAL
quenching thirst: ADIPSOUS
questioning: EROTETIC
questioning in a mock or in-

sincere way: QUIZZATORIAL
questioning or inquiry: SCISCITATION
questioning or interrogatory: PYSMATIC
quibble: QUILLET
quibbles, the raising of: CAVILLATION
quibbling or carping: RABULISTIC
quicksand: SYRTIS
quiet, to: ACCOY
quintessence: CLYSSUS
quiver, to: TRESSILATE

R

race, of the same: HOMOPHYLIC

races, comprised of two: BIGENTIAL

raging or furious: FURABUND

rain, pert. to: HYETAL

rain, pert. to: PLUVIAL

rain or mud, to befoul with: BEDRABBLE

rain or storm clouds, bringing: NIMBIFEROUS

ram, butting like a: PETULCOUS

ramble, rove, or stroll, to: SPATIATE

ramble through, to: PERVAGATE

ramlike butting, a: ARIETATION

rank or position, high: CELSITUDE

ransom, payment of: LUITION

rape: STUPRATION

raptures, given to: ARREPTITIOUS

rationalize one's opinions or beliefs, to: THOB

readiness or preparation: PROCINCT

read through, to: PERLEGATE

ready or prepared, not: IMPROMPT

reasoning, false: CROCODILITY

reasoning, pert. to Socratic: HEBAMIC

rebirth or revival: PALINGENESY

reborn: REDIVIVUS

reborn, capable of being: RENASCIBLE

rebuke, chiding, or reproof: INCREPATION

receptive to all aspects of thought or truth, one who is: OMNIST

recklessness, foolish daring or willful: HARDYDARDY

reclining: DECUBATION

recognition or acknowledgment: AGNITION

recognized, easily: KENSPECKLE

recorded, not: IMPERSCRIPTABLE

recur constantly or persist, to: PERSEVERATE

reddish: RUBEDINOUS

reddish or golden light, glittering with: RUTILANT

refined or graceful, mentally: SPIRITUEL

refined or subtle in expression, overly: ALEMBICATED

refresh or comfort, to: FOCILLATE

refresh or revive, to: REFOCILLATE

refusal that is pretended of something one wants: ACCISMUS

refuse or deny, to: DENE-
GATE
region, a description or tour
of a: PERIEGESIS
register or enroll, to: IM-
BREVIATE
regretful about something
unattained earlier, one
who is: WOULD-HAVE-
BEEN
reigning or dominant: REG-
NANT
reiterate or repeat, to: IN-
GEMINATE
reject as spurious, to: ATHE-
TIZE
reject or condemn, to:
ASPERNATE
reject strongly, to: RESPUE
rejoicing or celebrating together: CONGAUDENCE
rekindle or relight, to: RE-
LUME
related by marriage: AFFI-
NAL
related on the mother's
side: ENATIC
relationship, a close:
PROXYSM
relied upon, one who can
be: SURESBY
relieve or disembarrass, to:
DEBARRASS
relieving weariness: ACOPIC

relight or rekindle, to: RE-
LUME
religious, extremely: RELIGI-
OSE
religious, zealously: EPIDEIS-
TIC
religious emotion from meditating on God: THEO-
PATHY
religious insanity: THEOMA-
NIA
religious rite: HIERURGY
relinquishing or resignation:
DEMISSION
remedy, all-purpose: CA-
THOLICON
remedy or drug good for
many things: POLY-
CHRESTY
reminder or rule that is cautionary: CAUTELA
remorse or repentance, incapable of: IMPENITIBLE
remove (oneself) to a distance, to: ELOIN
renewal or restoration: IN-
STAURATION
rent out, to: ABLOCATE
repay or reward, to: RE-
GRATE
repeatedly occur or persist,
to: PERSEVERATE
repeating, to keep: PERSEV-
ERATE

repeat or reiterate, to: IN-
GEMINATE
repentence or remorse, incapable of: IMPENITIBLE
repetition, needless verbal:
BATTOLOGY
represent, portray, or depict
artistically, to: EXICONIZE
reproof, chiding, or rebuke:
INCREPATION
reputation, honor, or credit:
IZZAT
requited love: REDAMATION
residence to foreigners, generally forbidding: XENE-
LASIA
resignation or relinquishing:
DEMISSION
resistant or constantly opposed: RENITENT
respectable, moral, or well-
mannered: MORATE
respects or compliments,
one's: BAISEMAINS
restoration or renewal: IN-
STAURATION
restorative: ROBORANT
restraining or holding with
the hands: MANUTENTION
restrict, to: ASTRICT
resultant secondary phenomenon: EPIPHENOMENON
resulting as a consequence:
CONSECTARY
result or effect: CAUSATUM

retreat or a going back: RE-
CULADE
returning of love: REDAMA-
TION
reveal, to: PROPALE
revealing or unveiling, an:
ANACALYPSIS
reveal or disclose, to: PA-
TEFY
revelations, to prevent or
punish: MORGANIZE
revenge in kind or an eye
for an eye, pert. to: TALI-
ONIC
revenge: ULTION
revival or rebirth: PALINGEN-
ESY
revive, liable to: REDI-
VIVOUS
revive or refresh, to: REFO-
CILLATE
reward, to: PREMIATE
reward or repay, to: RE-
GRATE
rewrite, to: RESCRIBE
rich, becoming: DITATION
rich, preoccupied with becoming: CHREMATISTIC
rich, the process of becoming: LUCRIFACTION
rich and complete: LOCU-
PLETE
rich or sumptuous: OPIP-
AROUS
ride away, to: ABEQUITATE

rider, horse: PRICKER
ridicule or mock, to: ILLUDE
right from left, able to distinguish: CHIROGNOSTIC
rights, equal political: ISONOMY
rink, an ice skating: GLACIARIUM
riotous or wild: RAGMATICAL
ripe, rottenly: FRACID
rip to pieces, to: DILANIATE
risk or danger, to expose to: PERICLITATE
river, pert. to a: AMNIC
roads, without: INVIOUS
roads or ways, having many: MULTIVIOUS
roaring or bellowing: BOATION
roasting or baking: ASSATION
rolling toward, a: ADVOLUTION
roots, to pull up by the: ABERUNCATE
rope, hanging from a: FUNIPENDULOUS
rope, to walk or dance on a: FUNAMBULATE
rope noose, armed with a: LAQUEARIAN
rottenly ripe: FRACID
rouged, highly: RADDLED
rough or rugged: ASPEROUS
rough or rugged: SALEBROUS
roundabout: AMBAGIOUS

rove, ramble, or stroll, to: SPATIATE
royal or kingly: BASILIC
rubbish: PALTREMENT
rubbing (ointment) in: INFRICTION
rub linament on, to: EMBROCATE
rub thoroughly, to: PERFRICATE
rugged or rough: ASPEROUS
rugged or rough: SALEBROUS
rule, total or universal: OMNIREGENCY
ruler of the world: KOSMOKRATOR
rule of the numerical majority: ARITHMOCRACY
rule or domination, under: DITIONARY
rumbling in the bowels: GURGULATION
rump or posterior: PODEX
run or flow together, to cause to: CORRIVATE
running or driving toward, a: APPULSE
runny nose: DEFLUXION
rural: AGRESTIC
rural or rustic: VILLATIC
rushed or overly hasty: PREPROPEROUS
rust, affected by: RUBIGENOUS
rust-colored: RUBIGENOUS
rustic or rural: VILLATIC

S

sacred rite: HIERURGY
sacrifice of women: GYNE-
THUSIA
sacrifice or sacrificing: LITA-
TION
sacrificial killing: MACTA-
TION
sad, a little: SUBTRIST
sad, making forever: TRO-
PHONIAN
sadden, to: CONTRIST
sad or sorrowful: DOLENT
salads, used in: ACETARIOUS
salivate, causing one to: SI-
ALOGIC
salt, containing: SALIFEROUS
salt, pert. to: HALIMOUS
salty, slightly: SALSUGINOUS
salvation, pert. to: SOTERIAL
same kind, of the: CONGEN-
EROUS
same period or equal age, of
the: EQUAEVAL
same time, coming into existence at the: COETANEOUS
sanctuary or shrine: DELU-
BRUM
sand-loving: AMMOPHILOUS
sane, legally: CAPAX

satisfaction or amends:
ASSETH
satisfied or pleased: BENE-
PLACIT
satyiasis: TENTIGO
satyr: CAPRIPEDE
saucy or impudent: MAL-
APERT
savage or beastlike: THER-
EOID
savage with one's teeth, to:
LANIATE
sawdust, like: SCOBICULAR
saying enough or enough
said: SATISDICTION
scare a baby, something to:
SCAREBABE
scarlike: ULOID
scented: OLENT
scholars, intellectuals, or
literati: CLERISY
scientific or technical name:
ONYM
scissors, a pair of: FORFEX
scoffing, gently: SUBDER-
ISORIOUS
scolding or criticism, tedious: JOBATION
scolding or quarreling: RIXA-
TION

scope, large or wide in: AM-
PLIVAGANT
scorned, to be: DERISABLE
sculpture or picture of, to
make a: EFFIGIATE
scurrilous or foulmouthed:
SPURCIDICAL
scurrilous or obscene: FES-
CINNINE
sea: AEQUOR
sea, a description of the:
HALIOGRAPHY
sea, pert. to the: AEQUORIAL
sea, produced in the: MA-
RIGENOUS
sea breeze: VIRASON
seal or seal up, to: SIGIL-
LATE
search into or investigate,
to: INDAGATE
search through, to: PER-
QUEST
sea-sunken goods (with the
spot marked): LAGAN
seclusion or indoors, done
or carried on in: UM-
BRATILE
secondary and resultant
phenomenon:
EPIPHENOMENON
second marriage: DEUTEROG-
AMY
secret, private, or underhand: CLANCULAR

secrets: PENETRALIA
secret thoughts, apt to reveal: PRODITORIOUS
sedative, acting as a: ANTI-
ORGASTIC
sediment or dregs: FAEX
see, delightful to:
SIGHTSOME
see, eager to: SPECTABUN-
DAL
seeable to the naked eye:
MACROMERITIC
seeker, applicant, or candidate: PETITOR
seems to exist, something
that only: TANQUAM
seen, things that ought to
be: VIDENDA
seen or observed, a thing to
be: OBSERVANDUM
seen through, easily: TRAN-
SPICUOUS
seismic: TERREMOTIVE
seizable or graspable: PRE-
HENSIBLE
select or excellent: EXHIMI-
OUS
self-aggrandizement or vainglory, the love or pursuit
of: KENODOXY
self-controlled or abstinent:
ENCRATIC
self-control or moderation:
SOPHROSYNE

selfhood or individuality:
SEITY

selfhood or self-identity: IP-
SEITY

self-identity or selfhood: IP-
SEITY

self-indulgent or pleasure-
loving: APOLAUSTIC

self-love or narcissism: AU-
TOPHILIA

self-worship: AUTOLATRY

self-worshiping: EGOLA-
TROUS

sell for profit, to: CAUPO-
NATE

send away or abroad, to:
ABLEGATE

senility: CADUCITY

senility, premature: PROGE-
RIA

senior citizens, pert. to the
medical treatment of:
GEROCOMICAL

senseless or tasteless: IN-
FRUNITE

senses, brought back to
one's: RESIPISCENT

senses, out of one's: EX-
SENSED

sensibility: ESTHESIA

sensual: EPITHUMETIC

sensualist: ACOLAUST

sensual or luxurious living:
EPICURITY

sentence arrangement, confused: SYNCHYSIS

sentence, judgment, or penalty: JUISE

sententious: GNOMOLOGIC

separable pieces, take-
apartable or having: CLAS-
TIC

separate or come apart, causing to: DIVELLENT

separating or characterized
by separation: SCHIZTIC

separation: SEJUNCTION

separationlike or separating:
SCHIZTIC

series of chance occur-
rences: CHAPTER OF ACCI-
DENTS

servant: VADELECT

set off or distinguish, to: DIS-
PUNCT

settled or agreed to: PACTI-
TIOUS

seven days in duration or
weekly: HEBDOMADAL

several years, lasting for:
PLURENNIAL

severed or disconnected: AB-
JUNCT

severely or inflexibly just:
RHADAMANTHINE

severing of peaceful relations: DIFFIDATION

sewn: SUTILE

sexual craving for women: GYNAECOCOENIC

sexual desire, lacking: ANAPHRODITOUS

sexual intercourse: CONCUBITUS

sexual intercourse: PAREUNIA

sexual intercourse, pert. to: SUBAGITATORY

sexual intercourse, to have: SUBAGITATE

sexually attracted to either sex: AMPHIEROTIC

sexual object, loving another as a: ALLOEROTICISM

sexual pleasure: VOLUPTY

shadow, casting a long: MACROSCIAN

shadow over, to cast a: OBTENEBRATE

shadows, dispersing or dispelling: SCIALYTIC

shady place or a cool walkway: FRESCADE

shake violently, to: CONQUASSATE

shaking, a severe: SQUASSATION

shaking, violent: SUCCUSSION

shameful: PUDENDOUS

shameful or ashamed: HONTOUS

shamelessness: IMPUDICITY

shaped well: EUMORPHOUS

shared feeling: COMPATHY

shared meal: SYSSITION

sharks, fear of: GALEOPHOBIA

sharp-pointed: ACUATE

shelter along the way, a place of: DIVERSORY

sherry: XERES

shining around: CIRCUMFULGENT

shining at night: NOCTILUCOUS

shining between others: INTERLUCENT

shining, bright, or lustrous: NITID

ship collision, intentional: ALLISION

shipwreck, causing: NAUFRAGOUS

shipwreck, in danger of: NAUFRAGEOUS

shipwrecked person: NAUFRAGUE

shirt, wearing one on the outside: CAMISATED

shock: PERCULSION

shoe: SUBPEDITAL

shopkeepers: CAPELOCRACY

shore, bank, or coast: RIVAGE

short in stature: IMPROCEROUS

short-legged: BRACHYSKELIC

short-lived, anything:
EPHEMERON
short-winded or breathing
strenuously: PURSY
short time or moment:
STOUND
showily, to display: VENDI-
TATE
showing off: APOPATHETIC
show of affection: EMPRESSE-
MENT
shrillness of voice: OXYPHO-
NIA
shrine or sanctuary: DELU-
BRUM
shudder at, to: PERHORRESCE
shy or bashful: DAPHNEAN
shy or bashful: VERECUND
sickbed, confinement to a:
DECUMBITURE
sickly or delicate: MALADIVE
sickness: EGRITUDE
sickness that is imaginary:
HUMDUDGEON
side, written on one only:
ANOPISTHOGRAPHIC
side by side, running: PARA-
DROMIC
side dishes: ENTREMETS
side or back entrance: POS-
TERN
siesta: MERIDIATION
sifting: CRIBATION
sighing or breathing heavily: SUSPIRIOUS

signature, a flourish made at
the end of a: PARAPH
signature for another person: ALLOGRAPH
signs or abbreviations representing words: SIGLA
silent: CONTICENT
silent, inclined to be: SI-
LENTIOUS
silent, obstinately: OBMUTES-
CENT
silken: BOMBYCINE
silly, foolish, or trifling: DE-
SIPIENT
similar, things that are alike
or: SIMILIA
similar in taste or flavor:
CONGUSTABLE
simultaneously coming into
existence: COETANEOUS
sin, liable to: PECCABLE
sin, without: IMPECCANT
sinful: PECCAMINOUS
sip or taste, to: DELIBATE
sits in or upon, one who: IN-
SESSOR
six-fingeredness: SEXDIGITISM
skeptical: PYRRHONIC
skeptical or doubting: APO-
RETIC
sketch or diagram, a careless: PERIGRAPH
skillful or able: HABILE
skin, a piece or shred of:
BLYPE

skin, having yellow: XAN-
THOUS

skin, pert. to: DERIC

skin, to bring goose bumps
to the: HORRIPILATE

skirmish: VELITATION

skull, having a high: HYPSI-
CEPHALIC

sky's pink or purple glow
after sunset: ANTI-
TWILIGHT

slackness, carelessness, or
negligence: LACHES

slander: TRADUCTION

slang, pert. to: ARGOTIC

slaughter: TRUCIDATION

slaughter of a people or nation: POPULICIDE

slaughter or massacre: BAT-
TUE

sleep, a place of: SOMNIFERY

sleep, a place to sleep: LIB-
KIN

sleep, causing: HYPNAGOGIC

sleep, something to prevent:
AGRYPNOTIC

sleep, to lull to: CONSOPITE

sleeping during the day: DI-
URNATION

sleepwalker: HYPNOBATE

sleight of hand or trickery:
ESCAMOTAGE

slimy: MUCULENT

slimy: ULIGINOUS

slimy or sticky, to make: EN-
GLEIM

slip, making a Freudian:
HETEROPHEMY

slothfulness: SEGNITY

sloth or idleness: IGNAVIA

slowness or sluggishness:
LENTITUDE

slowness or sluggishness:
LENTOR

slow or tardy: LATREDE

slow-stepping or sluggish:
TARDIGRADE

sluggishness or laziness: SEG-
NITY

sluggishness or slowness:
LENTITUDE

sluggishness or slowness:
LENTOR

sluggish or slow-stepping:
TARDIGRADE

slurred speech: SLURVIAN

sly or crafty: SUBDOLOUS

small, extremely: MINUTIS-
SIMIC

small-bodied: NANOID

small portion: SCANTLE

small quantity: QUANTULUM

small space, compressed
into a: POLYMICRIAN

small talk or chitchat: BA-
VARDAGE

smell, a burnt: EMPYREUMA

smell, having a good sense
of: NASUTE

smell, having a keen sense of: HYPEROSMIC

smell, without: AOSMIC

smell, without: INODOROUS

smellable: OSPHRETIC

smelling bad: MALEOLENT

smelling bad: OLID

smelling fragrant: OLENT

smelling like an animal: CAPRYLIC

smelling strongest at night: NOCTUOLUCENT

smells that are noxious from household conditions: OIKIOMIASMATA

smell that is strong and offensive: GRAVEOLENCE

smiling: SUBRIDENT

smoky or sooty: FULIGINOUS

smooth-talking: HYBLAEAN

snake charming, pert. to: PSYLLIC

snarl back, to: INTERGERN

snarling, growling, or grumbling: OGGANITION

snatch or take away, to: EREPT

sneering: MYCTERISM

sneezing: STERNUTATION

sneezing, causing: PTARMIC

snoring: STERTOROUS

snorting or snoring: RHONCHISONANT

snowy: NIVEOUS

soak or steep, to: INSUCCATE

soaring in spirit: ESSORANT

sob: SINGULT

social custom or convention: CONSUETUDE

social intercourse: ENTREGENT

socially awkward, tactless, or crude act: GAUCHERIE

Socratic reasoning, pert. to: HEBAMIC

soft, becoming: MOLLESCENT

soften, to: LENIFY

softening or soothing: DEMULCENT

soften or make tender, to: INTENERATE

softness or effeminacy: MOLLITUDE

soft-voiced: MALACOPHONOUS

solicit: WANTONIZE

solicitude or caring for: ACCURANCE

soliloquizing, prone to: SOLILOQUACIOUS

solitude, love of: APANTHROPY

somber or dingy: SUBFUSC

songwriter: ASMATOGRAPHER

soothe, to: ACCOY

soothing or calming: HESYCHASTIC

soothing or softening: DE-
MULCENT
sooty or smoky: FULIGINOUS
sorrow, deep: EGRIMONY
sorrowful or sad: DOLENT
sorrowful or mournful: LUC-
TUAL
sorrow or gloom, bringing:
LUCTIFEROUS
sorrow or mourning, mu-
tual: COLLUGENCY
soul, greatness of: MEGALO-
PSYCHY
sounding like a whisper, as
wind among leaves: PSITH-
URISM
sounding like blowing across
the mouth of a bottle:
AMPHORIC
sounding stately: GRANDISO-
NANT
sound that is grating, to
make a: GRIDE
sour juice: VERJUICE
southern: AUSTRAL
space, having no location
in: ILLOCAL
spank, to: BUMBASTE
sparkling or sputtering: EMI-
CATION
spatter with mud or dirt, to:
BELUTE
speak, able to: MEROPIC
speaker who is a haranguer

or preacher: CONCIONA-
TOR
speaking in a plain way:
PLANILOQUENT
speaking in different ways:
DIVERSILOQUENT
speaking learnedly: DOCTILO-
QUENT
speaking loudly: STENTORO-
PHONIC
speaking range:
TONGUESHOT
speak to, easy to go up to
and: PERAFFABLE
speculative thinker or theorist: NOTIONALIST
speech, filthy: BORBOROLOGY
speech, kindliness or considerateness in: BENEDICENCE
speech, pert. to: PHEMIC
speech (soliloquy), prone to
making a: SOLILOQUA-
CIOUS
speech, slurred: SLURVIAN
speech, smooth in:
HYBLAEAN
spell (on), to put a: ENSOR-
CELL
spending on food and drink,
lavish: ABLIGURITION
sphinxlike: SPHINGINE
spirit, a good: CALODEMON
spirit, soaring in: ESSORANT
spirits, somewhat depressed
or in low: HYPPISH

spiritual healing for the
   soul: PSYCHIASIS
spit, apt to: SPUTATIVE
spit out or cough up, to: EX-
   CREATE
spit out or ejected: EX-
   SPUTORY
spitting or hawking: SCREA-
   TION
spitting out: EXSPUITION
spitting while one is speaking: SIALOQUENT
spit upon, to: CONSPUE
splintery: ESQUILLOUS
splitting hairs: PILPULISTIC
spokesperson: PROLOCUTOR
spontaneous: ULTRONEOUS
spoonful (medicinally):
   COCHLEARE
spreading or opening
   widely: PATULOUS
spring, pert. to: VERTUMNAL
spring, pert. to early: PRIMA-
   VERAL
sprinkle, to: ASPERGE
spurious, to reject as: ATHE-
   TIZE
sputtering or sparkling: EMI-
   CATION
spy: OTACUST
squabble, quarrel, fretting,
   or bother: TRACASSERIE
squall or thunderstorm: BO-
   RASCO
squatly fat: FUBSY

squeeze and crush, to:
   SQUISS
squeeze or compress, to:
   CONSTRINGE
stagger or stumble, to: TITU-
   BATE
staircase landing, a small:
   HALFPACE
stammering: BALBUTIENT
stammering: BLESILOQUENT
stammering: TRAULISM
stamping the feet in disapproval: SUPPLOSION
stand, a place to: POU STO
starchy: AMYLACEOUS
starry: ASTRIFEROUS
startle, to: ABRAID
stately and Latinate in literary style: TOGATE
stately or dignified: TOGATE
stately sounding: GRANDISO-
   NANT
state or country, a petty: TO-
   PARCHY
stealing, given to: FURA-
   CIOUS
steel blue: CHALYBEUS
steep or hilly: CLIVOSE
steep or soak, to: INSUC-
   CATE
step by step or cautiously,
   proceeding: PEDETENTOUS
step by step or gradually:
   GRADATIM

stepmother, pert. to a:
NOVERCAL
stern or severe: TORVOUS
sticky and wet: VISCID
sticky or slimy, to make: EN-
GLEIM
stiff or numb, tending to
be: RIGESCENT
stimulating or tonic: ANABI-
OTIC
stinginess: EUCLIONISM
stinging or itching: URTI-
CANT
stinking: OLID
stocked plentifully: LOCU-
PLETE
stomach, a rumbling in the:
GURGULATION
stomach growling: BOR-
BORYGM
stomach or ears, a buzzing
in the: BOMBUS
stone, turning to: PETRES-
CENT
stone, written in: RUPES-
TRIAN
stone rounded off by the
wind: VENTIFACT
stop up or close, to: OBTU-
RATE
storefront nameplate: FACIA
storm or rain clouds, bringing: NIMBIFEROUS
stormy: ORAGIOUS
stormy: PROCELLOUS

story's moral: EPIMYTH
straight hair, having: EUTHY-
COMIC
straight line, walking in a:
RECTIGRADE
straightforward, not: AMBA-
GIOUS
straightforward or genuine:
JANNOCK
strained or futile humor:
WITZELSUCHT
strange or absurd thing or
person: QUOZ
strange or unusual: SEL-
COUTH
strangers, a hater of: MISOX-
ENE
stratagem or trick: BLENCH
straw-colored: STRAMINEOUS
straw yellow: FESTUCINE
strenuous effort: MOLIMEN
stretching and yawning:
PANDICULATION
strife or fighting: DIMICA-
TION
striking or impressive: FRAP-
PANT
stringed instruments, pert.
to: FIDICINAL
strip or lay bare, to: DENU-
DATE
stroll, rove, or ramble, to:
SPATIATE
stronger in influence,

power, or weight: PREPOL-
LENT
strong or lively seeming but
really weak: FORCIBLE-
FEEBLE
struggling, contention, or
wrangling: COLLUCTATION
struggling in opposition:
CONTRANITENT
struggling to overcome: LUC-
TATION
stubborn: PERVIVACIOUS
stubborn, extremely: ENTETE
student: EDUCAND
student, a fellow: CONDISCI-
PLE
student, unteachable as a:
INDOCIBLE
studio or workshop: BOT-
TEGA
study or thought, a place
for: PHRONTISTERY
stuffed with food: FARCTATE
stumble or stagger, to: TITU-
BATE
stunning or dazzling: FOU-
DROYANT
stupid, equally: UNASINOUS
stupidity and laziness, an opponent of: ANTISOCORDIST
stupidity or ignorance: CRAS-
SITUDE
stupid person: STUPEX
stuttering: BALBUTIENT
stuttering: BLESILOQUENT

stuttering: TRAULISM
subduer or conqueror: DEBEL-
LATOR
subscriber: ABONNE
subsequent: POSTLIMINOUS
subservient or sycophantic:
SEQUACIOUS
substitute: SUCCEDANEUM
subterranean or under-
ground: CATACHTHONIAN
subtle or refined in expression, overly: ALEMBI-
CATED
subtractive, lessening, or diminishing: ABLATITIOUS
success, one on the way to
socially or professionally:
PARVENANT
sudden, hasty, or unex-
pected: SUBITANEOUS
suddenly or hastily done or
made: SUBITARY
suffering, enduring: PERPES-
SION
suffering or pain, incapable
of: IMPASSIBLE
sugar, a depriving of: DESU-
CRATION
sugar candy: ALPHENIC
suitable or apt: IDONEOUS
summer, pert. to late: SEROT-
INAL
summon, to: ACCERSE
sumptuous (esp. regarding
meat): LAUTITIOUS

248

sumptuous or rich: OPIP-
AROUS
sum up concisely, to: COM-
PENDIATE
sun, to bask in the: APRI-
CATE
Sunday, pert. to: DOMINI-
CAL
Sunday clothes, dressed up
in one's: ENDIMANCHE
sung in a natural (rather
than falsetto) voice: DI
PETTO
sunken or collapsing in the
middle: COLLABENT
sunken-in-the-sea goods
(with the spot marked):
LAGAN
sunset glow (pink or purple)
of sky: ANTITWILIGHT
sunstroke: SIRIASIS
superior in influence,
power, or weight: PREPOL-
LENT
supernatural: HYPERPHYSICAL
supernatural powers, fear of:
DEISIDAIMONIA
supper-loving: COENACU-
LOUS
supplemental: ADSCITITIOUS
support: SUPPEDITOR
suppository: BOUGIE
suppression of the truth,
fraudulent: SURREPTION
surface, pert. to a: EPIPOLIC

surrender: CAPITULANT
surrender: DEDITION
swaggering: HUFTY-TUFTY
swallow up or gulp down,
to: INGURGITATE
swallowable whole: DEVORA-
TIVE
swallowing: DEGLUTITION
swear under oath, to: DE-
PONE
sweating, causing or accom-
panied by: INSUDATE
sweet, smelling: SUAVEO-
LENT
sweet potato: BATATA
swelling: TURGESCENT
swim, able to: NATILE
swollen of face because of
weeping: BEGRUTTEN
swoon or faint, tending to:
LIPOTHYMIC
swordfish: XIPH
sycophantic or parasitic:
GNATHONIC
sycophantic or subservient:
SEQUACIOUS
syllables, a word or more
than two: HYPERDISYL-
LABLE
symbols or abbreviations representing words: SIGLA
sympathy, an absence of:
DISSYMPATHY
synonym: POECILONYM
synthetic: SYSTATIC

T

table, central ornament on a: EPERGNE

tablet (pill): TROCHE

taciturn: SILENTIOUS

tailor: SARTOR

take-apartable or having separable parts: CLASTIC

take away or cancel, to: SUBLATE

take away or snatch, to: EREPT

talk, excessive: PLENILOQUENCE

talk, filthy: BORBOROLOGY

talk, foolish: ONOLOGY

talk, given to windy: VENTOSE

talkative: LINGACIOUS

talking in a smooth way: HYBLAEAN

talking windily: BLOVIATION

talk or behave foolishly, to: FOOTLE

talk that is rambling or evasive: ALIENILOQUY

talk too much, to: POLYLOGIZE

tallness: PROCERITY

tame, to: AMENAGE

tame or make mild, to: CICURATE

tar and feathers, consisting of: PLUMEOPICIAN

task, to apply oneself to a: ACCINGE

task or job: GERENDUM

task or job that is unpleasant and unavoidable: CORVEE

taste, conventional, bourgeois, or vulgar in: BIEDERMEIER

taste, having no detectable: INGUSTABLE

tasteless or senseless: INFRUNITE

taste or flavor, similar in: CONGUSTABLE

taste or knowledge (of something) that is slight: DELIBATION

taste or sip, to: DELIBATE

tasty: SAPID

tea, one who drinks too much: THEIC

teacher, pert. to a: DIDASCALIC

teaching, fast: TACHYDIDAXY

teacup, a tempest in a: BATRACHOMYOMACHY

tear away or pluck, to:
AVULSE

tearful or doleful: FLEBILE

tear to pieces, to: DILANI-
ATE

technical or scientific name:
ONYM

teeth, gnashing one's: FREN-
DENT

teeth, having: DENTIGEROUS

teeth, having yellow: XAN-
THODONTOUS

teeth, to savage with one's:
LANIATE

teeth (upper) that project,
having: GUBBERTUSHED

telephone message: TELE-
PHEME

temper, an outburst of: TIR-
RET

temporary: AD INTERIM

tempting or enticing to evil:
LENOCINANT

tenderize or soften, to: IN-
TENERATE

tenderness of affection:
CHERTE

tenfold: DECUPLE

tennis-playing: SPHAIRISTIC

tension, anxiety, or excitement, a state of: FAN-
TIGUE

tentative or experimental:
PEIRASTIC

terminal or closing: DESI-
NENT

terrify or dismay, to: CON-
STERNATE

testicles, lacking: ANOR-
CHOUS

thatched cottage: CHAU-
MIERE

theatricality or obvious playing to the crowd: CABO-
TINAGE

theorist or speculative
thinker: NOTIONALIST

thickened: INSPISSATED

thick-lipped: LABROSE

thickness: CRASSITUDE

thickness or density: SPISSI-
TUDE

thick or clotted: GRUMOUS

thick-set: SPUDDY

thick-skinned: PACHY-
DERMATOUS

thief, given to being a: FU-
RACIOUS

thin or lean: MACILENT

thin or slender, becoming:
GRACILESCENT

thin-skinned, delicately: LEP-
TOCHROUS

thing or person inquired
about: QUESITED

things of little value: TRAN-
TLES

things that are forbidden:
VETANDA

things that ought to be
seen: VIDENDA
things that shouldn't be
mentioned: TACENDA
things to be believed:
CREDENDA
thinker, a theorist or speculative: NOTIONALIST
thinking deeply or pensive:
COGITABUND
third downfall or "slip": TRI-
LAPSE
thirst-causing: DIPSETIC
thirst-quenching: ADIPSOUS
thirsty: SITIENT
this day, pert. to: HODIER-
NAL
thoughtless: INCOGITANT
thoughtless action: ETOUR-
DERIE
thought or study, a place
for: PHRONTISTERY
thoughts, expressed only in
one's: SUBVOCAL
thousandth: MILLESIMAL
thread, hanging by a: FILI-
PENDULOUS
threatening: MINACIOUS
threatening: MINITANT
threefold: TRIPLASIAN
three times a day: TERDIUR-
NAL
throb, to: QUOP
thumb and forefinger, the

space between the: PUR-
LICUE
thumb curled behind the
second finger, with the:
CUNNY-THUMB
thunder, a sound like distant: BRONTIDE
thunderstorm or squall: BO-
RASCO
ticklish (in dealing with):
QUISQUOSE
tie, link, or bond: VINCU-
LUM
tie up, to: ASTRICT
timber framework: CONTIG-
NATION
time, comparatively short
in: CURTATE
time, excessively on: PRE-
PUNCTUAL
time, preceding in: ANTE-
CEDANEOUS
time, preceding in: ANTE-
VENIENT
time, previous to a particular: PREPUNCTUAL
timed unfortunately: MELAN-
COUNTEROUS
timid or afraid: PAVID
tingling, to feel or cause an
unpleasant: PRINGLE
tiny, very: MINUTISSIMIC
tip or gratuity: BONAMANO
tiptoed: DIGITIGRADE

252

tired or faint, becoming: LANGUESCENT

tired or weary: LASSATE

tit for tat: DO UT DES

toastmaster or master or ceremonies: SYMPOSIARCH

toast to, to drink a: PROPINE

tobacco, bad-smelling: MUNDUNGUS

tobacco, coarse smoking: CANASTER

today, pert. to: HODIERNAL

toe, pert. to the big: HALLUCAL

toes, actions to keep people on their: PANTARAXIA

toes, having slender: LEPTODACTYLOUS

together, calling out: CONCLAMANT

together, celebrating or rejoicing: CONGAUDENCE

together, to cause to run or flow: CORRIVATE

together, to crowd or jam: CONTRUDE

tongue, pert. to the: GLOSSAL

tongue-kissing: CATAGLOTTISM

tongue-lashing: SISERARY

toothache: DENTAGRA

toothless: AGOMPHIOUS

toothless: EDENTULOUS

toothpick: DENTISCALP

top off, to cut the: OBTRUNCATE

torment or torture: CRUCIATION

torment or torture, to: DISCRUCIATE

torture, love of inflicting: PHALARISM

torture, the final or worst: QUESTION EXTRAORDINAIRE

torture or torment: CRUCIATION

torture or torment, to: DISCRUCIATE

toss and turn, to: JACTITATE

total or universal rule: OMNIREGENCY

touch, pert. to: HAPTIC

touch, to: ATTINGE

touch, using to determine where one is: TOPESTHESIA

touching or in contact with: ATTINGENT

touching, nearly: SUBCONTIGUOUS

touching or contact: TACTION

touching or fingering: CONTRECTATION

tour or circuit: PERIPLUS

tour or description of a region: PERIEGESIS

tragic: MELPOMENISH

tranquilizing or calming: PACATIVE

transcendent or unearthly: SUPERMONDANE

transform, to make different or: HETERIZE

transitoriness: CADUCITY

translator: METAPHRAST

transparent in water: HYDROPHANOUS

trap or ensnare, to: ILLAQUEATE

trashy: QUISQUILIAN

traveling about: VIAGGIATORY

traveling companion: SYNODITE

treading underfoot, a: CONCULCATION

treason: PERDUELLION

treat as if of trifling value, to: FLOCCIPEND

treat as on the same level, to: EQUIPARATE

tree, dwarf: ARBUSCLE

tree, fit-to-be-felled: CEDUOUS

tree boughs or branches: RAMAGE

tree-loving: DENDROPHILOUS

trees, living in: DENDROPHILOUS

trickery or sleight of hand: ESCAMOTAGE

trick or stratagem: BLENCH

tricky (in dealing with): QUISQUOSE

trifle: TRILLIBUB

trifling, foolish, or silly: DESIPIENT

trilled: HIRRIENT

trinket or bauble: FLAMFEW

trinker or puzzle, odd: TRANGAM

triumphant exultation or boasting: GLORIATION

trouble, full of: AERUMNOUS

trouble or contention, wanting: DIVERSIVOLENT

true, suggesting as what is false: FALSIDICAL

trumpet flourish or signal: TUCKET

truncated: PREMORSE

trust or belief, worthy of: FAITHWORTHY

truth, speaking the: VERILOQUOUS

truthful: VERIDICAL

twilight, morning: UGHTEN

twin or paired: JUMELLE

twisted and entangled: CONTORTUPLICATE

two days, lasting: BIDUOUS

two-edged or cutting both ways: ANSAL

two ways, leading: BIVIOUS

typical, not perfectly: HYPOTYPIC

U

ulcer, a little: ULCUSCULE
ulceration: HELCOSIS
unapproving: UNPLAUSIVE
unattainable ideal, a
    yearning for an: NYMPHO-
    LEPSY
unconsciousness: APSYCHIA
unconscientious: DISCON-
    SCIENT
uncouth: AGRESTIC
uncurl by moistening or
    steaming, to: DECATIZE
undefiled: INTEMERATE
underage, the state of be-
    ing: NONAGE
underfoot, a treading: CON-
    CULCATION
underground or subterra-
    nean: CATACHTHONIAN
underhand, secret, or pri-
    vate: CLANCULAR
understandable to most peo-
    ple, readily: EXOTERIC
understood, easily: TRAN-
    SPICUOUS
undoable, not: INDEFEASIBLE
undressed, partly: DISCINCT
undressed, partly: DISHA-
    BILLE
unearthly or transcendent:
    SUPERMONDANE

unemployed or idle: OTIANT
unequaled, the quality of be-
    ing: PHOENIXITY
unexpected: INOPINATE
unexpected, hasty, or sud-
    den: SUBITANEOUS
unfamiliar surroundings, in:
    DÉPAYSÉ
unfazability or intellectual
    detachment: ATARAXY
unfeeling or insensitive: IM-
    PASSIBLE
unforeseeable: IMPREVISIBLE
unhappiness, causing: IN-
    FELICIFIC
unhappiness that is inescap-
    able: ANHEDONIA
unified whole, molding into
    a: ESEMPLASTIC
uninformed or knowing lit-
    tle: PARVISCIENT
unison, calling out in: CON-
    CLAMANT
unite, blend, or grow to-
    gether, to: INOSCULATE
universal or total rule: OM-
    NIREGENCY
unkindness: IMBENIGNITY
unknowable: METAGNOS-
    TIC
unluckiness: SCAEVITY

unlucky or worthless thing:
AMBSACE
unmarried, living together:
CONCUBINAGE
unmelodious and grating:
SCRANNEL
unmentionable or unspeak-
able: INFAND
unmentionable things: TA-
CENDA
unmixed or pure: MERA-
CIOUS
unnamed: INNOMINATE
unnatural: ABSONANT
unpleasant: ILLEPID
unprepared or unready: IM-
PROMPT
unprofitable: IMPROFICUOUS
unprofitable or vain: FRUS-
TRANEOUS
unpronounced letter or letter combination: APH-
THONG
unready or unprepared: IM-
PROMPT
unreasonable: ABSONANT
unreasonableness: ALOGY
unrecorded: IMPER-
SCRIPTABLE
unrivaled, the quality of being: PHOENIXITY
unscrupulous: ANY-
LENGTHIAN
unspeakable or unmention-
able: INFAND

unsusceptible or immune, to
make: VASTATE
unteachable as a pupil: IN-
DOCIBLE
untruthful or fabricated:
COMMENTITIOUS
untying or unbinding: AB-
STRICTION
unusual or strange: SEL-
COUTH
unveiling or revealing, an:
ANACALYPSIS
unvoluntary giving: DA-
TION
unwilling, the state of being: NOLLEITY
unwillingness: NOLITION
unwise or foolish: INSIPIENT
unworldly or divine: SUPER-
MUNDANE
upbraid or censure, to: EX-
PROBATE
uproarious or noisy:
ROUTOUS
uproar or din, a confused:
TINTAMARRE
uproar or disturbance:
STRAMASH
uprooted: DERACINE
upward, turned or bent:
RESIMATED
urinate, to: MICTURATE
urinate, wanting or needing
to: MICTURIENT

urinating backward: RET-
ROMINGENT
urination: MICTION
urine or urination: EMICTION
urine and dung, composed
of: MERDURINOUS
useful, advantageous, or
profitable: PROFICUOUS

useful arts, the science of
the: CHREOTECHNICS
use or enjoyment: JOUIS-
SANCE
usury: FENERATION
utilitarian, practical, or
functional: BANAUSIC
uttermost or outermost: EXTI-
MATE

V

vague: NUBILOUS
vain about one's wealth:
PURSE-PROUD
vainglory: GLORIATION
vainglory or self-aggrandizement, the love or pursuit
of: KENODOXY
vain or unprofitable: FRUS-
TRANEOUS
valedictory: APOPEMPTIC
value, things of little: TRAN-
TLES
value, to treat as if of trifling: FLOCCIPEND
value little or consider
worthless, to: FLOCCIFY
vanity: KENODOXY
veiling or concealing: OB-
VELATION
venereal disease: CRINKUM
vengeance or plague: WANION

ventilate or blow through,
to: PERFLATE
verbal misinterpretation:
MISACCEPTATION
verbal repetition, needless:
BATTOLOGY
verbal wrangling: DIGLADIA-
TION
verse, a mania for writing:
METROMANIA
victory, in celebration of:
EPINICIAN
view, an ability to take a
general or overall: EN-
SYNOPTICITY
vigorous seeming but really
weak: FORCIBLE-FEEBLE
vintage, to harvest the: VEN-
DEMIATE
violated or broken: INFRACT
violate or deflower, to: CON-
STUPRATE

violent or acute, very: PER-
ACUTE
violent or cruel: HARAGEOUS
virgin: PARTHENIAN
virginity: PUCELAGE
visceral: SPLANCHNIC
visible: ASPECTABLE
visible or obvious: PHAN-
IC
visible to the naked eye:
MACROMERITIC
visual: SCOPIC
vital or living: ZOETIC
vitamin A: ERGUSIA
vocal (speaking) range:
TONGUESHOT
voice, having a high and
clear: HYPSOPHONOUS

voice, having a high or
loud: MEGALOPHONIC
voice, having a soft: MALA-
COPHONOUS
voice, loss of: ANAUDIA
voice, shrillness of: OXYPHONIA
vomit, to: PARBREAK
vomited matter: EXGORGITA-
TION
vomiting: ANACATHARSIS
voracious: ADEPHAGOUS
voting by a show of hands:
CHIROTONY
vow to be faithful and true,
a solemn: AFFIDATION
vulgar or second-rate artistically: BIEDERMEIER
vulnerable, constitutionally:
DIATHETIC

W

wagon or cart, pert. to a:
PLAUSTRAL
waiting in ambush for a victim: LOCHETIC
wakening: EXPERGEFACIENT
wake up, causing to: HYPNO-
POMPIC
waking up: EXPERRECTION
wail or lament, to: EJULATE
walk, able to: GRESSIBLE

walk about or wander, to:
OBAMBULATE
walk in front of, to: ANTE-
AMBULATE
walking in a straight line:
RECTIGRADE
walk or dance on a rope,
to: FUNAMBULATE
walkway or a shady place,
cool: FRESCADE

walled around: OBVALLATE

wall in, to: INTERMUR

wall in or around, to: CIR-
CUMMURE

wallowing: VOLUTATION

wand, magic: RHABDUS

wandering at night: NOC-
TIVAGANT

wandering from market to
market:
CIRCUMFORANEOUS

wandering over the world:
MUNDIVAGANT

wander or walk about, to:
OBAMBULATE

wanton or loose girl: NYSOT

war, a recital of wrongs before declaring: CLARIGA-
TION

war, hating: MISOPOLEMICAL

war, mighty in: BELLIPO-
TENT

war, pert. to the spoils of:
MANUBIARY

ward off or avert, to: AVER-
RUNCATE

warlike or battle-ready: BAT-
TAILOUS

warm, growing: INCALES-
CENT

warty: VERRUCOSE

washing or cleansing: CLYS-
MIC

wasp's nest: VESPIARY

waste matter, pert. to:
SPODOGENOUS

wasting away: TABESCENT

watch diligently, to: AD-
VIGILATE

watch, keeping: EXCUBANT

watched or observed, a
thing to be: OBSERVAN-
DUM

water, diluted with:
LYMPHATE

water, transparent in: HY-
DROPHANOUS

water drinker: AQUABIB

waterfall: CATADUPE

water into wine, a turning
of: BETHPHANY

watermelon or gourd: ANGU-
RIA

wavy hair, having: CYMOTRI-
CHOUS

wayside place of shelter: DI-
VERSORY

ways or roads, having many:
MULTIVIOUS

weak, physically: HY-
POSTHENIC

weaken or impair, to: LA-
BEFY

wealth, a lover of: PHILOPLU-
TARY

wealth, vain about one's:
PURSE-PROUD

wean from the breast, to:
ABLACTATE
weariness, relieving: ACOPIC
weariness or fatigue: DELAS-
SATION
wearing a shirt on the outside: CAMISATED
weather, an interval of fair:
SLATCH
wedding or marriage: CON-
FARREATION
week: SENNIGHT
weekly: SEPTIMANAL
weekly or seven days in duration: HEBDOMADAL
weep, not able to: ILLACHRY-
MABLE
weeping: PLORATION
weepy: LARMOYANT
weighable: POISABLE
weigh, consider, or balance,
to: TRUTINATE
weight, equal in: EQUIPON-
DERATE
welcome as a guest, to:
GESTEN
well-formed or -propor-
tioned: FEATOUS
well-made: AFFABROUS
well-mannered, moral, or respectable: MORATE
well-proportioned and graceful: TRETIS
well-shaped: EUMORPHOUS
wells, pert. to: PHREATIC

western or occidental:
HESPERIAN
western or occidental: PO-
NENT
wet and sticky: VISCID
wet or moist: UVID
wheedling or coaxing: SUP-
PALPATION
whereness: UBIETY
whimsical or capricious: VA-
GARIOUS
whinny, able to: HINNIBLE
whipping, fond of: PLAGOSE
whipping, pert. to punishment by: BACULINE
whisper, to: SIFFILATE
whispering: SUSURRANT
whispering sound, as of
wind among leaves: PSITH-
URISM
white, glowing: CANDENT
white magic: MAGIA
white magic: THEURGY
white people (derogatory):
ALBICULI
white person newly arrived
in India, the state of being a: GRIFFINAGE
whole, molding into a unified: ESEMPLASTIC
wicked, extremely: FACINO-
ROUS
wicked, extremely: SCELER-
ATE
wicked, vilely: FLAGITIOUS

wicked deed: MESHANTERY
wide or large in scope: AM-
PLIVAGANT
widowed: VIDUATE
width: LARGEOUR
wife, overly devoted to
one's: UXORIOUS
wife's belongings or property
that she legally retains:
PARAPHERNA
wild, living or growing in
the: AGRESTAL
wild beast, like a: FERINE
wild or riotous: RAGMATICAL
willingness: LIBENCE
willingness, lack of: NOLI-
TION
willingness, the state of lacking: NOLLEITY
winding maze: ANFRACTURE
window: VENTANNA
wind-rounded stone: VENTI-
FACT
windscreen: PARAVENT
windy talking: BLOVIATION
wine, a turning of water
into: BETHPHANY
wine, to drink: POCULATION
wine or liquor, the best:
QUADRIMUM
wink, to: NICTITATE
winking: CONNICTATION
winter retreat: HIBERNACLE
wintry: BRUMAL
wintry: HIBERNAL

wintry: HIEMAL
wiping the nose: EMUNC-
TION
wish, a devout: APPRECA-
TION
wishbone: FURCULA
wishful about something unattained earlier, one who
is: WOULD-HAVE-BEEN
witchcraft stabbing of a person's image: INVULTUA-
TION
withered or decayed: MAR-
CID
without a particular point
being made of: SUB SI-
LENTIO
witless: INSULSE
woman, a gossiping: COM-
MERE
woman, girl or young: JU-
VENCLE
woman, masculinity in a:
VIRAGINITY
woman's article of clothing:
BILIMENT
women, a sacrifice of: GYNE-
THUSIA
women, fond of: MULIEROSE
women, knowledge of:
GYNICS
women, pert. to: MULIEBRAL
women, sexual craving for:
GYNAECOCOENIC

261

women, very fond of: PHI-
LOGYNOUS
women in common, having:
GYNAECOCOENIC
wonders, working: MIRIFIC
wondrous: MIRANDOUS
wondrous or marvelous ob-
ject: STUPOR MUNDI
wood, injurious or destructive to: LIGNIPERDOUS
wood, made of: TREEN
wooing or a marriage pro-
posal: PROCATION
woolly hair, having: ULOTRI-
CHOUS
word, the taking of in a
wrong sense: MISACCEPTA-
TION
word having several mean-
ings: POLYSEMANT
word of more than two syllables: HYPERDISYLLABLE
wordplay, cleverness in using: LOGODAEDALY
words, fascinated by: LOGO-
FASCINATED
words, one who legislates in
matters regarding: LOGO-
GOGUE
work, enhancing abilities
for: ERGOGENIC
work, painstaking effort or:
OPEROSITY
worker interference with

the orderly process:
FREINAGE
workmanlike: AFFABROUS
work of all kinds, ready to
do: PANURGIC
workshop or studio: BOT-
TEGA
work together, to: COACT
world, wandering over the:
MUNDIVAGANT
world-destroying: MUNDI-
CIDIOUS
world ruler: KOSMOKRATOR
worriedly preoccupied or absentminded: DISTRAIT
worshiping oneself: EGOLA-
TROUS
worship of anything archaic:
ARCHAEOLATRY
worship of false gods: PSEU-
DOLATRY
worship of obscenity or
filth: AISCHROLATREIA
worship of oneself: AUTOLA-
TRY
worst element, government
by the: KAKISTOCRACY
worthless, to value little or
consider: FLOCCIFY
worthless or unlucky thing:
AMBSACE
worthless things: PALTRE-
MENT

worthy of trust or belief:
FAITHWORTHY
worthy to be chosen: DELIGI-
BLE
would-have-liked-to-have-
been person: WOULD-
HAVE-BEEN
wounding: VULNIFIC
wrangling, struggling, or
contention:
COLLUCTATION
wrangling, verbal: DIGLATIA-
TION
wrinkleless: ERUGATE
write in reply, to: RESCRIBE

writing: CHARACTERY
writing, fond of: SCRIBA-
CEOUS
writing, to put in: REDACT
writing for another person:
ALLOGRAPH
writing that's good on a minor subject: ADOXOGRA-
PHY
written on only one side:
ANOPISTHOGRAPHIC
wrong belief, opinion, or
doctrine: CACODOXY
wrongs, a recital of before
declaring war: CLARIGA-
TION

Y

yawn, to: OSCITATE
yawning and stretching:
PANDICULATION
yawning or drowsy: OSCI-
TANT
yawning or gaping: HIANT
yearly or annual:
QUOTENNIAL
yearning for an unattainable
ideal: NYMPHOLEPSY
yearning or desire: APPE-
TITION
yearning or loss, a feeling
of: DESIDERIUM

years, lasting for several:
PLURENNIAL
yellow, straw: FESTUCINE
yellow, turning pale: FLAVES-
CENT
yellowing: LUTESCENT
yellow-skinned: XANTHOUS
yesterday, pert. to: HESTERNAL
yolk of an egg: VITELLUS
young: BREPHIC
young, growing: JUVENES-
CENT
young man, being a: EPHE-
BIC

young woman, girl or: JU-
  VENCLE
youthful appearance: AGERA-
  SIA

youth, inexperience, or
greenness: VIRIDITY

Z

zeal: CALENTURE

zeal, fanatical: ZELOTYPIA